Consumption Matters

A selection of previous *Sociological Review* Monographs

Life and Work History Analyses[†]
ed. Shirley Dex

The Sociology of Monsters[†]
ed. John Law

Sport, Leisure and Social Relations[†]
eds John Horne, David Jary and Alan Tomlinson

Gender and Bureaucracy*
eds Mike Savage and Anne Witz

The Sociology of Death: theory, culture, practice*
ed. David Clark

The Cultures of Computing
ed. Susan Leigh Star

Theorizing Museums*
ed. Sharon Macdonald and Gordon Fyfe

[†] Available from The Sociological Review Office, Keele University, Keele, Staffs ST5 5BG.
* Available from Marston Book Services, PO Box 270, Abingdon, Oxon OX14 4YW.

Consumption Matters

The production and experience of consumption

Edited by Stephen Edgell, Kevin Hetherington and Alan Warde

Blackwell Publishers/The Sociological Review

Copyright © The Editorial Board of the Sociological Review 1996

First published in 1996

Blackwell Publishers
108 Cowley Road, Oxford OX4 1JF, UK

and
238 Main Street,
Cambridge, MA 02142, USA

British Library Cataloguing in Publication Data

A CIP catalogue record for this book is available from the British Library

Library of Congress Cataloging-in-Publication Data
Consumption matters: the production and experience of consumption /
edited by Stephen Edgell, Kevin Hetherington and Alan Warde.
p. cm.—(Sociological review monograph; 44)
Includes bibliographical references and index.
ISBN 0–631–20350–8 (alk. paper)
1. Consumption (Economics)—Social aspects. I. Edgell, Stephen.
II. Hetherington, Kevin. III. Warde, Alan. IV. Series.
HM15.S545 no. 44 [HC79.C6] 306.3—dc20 96–45997

Printed in Great Britain by Whitstable Litho Ltd., Whitstable, Kent
This book is printed on acid-free paper.

Contents

Contents

Introduction: consumption matters

Stephen Edgell and Kevin Hetherington

The concept consumption is applied to a bewildering range of goods and services—everything from art to shopping, to watching television, receiving welfare and visiting a zoo. It also figures prominently in accounts of political change, economic transformation and cultural fragmentation. Consumption clearly matters, some would argue more than ever before, but its importance *viz-a-viz* other activities, notably employment, in what way or ways, and to whom, is less than transparent.

The chapters included in this volume arose out of an ESRC funded interdisciplinary seminar series concerned with just these points; it was entitled 'Conceptualizing Consumption Issues' and took place between 1994–6. The seminars were organized by colleagues from the Departments of Sociology at the Universities of Salford and Lancaster and the Department of Sociology and Social Anthropology, Keele University. The series involved thirty-two presentations by social scientists from a variety of disciplines, including political science, anthropology, cultural studies, and social policy, as well as sociology. The selection included here consists of revised versions of papers first presented in this series or chapters that have been commissioned for this volume.

One of the main aims of the seminar programme was to publish a range of papers which reflected the diversity and strengths of recent theoretical and empirical research on consumption, especially by sociologists, that would be of interest to social scientists and advanced students. As such, this monograph seeks to build upon recent collections of papers on the sociology of consumption, edited by Warde (1990), Burrows and Marsh (1992), and the multi-disciplinary volume by Miller (1995). The ESRC seminars covered all aspects of consumption, from provision to use and meaning. Hence this collection is divided into two overlapping parts; the production of consumption and the experience of consumption.

The Production of Consumption

A useful starting point for consideration of the links between production and consumption is Warde's ideal-type model of cycles of production and consumption (1990, 1992). This approach provides a theoretical framework with reference to which past research can be reviewed and future empirical projects can be mapped. Also, it does not avoid the production *versus* consumption problematic, but begins to resolve it by recognizing that the way goods and services are produced can affect, although not in any simple 'determinist' way, the process of consumption and should therefore be considered as integral to it. Thus, it not only reveals what has been called the 'productivist bias' (Urry, 1990:277) of social science, but represents an alternative to the extent that as 'consumers' we are all 'economically active', whereas it has been estimated that in 1996 as 'producers', only 73 per cent of adult men and 54 per cent of adult women will be 'economically active' (Hakim, 1993). Arguably, there is no better indicator of the productivist bias of the social sciences, especially neo-classical economics, than the conventional definition of economic activity which equates it with labour force participation for pay and/or profit. Moreover, in marked contrast to Warde's model, such an approach privileges paid work over unpaid work and therefore tends to overlook work in the household, much of which is concerned with consumption and still heavily dependent upon female labour. Thus, this taken-for-granted meaning of the term 'economically active', is theoretically flawed and empirically limited. Conversely, the cycles of production and consumption approach to economic activity is theoretically more complete and empirically more inclusive.

In Table 1, the links between mode of provision, conditions of access, manner of delivery, and the final environment or experience of consumption, 'negative as well as positive' (Warde, 1992:20), are meant to be read as tendencies.

Table 1 distinguishes four modes of provision which are related to four stages within any one production/consumption cycle. Such an ideal-type formulation does not exclude the possibility of mixed cycles. For example, the market and state modes of provi-

Table 1 Cycles of production/consumption

Mode of Provision	Access/Social Relations	Manner of Delivery	Experience of Consumption
Market	Price/Exchange	Managerial	Customer/Consumer
State	Need/Right	Professional	Citizen/Client
Household	Family/Obligation	Family	Self/Fam./Kinship
Communal	Network/Reciprocity	Volunteer	Friend/Neighbour/ Acquaintance

Source: Expanded and amended version of Warde (1992)

sion may be equally bureaucratic in terms of delivery, and the consumption experience of the household and communal modes may be qualitatively similar. Notwithstanding the attempt by market and state providers of goods and services to personalize the production/consumption process ('family' restaurants, paternalistic employers, the use of first names in banks, etc), this model could be usefully sub-divided into impersonal/formal (market and state) and personal/informal (household and communal) cycles for certain research purposes. For instance, in the case of those interested in the historical trend in favour of impersonal production/consumption cycles.

All the papers in this volume can be located, to a greater or lesser extent, within this framework, thereby illustrating its comprehensiveness. Thus, Baldock and Ungerson's evaluation of the recently introduced changes in the provision and delivery of community care reveals, among other things, the complexity of the new mixed economy of welfare, especially from the perspective of the consumer. The paper by Dowding and Dunleavy focuses on two of the main approaches to analysing the public-private divide and as such is more concerned with the earlier rather than the later stages of formal cycles. Clarke also addresses the issue of changes in state provision, but from the standpoint of how it has been represented politically. Ford and Rowlingson too focus on the production end of the above *schema* and are concerned with female access to credit with reference to the household/neighbourhood/market nexus of relationships. The paper by Crompton connects with both 'ends', as it were, of the above ideal-typical model, in as much as it discusses the social significance of class and consumption processes.

Although all the papers in this part of this volume are essentially concerned with the early stages in the cycle of production/consumption, the first three focus on the shrinking and changing nature of state provision. More specifically, the papers by Baldock and Ungerson, Dowding and Dunleavy, and Clarke, raise serious doubts about the continued usefulness of the distinction between public and private provision. Arguably, they present a strong case, along with other recent research on the transformation of state provision (eg Flynn *et al.* 1996), for the obsolescence of this historical distinction, at least in Britain, if not elsewhere. This suggests that the framework outlined in Table 1 is in need of major revision on the grounds that direct provision of goods and services by the state has been transformed due to privatization, broadly defined (Edgell and Duke, 1991), and what has remained nominally under the *aegis* of the state has become more commercialized and fragmented (eg charges, internal markets, quasi-markets, etc.) and therefore almost indistinguishable in certain respects from market provision.

Thus, to the extent that all forms of state provided goods and services have been contaminated by market processes, the old category of 'pure' state provision ceases to be of much relevance. Hence, a revised version of the above model would need to recognize the emergence of a new mode of provision, that of marketized-state provision, albeit characterized by great heterogeneity, whilst retaining the other modes of provision. In brief, the growth of marketized-state provision and the variable forms it takes, is a matter of considerable social, economic and political significance for individuals. In contexts where the language of the market place increasingly prevails, terms such as 'customer' implies choice, competition and payment, which in turn suggests that the public/private divide has become indistinct at the cost of what was implied by the former, namely, needs and rights.

In addition to drawing attention to the increased complexity and tensions within the marketized-state mode, the chapters in this section shed light on some of the consequences of this transformation of state provision for the household and the under researched voluntary sector, and particularly therefore for women. It would seem that the more that the state withdraws from direct provision on a universalistic basis, the greater the contribution of females to production/consumption cycles, not only in an unpaid capacity in the home and/or neighbourhood, but also in a (poorly) paid privatized health and welfare system.

4

The Experience of Consumption

If there is one overall theme running through all the chapters in this second section, it is a critique of an underlying individualism within the study of the experience of consuming. These critiques ranged from challenging the methodological individualism of economistic studies and rational choice approaches to consumer practices (Falk); critiques of postmodern assumptions about the decline of class, as a measure of social activity and suggestions of consumer practices of self-directed expressions of agency freed from any structuring social relations (Harbottle; Werbner); rejection of a modernist view of the self as an essentialist category outside of the process of consuming (Munro); to positive, if sometimes critical, engagements with theories of the processes of consuming which suggest a structurally determining role for social relations, notably through the work of Bourdieu (Allatt; Bagnall; Longhurst and Savage). The general conclusion drawn by all of these chapters is that social relations shape the experience of consuming and that the social construction of the consumer is a consequence of these processes.

In contrast to economists' assumptions of rational choice and postmodern arguments on the dislocation of individuals from social relations as agents with the ability to create their own identities through consumer practices, these chapters recognize consumer practices as social practices that have a distinctly performative mode to them. Starting from the consumption end of the (modified) model of cycles of production/consumption, and avoiding an overly individualistic conception of the process of consumption, the chapters in this section of the volume all emphasize that social relations shape the experience of consumption.

In Werbner's discussion of gift-giving at Christmas, she suggests that gifting involves the construction of a moral economy organized around honour and debt (expressed in Veblen and Mauss as potlatch, and in Bourdieu as symbolic violence) and the reproduction of social hierarchies both within the family and at a national level. For Werbner, the practices of consumption, expressed in gifting as well as through the symbolism of Father Christmas, the Pantomime, the Queen's speech, and charity giving during the 'festive season', construct Christmas as an agnostic struggle for distinction that maintain hierarchies between parents and children, between families, between rich and poor, and around the issues of ethnicity and religion where non-Christians are excluded from the performance of the 'nation' at Christmas time.

In Allatt's chapter the practice of consuming private schooling reveals some similar issues to those raised by Werbner. Drawing explicitly on Bourdieu, Allatt shows how parental choices about sending their children to private schools have to be seen not as individual choices, but as means of reproducing middle-class families who are able to mobilize high levels of economic and social capital in obtaining the education they want for their children. In doing so, hierarchies and relations of power within families are reproduced via parental sacrifice and children's obligations to reciprocate through hard work at school, and beyond, to 'repay' their parents. Thus, middle-class parental 'choice' in the emergent quasi-market of education is rooted in the economy and culture of the family over time. Moreover, the experience of the consumption of education involves a considerable amount of private and public work before it can be realized in terms of the outcomes and identities of all those involved in the process.

The construction of social identities and the critique of the position that the process of consuming is only about individual choice is addressed in other contributions. In a broadly historical chapter, Falk argues that the configuration of health and its relationship to identity has become an important component of modern societies. Health becomes a life project organized around risk avoidance and longevity that is performed through a number of symbolic practices that involve the consumption of so called protective substances such as vitamin pills. Consumption for Falk is an 'other directed' performance in which identification, rather than self-identity *per se*, becomes the means through which the performative regimens of diet and health are socially validated.

The social significance of ingesting certain kinds of products by a specific social group, in this instance Iranian migrant women, is also considered by Harbottle. Although the emphasis here is also on the experience of consumption, considerable attention is given to the provisioning dimension of the process. Similarly, the chapter by Bagnall on how the consumption of two heritage sites are experienced by visitors involves the examination of both the production and consumption processes at work. However, in keeping with the rest of this section, Bagnall focuses on what visitors bring to the sites rather than what is provided for them.

These various critiques of individualism and of the practices of consumption, being all about 'individual choice', follow through into a further theme that is developed in this part of the volume. The process of consumption, as these chapters make clear, cannot be separated from the social construction of the consumer. For example in Werbner's discussion of Christmas, these social identities are performed through hierarchical relationships that are in turn symbolically reproduced in the antagonistic battles over giving. Identities are located within these hierarchies for Werbner and cannot be extracted from them even where giving is perceived as an individual act of love, recognition or charity. Again, an issue similarly conveyed in Allatt's discussion of relations between generations over schooling.

In an innovative chapter, which draws on the work of Strathern, Munro explores issues of self through a discussion of the consumption thesis. For Munro, it is not just identities that are constituted through consumption but the self as well. He criticises what he calls a production view of the self. In contrast to those who regard consumption as a system of communication, for Munro the self is constituted through the practices of consumption rather than existing prior to it. The self exists in extension. It is constituted in the world of goods (and services) that are consumed.

The paper by Longhurst and Savage reviews critically and constructively the most important contemporary sociologist of consumption, Bourdieu. They discuss how his consumption paradigm has influenced both those concerned with the relationship between class (production) and variations in consumption (notably American sociologists), and those who have focused more on contemporary cultural change (consumption experiences) and especially the emergence of a consumer culture in Britain. As Longhurst and Savage indicate, the papers presented in the seminar series as a whole, and those included in this section, reflect this pattern of appropriation.

The final contribution by Warde is not only concerned with the future of the sociology of consumption with reference to all the chapters in this volume, but does so in the context of current social scientific research on, and overviews of, consumption in Britain. Needless to say, the final two chapters are more concerned than most with pointing to some possible directions for consumption research.

7

Acknowledgements

We wish to thank Rob Flynn, Brian Longhurst and Alan Warde for their helpful comments on an earlier draft of this Introduction. The usual disclaimers hold.

Notes

1 The core participants from the three Departments involved in the seminar series were; Stephen Edgell, Rob Flynn, Brian Longhurst and Greg Smith (University of Salford), Celia Lury, Wendy Olsen and Alan Warde (Lancaster University), Gordon Fyfe and Kevin Hetherington (Keele University), plus Mike Savage (originally of Keele University, now at Manchester University).

References

Burrows, R. and Marsh, C., eds, (1992) *Consumption and Class*, London: Macmillan.

Edgell, S. and Duke, V., (1991) *A Measure of Thatcherism: A Sociology of Britain*, London: HarperCollins.

Flynn, R., Williams, G. and Pickard, S., (1996) *Markets and Networks: Contracting in Community Health Services*, Buckingham: Open University Press.

Hakim, C., (1993) 'The myth of rising female employment', *Work, Employment and Society*, Vol. 7:97–120.

Miller, D., ed., (1995) *Acknowledging Consumption: A Review of New Studies*, London: Routledge.

Urry, J., (1990) 'Work, production and social relations', *Work, Employment and Society*, Vol. 4:271–280.

Warde, A., (1990) 'Introduction to the sociology of consumption', *Sociology*, Vol. 24:1–4.

Warde, A., (1992) 'Notes on the relationship between production and consumption' in R. Burrows and C. Marsh (eds) *Consumption and Class*, London: Macmillan:15–31.

Part I
The Production of Consumption

Becoming a consumer of care: developing a sociological account of the 'new community care'

John Baldock and Clare Ungerson

Abstract

The chapter evaluates the reformed arrangements for the management and delivery of social care following the *NHS and Community Care Act 1990* using a framework drawn from economic sociology. Research findings describing how a group of newly disabled older people fared as consumers of the services are summarized. An explanatory account is given drawing upon concepts and theory to be found in the growing literature on the sociology of economic life, particularly studies of consumption. The central conclusion is that it is difficult to account for the effects of the recent reforms on community care consumers without situating them within a context of existing social relations and institutions. If the reforms are to succeed they must change not just the practical mechanics of service funding and delivery but deeply embedded values and behavioural norms.

Introduction

This chapter is a preliminary exercise in using a framework drawn from economic sociology to evaluate what has been called the 'new community care'. The term refers to the reformed arrangements for the management and delivery of social care following the *NHS and Community Care Act 1990*. We seek to explain research findings which describe how a group of newly disabled older people fared as consumers of the services available under the new arrangements. The explanations we offer draw upon concepts and theory to be found in the growing literature on the sociology of economic life, particularly studies of consumption. Our central conclusion is that it is difficult to account for the effects of the recent reforms on community care consumers without situating them within a context of existing social relations and institutions. If our analysis is right then the new community care is much more ambitious than it first appeared; for to succeed it must change not just the practical mechanics of service funding and delivery but it will need to bring about shifts in deeply embedded values and behavioural norms.

The empirical findings, upon which this argument is based, followed a small sample of 32 people who had suffered a stroke and then recovered sufficiently to be discharged from hospital to return home. A full account is to be found in Baldock and Ungerson (1993, 1994a, 1994b). Each stroke sufferer, together with their families and carers, was followed for six months. We observed three patterns of outcome which this paper seeks to explain:

i)   All of our sample were the recipients of, or effectively the consumers of, a relatively homogeneous product; care assessment followed by care management provided by the local social services department. However, in all but a few of the cases, the accounts they gave us of this experience were hugely at variance with the formal definitions of the service they had received. In particular the language and terminology the people in our sample used were not at all the same as those used in policy documents that described what they were getting.

ii) The vast majority of our sample experienced great difficulty in adjusting to and accepting the help that constituted their 'care in the community'. The nature and variety of these difficulties could not be explained in terms of the 'usual' variables; service received, level of disability, age, and income.

iii) At the end of the six months we observed that the people in our sample had moved to a variety of arrangements for, or 'solutions' to, their care needs and these again could not readily be explained simply in terms of their disabilities or the services they had been offered.

These were not expected results. The intention had been to use a small sample to explore the range of implementation problems—almost at the level of 'hiccups' and teething problems—that were likely to occur in the early stages of what were fairly radical changes of policy for community care. We would not have been surprised to discover a pattern of relatively small, technical malfunctions in the implementation process. Instead we found fundamental problems at level of meaning, expectation and social behaviour. We interviewed the stroke sufferers and their carers, where they existed, three times; when the stroke survivors first went home from hospital, at three months and at six months. This was a deliberately small sample (32) in order to allow as full as possible an exploration of what was happening in the interviewees' own terms. The object of this study was a classic qualitative search for 'validity at the expense of reliability' (Newby, 1977). The interviews were structured round a range of open-ended questions designed to explore as widely as possible the sample's circumstances and concerns, to capture the experiences of a return home with new dependencies and to understand what was important in the accounts of the services received. The interviews took place between June 1991 and December 1992 and were recorded and later transcribed.

Instead of speaking of practical difficulties which might be related to service provision and coordination, all those in our sample described the process of adaption after stroke in terms of a major revision of what might loosely be called their 'life-style'. In particular they described substantial changes in their spending priorities, how they arranged their incomes, what they bought and from whom, and the difficulties they had in justifying and accepting these changes. Most of these accounts were given in the context of the relationships that they entailed; with family, friends, professionals, voluntary and commercial providers. Hence, in seeking to give some structure and order to these accounts we have been drawn to the work of sociologists who have studied economic life and the pattern and meaning of consumption choices. Our use of this literature is necessarily somewhat eclectic and hence our conclusions are tentative. They are:

i) That it is useful to reconceptualize the community care reforms introduced by the 1990 Act in terms of their implications for social relations and institutions. Our sample described how, in order to obtain the support services they required, they had been confronted by a need to change both their patterns of life, particularly in terms of how they interacted with people in their family and social networks, and deeply held assumptions about the proper and accepted ways to behave. Seen in these terms the reforms are much more demanding, or audacious and arrogant, depending on one's point of view, than the official accounts imply.

ii) That social care is a particularly complex commodity and that the consequences of changing the conditions under which it is given, bought and sold—changes central to the reforms—can be better understood if one applies some of the insights of the sociology of consumption.

iii) That, in order to explain the choices made by the people in our sample, it is necessary to go beyond a treatment of them as mere utility-maximizing consumers facing a re-ordered set of suppliers—which is how the policy designers would appear to have seen them (Griffiths, 1989: Cm 849, 1989)—and to present a more socially embedded and differentiated account which takes account of habits, preferences and values and of the social contexts that have generated them.

The 'New Community Care'

The scale and distinctiveness of the changes in what Social Administration researchers have traditionally called 'the personal social services' can hardly be exaggerated. Most industrial nations have been seeking ways to deal with the growing numbers of older people who will need relatively long term health and social care. The late 1980s and early 1990s have seen a rash of major reform legislation across Europe (Sweden, the Netherlands, Germany, Italy, France, Austria as well as the UK; Baldock and Evers, 1991) which has sought in different ways to determine where the resources for care will come from and to ensure that more of that care will be provided in peoples' own homes in the community rather than in institutions (partly because there is evidence that homecare is what people want and partly because governments hope it will be cheaper).

However, the manner of the reform process in Britain stands out sharply from our European neighbours. In Sweden, for example, legislation grew out of a long and open debate, cast in terms of welfarist principles, and neatly representing the social democratic model of social politics (Esping Anderson, 1990). In Germany the corporatist tradition has been well demonstrated in similarly open discussions about where the additional costs of financing a social insurance solution to the *Pflegenotstand* (care crisis) should fall (Dieck, 1994). In Britain, on the other hand, we have seen reform driven by dictat rather than by negotiation and characterized by secrecy rather than openness. A year of government silence followed the Griffiths Report (1988). The White Paper that eventually emerged in 1989 was generous with ideological exhortation but very short on detail, particularly as to whether there would be any increase in expenditure to meet the new goals. Indeed it was not until well after the National Health Service and Community Care Act was passed (December 1990) that the local authorities learnt how much money they were to have in order to implement it (July 1992). They discovered, in effect, that social care was to be cash limited and based on existing *per-capita* levels of expenditure rather than being a commitment of greater resources. Indeed, if one takes account of the continuing reductions in longstay beds in National Health service hospitals that have occurred over the last fifteen years, the new community care in Britain amounts to a planned reduction in public expenditure. The 'reform' process had been a textbook example of the highly centralized process of policy-making in Britain.

The new community care in Britain marks a radical shift from the past. It is widely accepted within the professional community that the implementation in England and Wales of those sections of the legislation which deal with the support of adults in the community will require that 'a revolution take place over the next decade in the way social services operate' (*Audit Commission*, 1992:1). The nature of this revolution is not merely administrative and organizational; in addition 'changing from the traditional role requires a cultural revolution . . . . (amongst social services staff) major changes in attitude are needed' (*ibid*:19). Central government recognition of the scale of the changes required of the public services is evidenced by the quite unprecedented level of support provided to local authority social services departments by the Department of Health, the Social Services Inspectorate and the Audit Commission in the form of publications, letters of guidance and collaborative training and monitoring exercises.

However, it may not just be the services that are having to adapt but also those who use and consume them. Indeed, as the Audit Commission itself points out, 'the new approach to community care focuses on the service user, not the service' (1992:1). The spirit of the reforms is explicitly consumerist; users will be empowered, they will be able to express their needs, they will exercise choice, suppliers will compete to obtain their custom in a 'mixed economy of care' (Cm 849, 1989: section 3.4). The Act effectively requires the creation of a more mixed-economy of care by insisting that some 85 per cent of the new care budget (monies transferred from the social security budget) is spent outside the public sector using private and voluntary care suppliers. It is this aspect of the legislation that has led to increased discussion about consumerism and partnership in social care. The legislation also appears to give dependent people and their carers new rights. Local social services must provide dependent people with a needs-based assessment and they must consult with them and their carers about the provision of care. It is these aspects that have led to debate about participation, consultation and empowerment. However, the Act does not give a right to care, only a right to assessment. Cash limits are likely to force local authorities to complement needs-based rationing with more explicit means-testing. Traditionally the principle determining the allocation of local personal social services has been one of need rather than income. Some LAs continue to insist this remains the case for community care services. Many, however, are being forced to offer no more than advice to people above fairly minimal income thresholds. An increasing majority of people will have to seek their care in the private, voluntary and informal sectors.

Yet relatively little attention has been paid to whether the public are likely to find the new community care system acceptable and useable and to investigating how far people will have to change their expectations and behaviour in order to benefit from the new arrangements. Despite the rhetoric of consumerism, not much effort had gone into discovering the consumer response to the new community care product.

Moving across the map of care

Amongst the choices or decisions that the people in our sample appeared to find difficult, at least initially, were: paying independent professionals such as physiotherapists; buying private home help; asking family, friends and neighbours for assistance; paying neighbours and friends; paying members of their own families; joining voluntary groups and taking advantage of voluntary services such as speech therapy. In a more general sense these people often found it hard to grasp or to accept that unless they initiated the use of some of these options nothing else would happen. For some their inaction was explained by a form of resignation or fatalism but for others apathy was not the problem but rather

16

uncertainty or fear that these sorts of consumption decisions would in some sense be unwise, inappropriate or risky.

Amongst the choices made more readily and frequently were: paying for and arranging forms of transport; paying for alterations and extra equipment for their homes (extensions, alterations, stair lifts); paying for help in the garden; and negotiating those parts of free NHS services that they wanted and avoiding those they did not. In these cases our samples were less surprised that they needed to act and make choices, in other words they expected to behave as consumers.

This is inevitably a very crude summary of complex and evolving patterns of care consumption. Where some people had difficulty others seemed to find the same choices easy and obvious, but overall the journeys people made, as consumers, across the map of care were slow, painful and oddly constrained.

It might be observed that most of the difficulties had to do with making payments to others and so a certain reluctance could be thought to be rather inevitable. However, payment itself was rarely the problem. People in this sample were ready to change their spending patterns. The shock of a stroke is deep; the impact on daily household routines is substantial when people return home to find they can no longer do many of the ordinary things (dress, bathe, drive, talk) that they hitherto had done without a thought. In the face of this trauma people were ready to make big adjustments to their spending patterns and to draw on long held savings. In a number of cases they made substantial, and possibly unwise, expenditure decisions almost as a reflex action. Spending money itself was not the problem.

Yet our sample was not, with the odd exception, a prosperous one. Retirement, for this generation at least, is a great leveller. Out of 32 households, while 28 owned their home, only 6 appeared to have net incomes over £150 a week (June 1991 to December 1992) and 12 couples lived on no more than the basic retirement pension and disability allowances. Yet, by the end of the six months, a shift of expenditure of the order of £30 a week in order to meet some of their new care needs was not uncommon amongst even those on the lowest incomes. The obstacles to payment for care were rarely explained to us in terms of poverty; rather they had to do with issues of habit, appropriateness and principle. It is these issues we explore in the rest of this paper.

The sociology of consumption

The developing sociology of consumption owes its origins to questions that initially arose in other arenas of empirical and theoretical investigation; from studies of stratification, of political action and voting behaviour, of social and psychological motivation, of the evolution of cultural forms (Dunleavy, 1980; Saunders, 1984, 1986; Cross, 1993; Miller, 1987). To a large extent we, in seeking to understand our data, have stumbled across consumption theory for parallel reasons; from a welfare perspective we were searching for an explanation as to why so many of our sample found the consumption of care so difficult to arrange and to benefit from. There is a bewildering variety of theory to choose from. Moreover it is clear that the sociology of consumption no longer serves only to answer questions from outside itself. It has become sufficient unto itself, that is to say further theoretical and descriptive elaboration are pursued for their own intrinsic value and not necessarily to answer questions from beyond its boundaries. A large part of this elaboration involves unpacking the capacious idea of consumption itself and classifying its variety of forms, contexts and meanings. Many of these developments have obvious relevance to understanding the consumption of care and suggest illuminating ways explaining the processes by which care is received by people. Any selection we make of from the growing literature is somewhat arbitrary.

The central idea that has informed our analysis is the concept of 'embeddedness' (Granovetter, 1985). It is clear that the preferences of our sample, and hence the choices they found they could or could not make, were inseparable from the relationships and the social institutions within which their lives were lived. Certainly, stroke forced change in this context. As Granovetter predicts, we did not find people responding mechanically—programmed like automatons by their pasts. But neither were they cool-headed seekers of the cheapest routes to maximum possible satisfaction. Negotiating their community care was not difficult because the new system was faulty in some organizational sense, but because of its very novelty and because it was so badly marketed. There was almost no awareness on the part of policy-makers and managers, of the social factors that would determine the new community care's acceptance—as distinct from the budgetary and administrative factors that preoccupied them.

18

The second major idea we have drawn from the literature on consumption concerns the ways in which the very nature of good or service is socially constructed. It became obvious that care is a particularly complex good. It is notable, for example, that the consumption of care exhibits many of the features of the consumption of food and that food is often chosen to exhibit the complexity of processes of consumption. Like food, care (for those who depend on it to get through the day) is basic to survival itself. It can be a necessity rather than an option. It is similarly charged with meaning and emotion. It is consumed in contexts which can be raw, brutal and demeaning (consider the poor house and its many institutional variants), while at other times, like food, care may serve as a luxurious or even religious celebration of love and commitment.

Warde (1990) has suggested that, for completeness, any account of consumption should consider at least four discrete elements in the process and he illustrates these largely by referring to food. The distinctions serve as well in a consideration of the consumption of care. They might be called 'the conditions of consumption' and we use them to explore the social complexity of care that was reflected in the accounts our sample gave us.

The conditions of consumption

i) *The process of production and provision*
Like food, care may be supplied for profit (and therefore be likely to exhibit degrees of systematization, routinization and bureaucratization), be produced within the household or be supplied directly or indirectly by the state.

ii) *The conditions of access*
Warde is still writing of food: 'The criteria of access to goods and services provided in . . . . different sectors are analytically distinct: purchasing [food care] availing myself of the labour of another household member and being in receipt of state-provided service entail diverse relations of access. Typically these three kinds of provisioning are governed, respectively, by the relations of market exchange, familial obligation and citizenship right. It is because services are produced under distinctive conditions and access to them is regulated accordingly, with subsequent consequences for their enjoyment, that the shifting

of service between sectors—from the state to the market sector, from the state to the household, or out of the household—is so important politically' (1990a:1–5).

iii) *The manner of delivery*
The service offered by different providers (private, for-profit suppliers, family members, or public sector employers) will vary in style, manner and perceived meaning and these differences become differences in the quality of the good itself.

iv) *The social environment of enjoyment*
'The social environment in which final consumption takes place [for example in the presence of strangers, or family or professionals] is an integral part of the experience but cannot be directly attributed to any other of the processes involved' (1990:4).

Part of the point is that some goods, indeed most goods, occupy a relatively stable and simple position in each Warde's 'elements in the process of consumption'. Take for example a highly standardized good like petrol; process of provision = sold by commercial suppliers; conditions of access = monetary payment; manner of delivery = little variation in petrol station forecourts (even self-service almost universal); environment of enjoyment = on public roads in a motor car (with some room for variation depending on the quality of your car and who you choose to travel with).

This is very much the pattern in a developed market economy such as Britain. We know the conditions of consumption and they remain relatively fixed and simple. Even quite complex goods are consumed under routinized and well-understood conditions. For example medical care, after nearly half a century of the National Health Service, is consumed under highly predictable conditions for most people; there's the GP and the local hospital and not much else in most people's experience (Busfield, 1990; Flynn, 1992:174–5).

As we have already said, there are other goods like food where the conditions of consumption are much more varied and complex (art, sex and alcohol are other commonly considered examples). It is these goods that are generally of more interest to the sociologists of consumption for they are interested in the social significance and cultural loading that comes with the variety. However, even in these more complex cases the conditions of consumption are relatively stable and fixed; they are just more varied and therefore take longer to learn and offer more choice for personal and social differentiation.

The more difficult cases occur when the conditions of consumption are both complex *and in flux* and this would seem to be true in the case of social care. For a variety of reasons the consumption of care is undergoing a period of uncertainty and change. The forces behind the change are many; government policy is only one and it is itself a response to many of the others—demographic change, the restructuring of family relationships, greater longevity and the growth of chronic dependence in old age (including that due to mental frailty such as Altzheimer's disease), labour market changes (particularly those affecting women), better housing and a preference for homecare. All these factors are forcing changes in the conditions of consumption of care for old people. Again the patterns of change can be considered in terms of Warde's four divisions:

The uncertain conditions of consumption of care in the community

The process of production and provision

Except for three particularly well-informed households in our sample, our stroke sufferers and their family carers all expressed themselves thoroughly confused about who was responsible for producing what care and in which manner. Where they had expected help from their GP it was not forthcoming; where they expected direct assistance from social services, they received instead enabling advice followed by approaches from commercial service-providers whose existence they had never even imagined. Even the day hospital, one of the more fixed beacons in this sea of change, operated in ways that surprised them. Only slowly did they begin to grasp the importance that private and voluntary assistance would have to play in their care.

In essence, they faced new confusions added to existing complexities. While the goal of the Conservative government's community care reforms is frequently described as seeking to create a mixed-economy of social care, even the key policy documents admit that the support of dependent people is already and always has been very varied (Cm 849, 1989; Audit Commission 1992;

Griffiths, 1988). A more complete description is to recognize that the new policies seek to reorder the already complex process of production and provision, replacing direct supply by the state with delegated and contracted-out services and substituting tax-financed entitlements with for-fee and for-profit provision. However, the shift to the new pattern is not distinct and well-focused. Rather, as we have already pointed out, the method of reform is not to establish a new but sharply defined set of responsibilities (as for example is happening in Germany and the Netherlands where the debate about care reform is precisely about the strict allocation of roles between state, private and voluntary sectors and the family), but to simply create a set of financial and regulatory conditions which will allow a different mixed economy of care to emerge.

Thus, for the moment, there is great uncertainty amongst care producers as to their roles in the new system and that uncertainty is to a large degree planned and deliberate. The reports of the new community care that are currently emerging from research evaluations (Lewis *et al.*, 1995; Pahl, 1994) and in the professional press (Community Care, 1994), document this confusion amongst service providers. What we discovered was an equal and parallel level of confusion amongst the current consumers of social care.

The conditions of access

One of the paradoxes of the new community care is that it is tending to substitute one form of citizenship, that built round a liberal conception of choice, for an established, more collectivist, entitlement to social services (Baldock and Evers, 1991; Offe, 1987). The justification is that some of the implicit state guarantees of the past (to publicly-provided home help, to longstay beds, to local authority residential homes) are simply no longer deliverable in the face of growing demand and costs. The new community care is monetizing the conditions of access in many areas—by obliging local authorities to contract out 85 per cent of their new social care budgets; by substituting payment for care allowances for the direct provision of services; by making the assessment of total social network support the key local authority function; and by means-testing most of the public out of entitlement to state-funded provision. The result is that access to social care is less built around a core of entitlements to state provision. Instead state provision has become a residual, fallback option once services accessed through payment, family obligation, neighbourly reciprocity and charity have been exhausted. The rules of access have been quietly and fundamentally changed.

This was a source of deep confusion for the people in our sample. They would often say to us things like: 'Well we thought we'd at least be entitled to a hour a week,' or 'We never expected them to stop the physio right away,' or 'I kept expecting social services would come round and sort it all out, but there was never a peep out of them'. The fundamental rules of access and the hierarchy of entitlement that they had internalized through a lifetime as citizens of the British welfare state had, from their point of view, suddenly been turned upside down. You could not start with what the state offered and then supplement it with family and private resources; rather you discovered that state assistance was secondary and contingent upon what you found for yourself. This basic confusion over the fundamental rules of access and entitlement may account for the degree of incomprehension and even non-recognition between the care-managers and members of our sample. The care-managers, having come through a barrage of retraining and organizational change over the last few years, had internalized the new rules and assumptions. Our elderly stroke sufferers and their spouses knew nothing of these changes. The two sides were simply were not talking the same language.

Professionals were not reported to have raised the issue of private expenditure in an explicit and systematic way. Public physiotherapists do not appear to discuss adding on more intensive private provision to the very limited time they tended to ration out to patients. Social workers might mention a private home-care agency or even pass on the name of the patient but not make it clear that they had done so. We came across no evidence that they had spent time discussing in detail the difficulties our sample had in dealing with the private sector—where private help could be obtained, how to negotiate over price and provision, how to establish the appropriate price with neighbours and friends who did odd jobs or who had been drawn into providing regular help. Similarly, doctors might say in passing, 'Oh you could get that privately but it will cost a bit', but seemed reluctant to get into any specific and helpful detail. As we have noted, our respondents tended to try to use our interviews with them as a way of exploring the difficulties they had encountered in becoming private care consumers. They would clearly have liked the interviewer to approve or comment on the solutions, in terms of source and price, that they had often struggled to reach; was this a good way to compensate a neighbour, had they been right to make such a request, would such a decision be disapproved of by the social workers or the day hospital?

The manner of delivery

The people in our sample found the manner of delivery of many of the services they began to use in their homes, or which it was suggested they should use, somewhat disturbing and uncomfortable. They were not sure what to expect, often disliked the way things were done and were uncertain to what extent their worries or reservations were legitimate.

One reason was that they had become accustomed to the manners of the national health service. Most of our sample of stroke sufferers had been inpatients in the stroke unit of the local hospital for many weeks. They had grown used to the slightly bossy but all-encompassing and reassuring care that entailed. To an extent they had become institutionalized. They were not used to exercising choice about the care they received. Also, because they were in hospital, they tended to attribute a degree of medical legitimacy to the mainly social and emotional care they received in the stroke unit.

Going home was looked forward to but deeply disturbing when it happened. When we interviewed our sample a week after they had arrived back home, many expressed a feeling of desertion. The care they then began to be offered was not delivered in the manner of the NHS hospital they were used to. The closest in style was the day-hospital some were attending. They felt comfortable there, though, after a few weeks most of them began to express concern about the fact that a day at the day hospital involved very little time actually getting treatment (such as physiotherapy) or seeing a doctor.

What most surprised people was the commercial manner of some of the community services they were introduced to. Some felt they had been given the 'hard sell' by local home help businesses put in touch with them by social services. Others found what the private suppliers offered rather limited: 'She offered shopping for food and that sort of thing. And I said well it was kind of her, but it didn't seem to me to be necessary put like that'. Others felt unwilling to trust the private sector: 'I'm sure you feel that with a government sponsored person there must be some integrity. They don't employ people without vetting them to some extent'. It took time for many of them to adjust to commercial relationships as ways of meeting needs that they had come to see as an area of public sector responsibility. In the end, however, most of our sample did make the necessary adjustments to a more commercial manner of delivery.

People had similar difficulties initially with voluntary sector provision, a source which after six months more were finding an essential part of their care. At the voluntary Stroke Association's speech therapy groups for example, the casualness about whether you came or not and who was in charge worried some; so did the unexpected mixture of paying for some things (lunch and transport) but not for others. These were not minor or marginal issues for people in our sample. Their strokes had made them feel vulnerable; the care they needed was fundamental to the quality of their lives, it was very personal and touched closely upon their sense of autonomy and identity.

Some care products have made the transition to being legitimate objects of independent consumerism. We came across frequent consideration of whether to buy a chair lift. This is product has apparently legitimated itself as a private purchase through many years of advertizing in home consumer magazines. It is also has many of the other characteristics that assist a care product to gain acceptance as a private purchase: it is fitted to the house and not the person and so does not require the hands-on contact that people believe should be the province of professionals; it can be used in private rather than in public (unlike an electric wheelchair for example), it is large, technical and contains manifest value (unlike some other aids for the disabled that look rather crude, home-made and poor value and unlike services such as physio- or speech-therapy where the value and skill involved is hard for people to grasp let alone agree to pay for).

The social environment of enjoyment

Most of the care consumed by our sample was consumed in their own homes, much of it in territory that had hitherto been private; in their bedrooms and their bathrooms. Here there were a whole series of complex adjustments to be made. Whether it was with spouse, or child, neighbour or professional home carer, in every case subtle and difficult adjustments to established social relationships were necessary.

('I feel like a baby,' said one distressed woman, and later her husband/carer echoed the sentiment: 'It's not the same. She's my wife but I have to do everything for her.' Another woman commented on the change involved in having to ask her fifteen-year-old nephew to help her in the toilet.)

Care comes into that class of goods that have the quality of having to be 'enjoyed' at the point of production—you can't take it home with you and consume it privately. This, together with the fact that without the care you may be quite stranded and helpless, means that the consumption of care can be a 'public' enactment of a dependent relationship. This is partly why professional rather than simple commercial suppliers are thought to be more appropriate in the provision of personal social services. It is also why many people prefer care to come from non-family sources (Wenger, 1984). The disability rights literature describes routes round this problem of dependent social relations in care (Morris, 1993). In this literature commercial relationships are actually seen as a solution rather than a problem because they permit control and autonomy by making disabled people the employers of their assistants. But that is an approach to consumption relations that takes time to learn and was not one that our newly dependent sample had had time to reach.

At first our stroke sufferers wished to avoid the cost of these adjustments and based a lot on their hopes of recovery and assumed much was temporary. Some did regain their full independence, but most had to make the difficult journey to the acceptance of new kinds of consumption in a place, their home, which in the past had been a haven of entirely voluntary and pleasant choices.

Different people, different journeys to care

In our interviews, the stroke survivors and their carers describe in great detail and in their own terms the journeys they made in the first six months after they left hospital. Some of these journeys ranged quite widely across the map of care, others did not move far at all. They had very varied starting points; some began on their own with little support while others were at the centre of households rich in caring resources. Similarly the journeys had varied end points; even when their needs appeared to an outsider to be relatively similar, people were dealing with them in quite different ways at the end of the six months.

Implicit in the new community care policy is that people's experience of exercising choice throughout their adult lives will be a resource in reaching solutions. They will be able to use their family and kinship network, their links with friends and neighbours, their experience of acting as consumers and shoppers in the market and their understanding of the public services in order to assert their needs and their preferences. Where they are uncertain, the implication is that it will be in connection with practical information about what is available and from where. They will then be able to use their accumulated skills as consumers in the market and as users of public services in order to make the care system work for them. In fact our research appears to show that our respondents' accumulated skills and understandings of the way things work operated as obstacles to rather than facilitated their new roles as consumers in the mixed economy of care.

What emerged from our interviews was confirmation that what people are prepared to buy or use is not a simple function of wants and an ability to pay. Advertisers have long been aware that the decision to make a purchase is determined by a very complex cocktail of habit, knowledge, values and perhaps most important of all, largely 'irrational' emotional responses. We found that there were similar cultural and emotional obstacles to effective participation in a care market. Even where people knew of services or products, needed them and could afford them, they still found the prospect of buying them uncomfortable or inappropriate in some way. These, what might be called loosely, cultural and psychological blocks to the full flowering of a care market, are complex and difficult to capture. People do not so much explain them; they are largely unaware of them, as demonstrated in their behaviour, in the choices they make and, often more importantly, in those they do not. A qualitative survey such as this is probably the only way to begin to tease out these behavioural phenomena but it remains an inexact process. What is offered below is an interpretation of what people told us they had done and not done.

'Habits of the Heart': the values that inform the search for social care

So far in this chapter we have treated the members of our sample as single group, suggesting that they all share, if in differing degrees of intensity, the same kinds of emotional distress and patterns of consumer behaviour. In this section we will try to incorporate into our account the considerable variety in outlook and expectations that also characterized our sample.

By the end of period they had, in each case, to some extent established care régimes that fitted with their expectations about what was right and possible, that were consonant with their preexisting scripts about how life is lived. They had also, in a variety of ways and to varying degrees, learnt and adapted to new ways of living their lives. As we hope we have shown, these were difficult lessons, or scripts, to learn and required, for some more than others, difficult adjustments. They had had to learn to do things that went 'against the grain' rather than with it.

How are we to characterize the varieties of 'script' according to which people reached decisions (or non-decisions) about how they would live with their new disabilities? We are not seeking to explicate their ideological commitments, such as support for freedom or justice, opposition to poverty or racial discrimination, but rather what sociologists have called 'norms' and 'intermediate values' which drive choice in their everyday lives. Here we would suggest the use of a term first used by Alexis de Tocqueville in his early 19th century study of America. He drew attention to what he termed the *mores* ('*moeurs*') of daily life. He characterized these as:

> Habits of the heart; notions, opinions and ideas that shape mental habits; the sum of moral and intellectual dispositions of people in society; not only ideas and opinions but habitual practices with respect to such things as religion, political participation and economic life. (Bellah *et al.*, 1988:37)

In a recent and very influential study of the culture and character of American life, a group of sociologists has built upon this idea to construct a typology of 'habits of the heart' (Bellah *et al.*, 1988). Here we attempt to use the same approach to capture the variety of behaviour in the care market amongst our sample.

Figure 1, 'Habits of the heart', describes the distinctions we wish to draw. It positions people along two axes. The horizontal axis describes the degree to which the stroke survivors and their carers expected their care to be provided from their own resources or from some kind of collective provision; it distinguishes an individualistic from a collectivist view of welfare. The

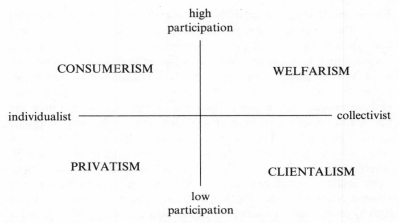

Figure 1 *Habits of the heart: modes of participation in the care market.*

vertical axis measures people's views of how active they would need to be in order to obtain services; it is a measure of participation. Thus, the diagram presents a model that distinguishes four types of disposition towards the provision of care at the beginning of our study; consumerism, welfarism, privatism and clientalism. What we are presenting are 'ideal types' of care consumers. Rarely were any of our sample solely of one category or another. The function of ideal types is to represent the theoretical range of individual examples. No particular individuals or households corresponded exactly to one or another of the categories; in fact most cases demonstrated elements of each. We shall characterize the qualities of each category by constructing cases that typify them but which are no more than composites of cases we found in our sample.

Consumerism

At its extreme this is a view that expects nothing from the state and intends to arrange care by actively buying it in the market or providing it out of household and family resources. There were relatively few examples of this view in our sample. Such people were not ignorant of public provision but were sceptical about whether it would suit them. They might doubt its quality but more often they found it inconvenient and time-consuming to use.

29

John Baldock and Clare Ungerson

For example they objected to the inflexibility of the day-hospital or, at the other extreme, the uncertainty about who would come and when in the case of public domiciliary services. Clearly this is a view which is easier to hold if one has enough money to pay for what one wants but it was not a position limited only to the better off in our sample. People in this category are used to the control and autonomy that being a customer brings and do not like the uncertainty about who is in charge that using voluntary or public services may bring. Thus we found some people with low incomes who would always prefer a private, for-payment arrangement where possible. For example one elderly couple, both of whom were disabled, appeared to have over the years established very reliable relations with a local taxi-driver, a local jobbing builder, a nearby grocer and a butcher (both of whom would deliver) and a number of neighbours who would do odd tasks for payment. For quite small amounts of money this couple appeared to be able to obtain very prompt and flexible attention which they could control. Their 'instincts' were always to use their own initiative. They did not wish to be indebted to anyone and they regarded the increasingly occasional visits of social workers or community nurses as almost purely social events. It must be added that these two people were immensely charming, even jolly; their 'business relationships' had a large non-commercial component.

Privatism

People who fell largely into this category did the least well in terms of support. Many sociologists have commented on the growth of what has been termed 'privatism' in British life (for a summary see Saunders, 1990:275–282). It is associated with owner occupation and thus, in retirement, quite often with moving to a new home in an unknown neighbourhood. Attention is 'devoted overwhelmingly to home and family based life rather than to sociability of a more widely-based kind' (Goldthorpe *et al.*, 1969:103). Privatism has also been closely associated with the growth of mass consumerism: 'Ordinary people now demand ever-increasing amounts of consumer goods which they place and use in their own homes. The result is that external and community facilities become marginal to their way of life (Saunders, 1990:277). This is a rather passive form of consumerism where most of the work is done by the producers and retailers and requires little initiative from consumers other than the act of purchase itself.

30

Such a privatized existence may work well when people are fit and the things they want are the products of mass consumerism. When they become ill and dependent and require products and services that are not available 'off the shelf' they have much more difficulty. In our sample these people had tended to refuse help when it was initially offered at the point of discharge. In some cases they very determinedly would not accept an assessment or any care management. They strongly valued their autonomy and would say things like 'we've never depended on other people. We've always looked after ourselves'. At home, as the months went by, we found them increasingly puzzled, embittered and, in some cases, frightened. Few of the skills and attitudes they had accumulated during their fit years seemed to serve them well now. What they needed was not advertised nor available in the ready way of the consumer goods they were used to buying. Neither were they accustomed to the ways of the voluntary and community-based support system. Some found their few unavoidable encounters with neighbours or voluntary help very difficult. For example, one carer-wife whose husband had always done the driving, found the process of negotiating her way round the local parish lift scheme quite excrutiating. She felt her privacy invaded, that she was having to beg and to justify her private choices. In seeking to take advantage of a private and market-based approach to home care, policy makers do not seem to have appreciated how impersonal and passive much of more conventional 'participation' in the market is.

Welfarism

This is a set of attitudes and an approach that is associated with such ideas as citizenship and welfare rights. These are people who believe in the welfare state and their right to use it. This implies the active pursuit of one's entitlements. People in this group tend to be educated, articulate and may well have worked in the public sector. The clearest example in our sample was a retired physiotherapist married to an ex-headmaster. She was impressively effective in obtaining the best of what was available in the public and voluntary sector. By the end of the six months she was attending the day-hospital three times weekly but only for so long as was required to receive the physiotherapy she wanted. She had used an NHS domiciliary dentist and an NHS chiropodist who also visited her at home. She attended the stroke club but had

31

refused an offer from a private domiciliary agency because she 'didn't like their money-making approach'. This stroke survivor's most outstanding, but very rare, characteristic was the way she had very explicitly participated in the assessment made by her case-manager. They had reached a clear agreement on what she needed, what she might need in the future and how she would go about contacting the social worker when necessary. However, much as this whole approach was in tune with a citizenship-based conception of welfare, it was equally obvious that if more than a very few people operated in this way the public sector would rapidly be overwhelmed.

Clientalism

This was a common approach amongst our elderly and often low-income sample. It is the 'traditional' way of using the welfare state; passive, accepting, patient and grateful. These people, unlike the privatists, did not refuse or question what was offered. They are accustomed to using what the welfare state offers, adjusting to its rigidities and accepting its omissions. It is a stance that works well where one's needs are high and manifestly so, such as where the stroke survivor was bed- or chair-bound. One does best if one does not get better; indeed more services will tend to appear the longer one is known to the services and less well one does. However, this approach also brings with it the classic and well-known disadvantages of public provision; it is inflexible and time-consuming. Those services one does receive (day-hospital, home care) are rigid in what they can provide and when.

At the same time the public provision leaves gaps. There were things it could not do; for example, put one to bed late. One wheelchair-bound stroke survivor preferred not to go to bed before about 11pm because otherwise her very frail husband would have to help her to the toilet during the night. Although a care assistant came each evening mainly to help the woman to bed, that is not in fact what happened. In other cases the classic inflexibility of public services was not a matter of timing but rather a bureaucratic inability to deal with a quite simple problem; for instance removing a carpet that made it impossible for an elderly woman to use her walking frame or, in another case, providing a much-promised bed-board that might have allowed the client to sleep and so greatly improve the quality of life of an elderly couple who still shared a double bed.

It was most commonly amongst those in our sample who most nearly fitted this category that we found the puzzling denial of having been assessed or even of having a care-manager where we now know one was very much involved. In its most extreme form, the passivity of this stance seems to hide from people even the organizing and planning that is being done for them. They find the ways of the welfare system and its staff unpredictable and do not attempt to understand or change them.

Conclusion

What has been misunderstood is that effective participation by needy people in the mixed economy of care requires that they change values and assumptions that are quite fundamental to how they have lived their daily lives hitherto and that these 'habits of the heart' are embedded in the social relationships and in the wider social institutions (the NHS) that have formed the context of peoples' lives. Policy makers, in designing the new community care, have tended to use frameworks which are largely incapable of grasping these social dimensions. Managerialist analysis is preoccupied which structures of incentives and lines of accountability (Griffiths, 1989). Economistic accounts (Audit Commission, 1992) focus on the efficiency of input mixes in obtaining tightly drawn outcomes. In neither case is there much awareness that the users of community care, or consumers as they are more often called these days, may not accept the product in the form that it is intended or even conceive of it in the same terms.

References

Audit Commission (1992), *The Community Care Revolution*, London: HMSO.

Baldock, J. and Evers, A., (1991) 'Citizenship and frail old people: changing patterns of provision in Europe', in N. Manning, ed., *Social Policy Review, 1990–1*, London: Longman.

Baldock, J. and Ungerson, C., (1993) 'Consumer perceptions of an emerging mixed economy of care' in A. Evers and I. Svetlik, eds, *Balancing Pluralism: new welfare mixes in care of the elderly*, Aldershot: Avebury.

Baldock, J. and Ungerson, C., (1994) 'A consumer view of the new community care: the homecare experiences of a sample of stroke survivors and their carers', *Care in Place*, Vol. 1, no. 2, pp. 85–97.

Baldock, J. and Ungerson, C., (1994) *Community Care and the Consumer: stroke victims and coping with dependency in the community*, York: Joseph Rowntree Foundation.

Bellah, R. *et al.* (1988) *Habits of the Heart: middle America observed*, London: Hutchison Education.

Busfield, J., (1990) 'Sectoral divisions in consumption: the case of medical care', *Sociology*, Vol. 24, no. 1, pp. 77–96.

Challis, D. and Davies, B. P., (1986) *Care Management in Community Care*, Aldershot: Gower.

Cm 849 (1989) *Caring for People: community care in the next decade and beyond*, London: HMSO.

Cross, G., (1993) *Time and Money: the making of consumer culture*, London and New York: Routledge.

Dieck, M., (1994) 'Reforming against the grain: longterm care in Germany' in R. Page and J. Baldock, eds, *Social Policy Review 6*, London: Social Policy Association.

Dunleavy, P., (1980) *Urban Political Analysis: the politics of collective consumption*, London: Macmillan.

Esping-Anderson, G., (1990) *The Three Worlds of Welfare Capitalism*, Oxford: Polity Press.

Flynn, R., (1992) *Structures of Control in Health Management*, London and New York: Routledge.

Goldthorpe, J. H., Lockwood, D., Bechofer, F. and Platt, J., (1969) *The Affluent Worker in the Class Structure*, Cambridge: Cambridge University Press.

Granovetter, M., (1985) 'Economic action and social structure: the problem of embeddedness', *American Journal of Sociology*, 91, pp. 481–510.

Griffiths, Sir Roy, (1988) *Community Care: agenda for action, a report to the Secretary of State for Social Services*, London: HMSO.

Lewis, J., Bernstock, P. and Bovell, V., (1995) 'The community care changes: unresolved tensions in policy and issues in implementation', *Journal of Social Policy*, Vol. 24, part 1, pp. 73–94.

Miller, D., (1987) *Material Culture and Mass Consumption*, Oxford: Basil Blackwell.

Morris, J., (1993) *Community Care or Independent Living*, York: Joseph Rowntree Foundation.

Newby, H., (1977) 'In the field: reflections on the study of Suffolk farm workers' in C. Bell and H. Newby, eds, *Doing Sociological Research*, London: Allen and Unwin.

Offe, C., (1987) 'Democracy against the welfare state: structural foundations of neo-conservative political opportunities', *Political Theory*, Vol. 5, no. 4, pp. 510–37.

Pahl, J., (1994) 'Like the job—but hate the organisation: social workers and managers in social services' in R. Page and J. Baldock, eds, *Social Policy Review 6*, London: Social Policy Association.

Saunders, P., (1984) 'Beyond housing classes: the sociological significance of private property rights in means of consumption', *International Journal of Urban and Regional Research*, no. 8, pp. 202–25.

Saunders, P., (1986) *Social Theory and the Urban Question*, 2nd edn. London: Hutchinson.

Saunders, P., (1990) *A Nation of Home Owners*, London: Unwin Hyman.

Taylor-Gooby, P. and Lawson, R., (1993) *Markets and Managers: new issues in the delivery of welfare*, Buckingham: Open University Press.

Warde, A., (1990) 'Introduction to the sociology of consumption', *Sociology*, Vol. 24 no. 1, pp. 1–4.

Wenger, G. C., (1984) *The Supportive Network: coping with old age*, London: Allen and Unwin.

35

Production, disbursement and consumption: the modes and modalities of goods and services

Keith Dowding and Patrick Dunleavy

Abstract

Two completely separate literatures have analysed government involvement in consumption; the collective consumption stream in urban
studies and neo-classical economics' account of public goods. Both
traditions have significantly converged in recent years, especially in
recognizing a differentiated spectrum of provision in place of previous
dichotomous categories. Collective consumption theories have poorly
explained consumption process trends, but captured many of the key
social and political causes of change. Public goods theories have
underpinned public policy shifts, and thus been congruent with the
direction of change, but poorly explained the social and political
dynamics involved. An integrated theory bridging both approaches
should better explain the relative autonomy of consumption processes.

More than a decade ago, Edmond Preteceille accurately observed
that:

> Traditional approaches to the study of collective facilities have
> always sought a criterion, or several criteria, which would
> enable them to make a clear distinction between the 'private'
> and the 'collective', and, having been unable to find one, have
> resigned themselves to the idea of more or less 'pure' 'collective
> goods'. Current terminology expresses this lack of agreement:
> collective goods, collective services, collective functions, market
> or non-market consumption, divisible or non-divisible entities'.
> (Preteceille and Terrail, 1985:127)

He went on to conclude that this search for a private/collective
dichotomy was doomed because: 'There is no single exclusive
form of the socialization of consumption, the collective/public

form—however vague and heterogenous one might take that "public" to be—but a variety of widely differing forms' (128). The suspicion that there is perhaps no discernible rationale to the scope or developments of 'public' provision in advanced industrial societies, has profound implications for two apparently separate literatures—first, the substantive explanation of 'socialized (collective) consumption' offered by neo-marxist and neo-Weberian accounts in urban sociology; and second the mainstream neo-classical economic approach to 'public' or 'collective goods'. Yet we argue here that the new eclecticism in forms of consumption has positive implications for both approaches, radically reducing the intellectual distance between them, and strongly suggesting a convergence on substantially the same theoretical objects and questions of concern. We briefly review the impact of some recent changes in consumption patterns before analysing each of the main literatures in turn.

The new eclecticism in contemporary consumption

Three connected developments over the last two decades have leant considerable force to the view that 'collective' and 'private' consumption are increasingly hard to distinguish—the strong and fairly consistent growth of all services; the continuing evolution of commodification processes; and the disaggregation of purchaser and provider roles within the public services sector consequent upon the spread of 'new public management' (NPM) practices.

Services growth has been an important influence on the economies of all advanced industrial societies. Unlike goods instantiated in physical products, services are notoriously difficult to define. Weber designated goods as 'non-human objects which are the potential source of utilities of whatever sort', and services as 'utilities derived from a human source, so far as this source consists in active conduct' (Weber, 1947:151). This residual form of definition still persists, as in *The Economist*'s dictum that services are 'anything sold in trade that could not be dropped on your foot' (quoted in Quinn, 1992:6).

The black box character of services has produced very important misconceptions amongst authors hailing a 'services revolution' and the coming of a 'post-industrial society' (Bell, 1974; Rostow, 1960). In fact the evidence suggests that services growth partly reflects a changing organizational division of labour in the production and marketing of *goods*, changes which disguise the long-run decline of previously important services (such as domestic service) and their replacement by consumer durables and 'do-it-yourself' equipment (Gershuny, 1978). Marxist accounts have argued plausibly that modern consumption frequently involves extended forms of disguised work, and that modern service arrangements usually substitute consumers' labour for producers' (for example, consumers fetch their own groceries, or serve their own petrol). Corporate management gurus are happy to admit, moreover, that self-service has repeatedly been the key to company growth (for instance, in fast food chains) (Quinn, 1992).

The sorry record of mis-diagnosis of services growth in the past has not stopped new generations of service enthusiasts talking in cornucopianist terms of 'an endless horizon' of economic development and the 'perpetual growth opportunities' in prospect, without reference to any difficulties from satiation, 'positionality', under-consumption and over-production crises, system limits (such as constant traffic/transit speeds in cities irrespective of the technologies employed), or environmental resource limits:

> 'The capacity of services to create value is limited only by the capacity of human imaginations to think up more important things to do with their time as intermediate customers or final customers—and the imaginations of others to think up better ways to serve their customers' health, financial, communications, transportation, entertainment, security, distribution, storage, lodging, gastronomic, education, design, information, comfort, cultural, environmental, public service and specialized knowledge needs'. (Quinn, 1992:436)

Behind the froth, there is some truth. Services focusing on new products (many of which, like financial futures and complex forms of asset holding, are really pseudo-products or even virtual-reality 'products') or new techniques and processes (in areas as diverse as enormously speeded-up financial trading, or cosmetic surgery) have important implications for society. Their cumulative impacts in restructuring advanced industrial economies have laid the basis for success in pioneering corporations. Old stereotypes of services as low-productivity, low investment, labour-intensive and non-export industries have been decisively challenged by innovations in service markets and the scale and pace of investment in service capital, especially information technology (Quinn, 1992:339–64).

Transformations in commodification processes lie at the heart of contemporary global change, which some critics see as the realization of a debased commercialized form of the Enlightenment ideal of a universal liberating civilization. In its place we have progressively established a kind of 'Macworld' capitalism, where product choices, whether for hamburgers or computers, are increasingly homogenized and standardized across all countries, and where systems and tastes are alike controlled and developed in a proprietary mode by large corporations—challenged only by the diverse (often repellent) forces of 'jihad', affirming local identities through struggle (Barber, 1991).

The scale of markets and competition has decisively escalated in some areas, screening out local solutions and corporations in favour of transnational companies, dominant brands and standardized solutions (Ritzer, 1993). Cultural barriers to product acceptance have crumbled even in areas where they once seemed insurmountable. In other cases increased preference-pooling has preserved or even enlarged the diversity of choices open to consumers in any one country, while at the same time routinizing the exotic so that it becomes familiar (often in subtly adapted forms). The result is that single-market choices expand, but the overall range or diversity of discrete choices across different countries' markets is reduced—another example of the flaws in claims of increasing choice (Dowding, 1992). Cross-national learning mechanisms also seem undeniably to have improved, with shortened diffusion of innovation times.

Paradoxically the bases of contemporary commodification processes, the foundations upon which are built huge corporate structures and personal fortunes, often seem surprisingly insubstantial. Large fast-food chains clearly embody new forms of Taylorist production, but in consumption terms they compete with numerous smaller, localized providers not just in terms of the intensive marketing of the few food lines they provide (Ritzer, 1993) but in terms of *how* customers are served. A key sales point is the speed and character of service, rather than the actual food products provided—whose quality is in most cases simply routine. Modern commodification processes focus increasingly on small aspects or 'characteristics' of goods (Lancaster, 1974) rather than goods themselves (considered as whole bundles or packages of multiple characteristics instantiated in a discrete physical product). These characteristics can be isolated and highlighted by technological management combined with intense marketing. Both

39

goods and services have increasingly been disaggregated into their component characteristics, and some features previously seen as unalterable or of minor importance have formed the focus of effort for corporations which now have global reach.

These private sector/civil society processes have had major implications for other areas of civil society and for the public sector—especially on the criteria we apply to government organizations in their treatment of citizens. A mass of existing research demonstrates that markets have tremendous significance in shaping social behaviour in general:

> The indirect effect of the market on the way we think is substantial. We assume without thought that goods are exchanged for precise money amounts and not given in the manner of exchange gift economies. We think of goods as individually and not collectively owned and that their usufruct pertains to their individual owners. We accept that we must earn our living in the labour market, that it is shameful to be dependent on kin, that the money in our pockets is exchangeable for commodities, and so forth. . . [W]hat we . . . think about often (but certainly not always) reflects what we have *learned* from the market. To a large extent the assumptions that we learn are, in fact, *causal theories* about ourselves and the institutions that affect our lives. (Lane, 1991:26)

Marketization trends in public services are likely to be particularly significant in breaking down historically strong beliefs about the separation of different 'spheres' of social life from each other, some areas appropriate to market allocations while in other areas of life society creates 'blocked exchanges' in order to insulate the allocation of goods from money or power influences (Walzer, 1985).

The strong drift in modern capitalism is for consumers to demand private-sector point-of-service standards in all their dealings with formal organizations, a standard with which government enterprises and public-service agencies find it very difficult to compete (Lane, 1983, 1986). Marketization of service characteristics gives these generalization and comparison effects an extra spiral, accentuating the push for the public services to compete increasingly in terms of point-of-service characteristics, something especially encouraged by New Right governments. At the same time the extent of personal interactions between government officials and citizens has been progressively reduced by cutbacks in government personnel and reliance on other means such as mail, telephone and, increasingly, electronic communications. The US federal government predicts that 85 per cent of its interactions with citizens will occur via electronic media by the year 2000, further fastening citizens' perceptions to impersonal indicators of government responsiveness and effectiveness (Margetts, 1995).

Disaggregating purchaser/provider roles in public services is often most visibly achieved by privatization. But it is much more widely under way through the breaking down of previously functionally integrated organizations into more fragmented patterns which has been characterized as a cross-national trend towards NPM (Dunleavy and Hood, 1994). Dunleavy (1994) argues that NPM focuses on three key changes—disaggregation, competition and incentivization, and that more than 31 different public service production innovations can be grouped together under these three headings. However it is achieved, disaggregation of purchaser/ provider roles (together with tagged consumer financing, increased performance indication, 'competition by comparison', quasi-markets etc) accentuates the focusing of public-service commodification processes onto characteristics. These changes partly reflect the unravelling of the Weberian rationalization process in a contemporary guise, where service quality and efficiency are measured and organized by what is easily quantifiable, given current capabilities in information technology, accounting practices and organizational forms. The changes partly reflect a strong ideological push by New Right governments pursuing their top-down, non-humanist version of NPM strategies. The current aim in Britain is to discover the core competencies of the state through residualization, contracting-out services until and unless the shoe pinches or a political backlash is triggered. Strategic non-core areas were once thought safe but no longer. The frenzy of public service restructuring and privatization in Britain and New Zealand, now spreading more widely in OECD countries, also reflects the continuing reverberations of the 'raging pandemic' of fear of bureaucracy in the 1980s (Kaufman, 1981). Once established, the enthusiasm for NPM has virtually all the characteristics of a 'policy boom' and a new ideology (Enteman, 1993). In many instances the organizational changes made may simply be symbolic, the adoption of rituals deemed legitimate by significant élites whether or not they have any effect (Meyer and Rowan, 1977). But whatever their origins, the cumulative impacts of NPM strategies on consumption processes have often been far-reaching.

The special characteristics of government may come to inhere less and less in physically observable or humanly populated organizations. 'Statehood' may become a minor feature of large-scale and centralized information systems, finance-raising programmes, budget-dissemination strategies, and rule-making procedures (Dunleavy, 1994; Margetts, 1995). The methods by which 'government' structures then interact with the parallel or rival systems of corporations, individuals, voluntary associations and other elements of civil society will also change radically, especially with the growth of electronically mediated communication.

The radical quality of the shifts in the private sector globally, and in the public sector in many (but not all) advanced industrial societies, seems to confirm the observation that: 'The socialization of consumption can no more be assimilated into any linear movement towards progress than can the socialization of production' (Preteceille and Terrail, 1985:127). These changes have had corrosive effects on the two main approaches to analysing public/private sector consumption boundaries, to which we now turn.

The socialized consumption approach

The collective consumption approach originated in the work of Castells and French neo-Marxist urban sociology in the mid to late 1970s. It was taken up, extended and de-Marxified in Britain by a range of writers operating in a basically Weberian framework. Yet despite their differences all the authors involved in this approach shared three basic concerns. The first was an effort to explain the location of the public/private, state intervention/civil society boundary in terms of the substantive development of social forces and the operations of economic growth processes. This boundary was not seen in formalistic terms (as it is in the neo-classical approach to collective goods), but instead as an important reflection both of social change and contestation between classes, class fractions or key interest groups.

The second shared concern was a conviction that the arena of consumption processes is inherently an analytically important and synthetically separable part of social life, whose dynamics can by no means be read off from the study of production processes and locations in the way that most Marxist and liberal sociology at that time assumed. This partial autonomy of consumption processes is dramatized and accentuated in the case of those consumption processes where the state intervenes to determine how much or what type of consumption occurs. This anti-productivist argument is that there is something common and unique about those areas where consumption is organized or subsidized by government—these areas stand out in comparison with the market society norm that 'what you pay is what you get':

'The increase in socialized consumption provisions has a potent effect in restructuring the bases of social inequalities. Access both to material and to symbolic "goods" is no longer a simple linear corollary of income. The linkage between production processes, "achievement", income and consumption which is central to neo-classical accounts of the welfare-maximizing operations of market systems is attenuated by the introduction of criteria related to "need", "merit", "entitlement" and other non-market criteria. Similarly political access and resources become more important in determining access to consumption, because of spatial variations in political control over local state resources'. (Dunleavy, 1986:138)

The third common concern was an attempt to decode and relate this uniqueness and shared character to the specific dynamics of urban development in advanced capitalism. Castells stressed collective consumption as a definable and legitimate object of study, and as a mode of countering the otherwise pervasive and insidious 'urban ideology', the physicalizing, environmentalizing, deterministic reduction of social behaviour to locational or built environment stimuli. Although roundly attacked by productivist authors, especially Marxists and quasi-Marxists, the legitimacy and importance of this argument has never been impugned. The disappointing, if not pathetic, history of subsequent efforts to identify an equivalent localist basis for urban studies neatly validates Castells's argument, leaving the urban ideology strongly entrenched and unchallenged.

None the less it is important to acknowledge that the collective consumption approach has not continued to develop in a unified way since the mid-1980s, and has shown some signs of overall loss of direction and vigour. If we look at the later output of this approach, that which succeeded its golden age in the late 1970s, it falls into four main groups which are partly divergent and fragmenting. Main themes have been; the close linkage of consumption to production; the role of collective consumption in economics development; the importance of sectoral conflicts in political realignments; and a more general effort to connect collective consumption into a more discrete sociology of consumption. We consider each in turn.

Linking consumption closely to production is a prominent theme of Preteceille and Terrail (1985). They stress the requirement for a definite approach to consumption processes as intrinsically important elements in the structure of capitalist social relations, but they adopt a purist Marxist line, arguing that class struggles and structuration must be the dominant influences upon consumption processes as well. Terrail (Chs. 1 and 2) is especially critical of bourgeois authors who affirm the independence of consumption processes from class ones, seeing in them a continuous struggle to affirm status differences, or a complex cumulation of signs and symbolism which relates scarcely at all to an underlying structure of social needs.

The role of collective consumption in economic development emerges as the dominant intellectual impetus behind a very detailed empirical study of the importance of public housing to the economic success of Hong Kong and Singapore (Castells, Coh and Kwok, 1990). Its conclusions emphatically keep faith with Castells' earlier work, albeit translated to a context of transition towards advanced capitalism, and the self-definition of two unusual states, almost city-states:

'Through its combined economic and social effects, public housing appears to be a major structural element in the models of development of both Hong Kong and Singapore . . . On average and over the whole period, their growth rates have been the highest in the world . . . The role of the state in intervening both in the general conditions of production and in the process of collective consumption, seems to be a fundamental element underlying some of the most successful processes of development in modern history . . . We observe a virtuous circle, linking provision of housing and public goods to the generation of resources through the competitiveness of a private sector partly subsidized by state policy. . . The connection between private production and collective consumption, between the urbanization process and the competitiveness of manufacturing, was only possible because of the deliberate action of the state'. (Castells *et al.*, 1990:330–1)

Many questions are left unanswered in this study and it is not consistent with some of Castells's other work on social movements, urbanization and growth processes in America, where collective consumption disappears into the background of explaining urban politics, and the focus on economic development was more on informatics and landtronics (Castells 1983, 1985). Is *The Shek Kip Mei Syndrome* therefore only a hangover from the collective consumption orthodoxy of the 1970s? Or is it instead an implicit repositioning of the role of collective consumption, now seen as a key element of the transition to modernization, but not an integral component of post-industrial change?

The political importance of sectoral conflicts is argued by Edgell and Duke (1991) and Dunleavy (1986). *Sectors* are defined as cross-class, economically and materially based differences between public and private employees, public and private consumption, and employment/own-account work versus state dependency. The sweep of the sectoral concept, and the challenge it poses to orthodox Marxist and Weberian class-based approaches, is still only dimly perceived by many sociologists. In Marshall's otherwise useful dictionary of sociology (1993), for example, production sectors and income sectors go unrecognized and only consumption sectors are acknowledged.

The scope of this now wide-ranging approach is captured by Edgell and Duke (1991) where the impact of the traumatic 1980s decade on two areas near Manchester is charted in great detail. Ironically, given the orientation of the collective consumption approach towards defining the urban field non-spatially and non-institutionally, this book is the best-focused work in a community studies tradition in Britain for more than two decades. A more synoptic picture can be gleaned from Dunleavy's (1986) figure linking 'socialized consumption' (an expanded form of the original collective consumption category) with production locations, professionalization and compulsory consumption, and with the political dynamics of welfare-state cutbacks (Figure 1).

The sectoral model's insistence on a simplifying public/private orientation to political life, an invasive and powerful ideological construct which has decisively called into question both the left/right political spectrum and associated class-based alignments, has chimed very well with the development of politics in a wide range of countries, especially the UK, the USA, Australia, New Zealand, Denmark and Sweden, and potentially in Germany and Italy. It has been less successful in countries where ethnicity and

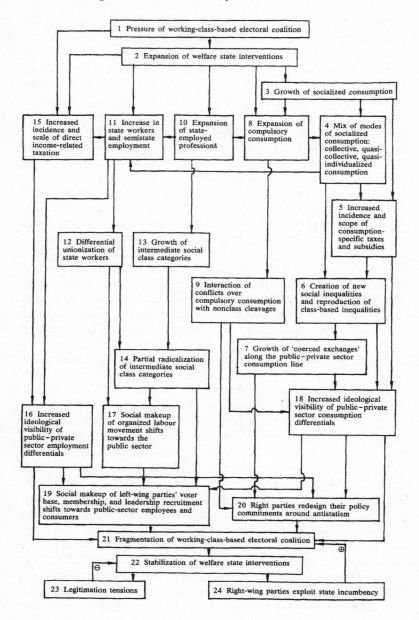

Figure 1 *Influences which make the expansion of the welfare state politically self-stabilizing.*

other cleavages predominate, although even here sectoral divisions often interact with ethnicity in important ways, as in Belgium. At the very least, sectoral conflicts have become part of a standard repertoire of cleavages which political scientists and sociologists can identify cross-nationally. Their importance seems unlikely to diminish in the future as the new public management agenda is played out across more OECD countries, and as the processes of social stigmatization and increasing social inequality combine with the continuous emergence of new goods and services, and new threats or risks triggering state intervention (such as AIDS, or drug-resistant versions of major diseases).

This strand's emphasis on the primacy of political direction has also begun to yield interesting connections with some post-modernist themes, especially the stress which Foucault placed upon the 'disciplinary gaze' in modern social formations. A recent study by Davina Cooper (1995) of the political dynamics and imperatives behind the UK state's (probably doomed) efforts to shore up compulsory religious worship in state schools demonstrates the extraordinarily close connection between party politics and collective consumption practices at a very detailed level. It also builds on the connection between socialized and compulsory consumption suggested in Figure 1, and their close inter-relationship with professionalism, a key Foucauldian concern.

Placing collective consumption within a more general sociology of consumption has been proposed in outline form by Saunders (1988) and partly filled in by essays collected by Otnes (1988). A variety of pathways is suggested. One is the study of the social psychology of consumption—recently masterfully surveyed in liberal vein by Lane (1991), while Lane (1983 and 1986) compares people's perceptions of their treatment in markets and by state agencies. A second pathway is to follow Bourdieu and Buadrillard in developing the study of consumption as social differentiation, perhaps as the primary means of class structures being defined and made apparent. Attention here focuses less on the residualization dynamics which concern sectoral theory, and more with the emergence of wants and needs at the top of social hierarchies. A more group-focused and pluralist picture of complex processes which link consumption with the inscription of identities is provided in post-modernist urban studies (eg Davies, 1990). Attention to the potential for 'dissatisfaction' is suggested as a key focus by Hirschman (1982), where it forms a key part of the argument for the cyclical process between private materialism

47

and a range of public affairs agendas (some of which, some of the time, might be consumption focused, of which in turn, in part—but only a part—may be socially progressive).

The problem here is the recurrent one in urban studies; the processes described cease to have any clear 'urban' referent, and become instead quite general analyses of social development or modern social life. Some of the themes are perfectly capable of specific urban instantiation—for example, the fragmentation of contemporary commodification processes to focus more and more on characteristics, and the cumulation of signs and symbols and identities in advanced industrial societies which separate 'needs' from actual consumption.

These divergences within the collective consumption approach undoubtedly reflect the impact of social and political changes in the last decade and a half. There is no clear boundary for 'collective' or socialized consumption in the post-privatization, NPM welfare state. And the sectoral approach's stress on overarching public/private polarities (albeit ideologically constituted in arbitrary forms) fits closely with changes in formal, party politics in advanced industrial countries. But it contrasts strongly with the post-modernist emphasis on multiple identities and constant variegation (variegation which matters greatly at the level of social movements and interest groups, but not in party competition). Nor has the collective consumption approach yet developed a satisfactory interface between its traditional 'amenity' and 'social needs' orientated approach and the growing importance of environmental politics and green ideologies (dismissed as sentimental bourgeois vaporizing in one chapter of Castells (1980)). None the less the approach still seems viable, lively, offering a coherent focus on as yet unsolved analytic problems, and still close to the central dynamics of political and social change.

The collective goods approach

The collective goods approach was initiated by Paul Samuelson as part of a wider 1950s effort to establish the competence of welfare economics and associated analytic contrivances (such as cost-benefit analysis) to handle non-market issues. Its initial purpose was to define a clear economic rationale for the empirically observable extended role of governments. But the concept has also been picked up and turned around by new right economists, in whose hands it becomes a weapon to declare illegitimate all forms of state intervention which do not neatly conform to the 'collective goods' model. The predicament is that few if any examples of 'pure' collective goods can be identified—even the famous lighthouse example is subject to multiple interpretations (Coase, 1974). This high level of contestation reflects increasingly appreciated problems in the under-specification of the 'collective goods' concept from the outset, and in the features on which it is supposedly based, so much so that some authors have called for the whole notion to be scrapped as impracticable and incapable of any adequate specification (Malkin and Wildavsky, 1991).

In fact the modality of the collective/private distinction has not been grasped. Whether 'a good' (used here to mean only something desired, which may physically be either a good or a service) may be fitted by liberal theorists into the collective-good or the private-good category depends upon a number of characteristics which belong to goods and services by virtue of various other characteristics of society. The current state of technology, the nature and degree of material equality, market conditions, and demand and supply, all affect the characteristics of goods and services. The characterization of goods and services as collective or private is not one of strict necessity (true in all possible worlds) but is place- and time-specific. A given good, 'correctly' identified as collective in one possible world, may be 'correctly' identified as private in a different possible world because of features which are not strictly characteristics of the good itself. The technical characteristics of goods are dependent upon current technology and other demand and supply conditions. In 1950 it was not technically feasible (or at least only prohibitively expensively so) to exclude any individual with a television from receiving a usable signal. Today, not only is it technically feasible, it is also relatively cheap.[1] Similarly, the economic feasibility of excluding individuals from using the facilities of a park depends upon the technical possibilities of monitoring entrants, average wage costs of employing park wardens, and the relative wealth of the local population. The latter is important since if there is no demand to pay the entrance fee determined by the costs of exclusion, excluding people is not worthwhile. Thus to discuss goods and services in a vacuum, as though the discussion holds for all places and times, or across all logically possible worlds is to ignore the very modalities which characterize the goods in question.[2] The technical characteristics of goods at any given moment in time are highly relevant to government intervention and regulation—indeed technical characteristics can often help to explain why government intervened. But arguments to the effect that the question is a technical rather than a normative one are a hangover from the logical positivism that still underlies much of economics. Liberal demands for government intervention may or may not be ethically grounded, but to hide normative desires for a certain type of society rather than another under the cloak of 'ethically neutral' technical characteristics is misleading and, moreover, open to empirical falsification once technology changes. Indeed much of the liberal retreat over government intervention since the late 1970s throughout the developed world has occurred since technological changes have enabled markets to provide goods and services that capitalists would once have shunned as unprofitable.

It is clear from the divergent uses of the collective goods approach that it does not denote any simple set of dichotomous concepts—collective versus private goods—as economics dictionaries and textbooks aver. Instead there are multiplicity of different concepts, with 'pure collective goods' as a small if not empty set. We demonstrate the range of concepts involved in two ways, first focusing on various theoretical features of goods and how they combine, and secondly considering more applied analyses.

Theoretical features associated with collective goods

These features are diverse and combine in many different possible ways, as Figure 2 shows. We review: (1) indivisibility, (2) jointness of supply, (3) degree of 'discreteness'; (4) non-excludability; and (5) 'crowdability'.[3] Strictly speaking only indivisibility, jointness of supply and non-excludability might be seen as 'defining' features of public goods, with crowdability and degree of discreteness as associated features. Explaining the diagram in strict sequential format is difficult, for many of the concepts hang together so intimately that each is explicable only in terms of the others. Readers should therefore persevere if terms are used before they are fully explained.

The logical relationship between the different characteristics of goods and services is shown in Figure 2 which is a comprehensive categorization of goods and services. Note the difference between implications (logical possibilities) and entailments (logical necessities). Confusion surrounding analysis of collective aspects of

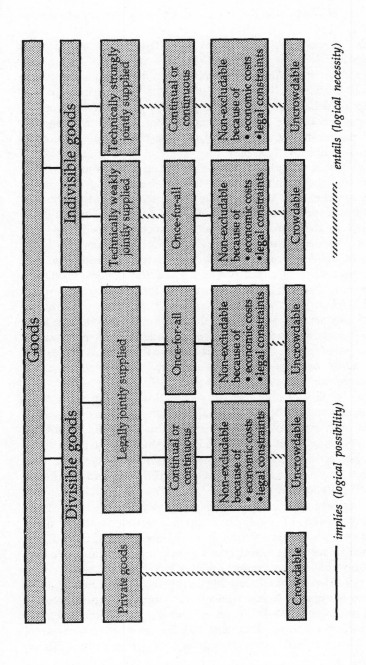

Figure 2 *The main characteristics of types of goods and services*

goods comes about because their respective modalities are misunderstood.

(1) *Indivisibility* is the condition that a good cannot be further sub-divided. However, all goods have a smallest unit which cannot be further subdivided except perhaps numeraire goods used in monetary exchange (Buchanan, 1968:51). A better way of distinguishing divisible from indivisible goods is that indivisible goods are one which can be *shared* but not *shared out*. We may share a house, but we share out the supply of houses. A house is indivisible, but it is not jointly supplied.[4]

Goods which are jointly supplied for legal reasons are divisible. By law the police should treat all crimes equally. Many police services are divisible. Yet they may refuse to help find the burglar of one house whilst investigating another robbery. The ability of the police to charge for specific services such as crowd control at public events demonstrates the divisibility of their services. Other aspects of policing are not divisible. Deterrence is often an indivisible externality of other services. Even the mafia's protection services can have this indivisible quality, though they may try to advertise whom they protect and whom they do not (Gambetta 1993). Many services which appear private have a collective good externality—as with fire services, refuse collection, or professional supervision of people taking antibiotics—which tends to lead to more efficient production through collective disbursement (that is, subsidization or financing).

The divisibility of police services also allows geographical divisibility where spatial boundaries (often with some haziness at the margins) may be drawn at will, some areas receiving a different level of policing from others. Studies which support more localized police services have tended to consider private rather than collective good (or externality) aspects (Ostrom and Whitaker, 1973, 1974; Parks and Ostrom, 1973, 1981).

(2) *Jointness of supply* was Samuelson's (1954, 1955, 1958) defining condition of a collective good. In his work and in many economics texts its description is positively enigmatic, and it is very hard to see what exactly jointness of supply means. We take it to imply that the consumption of a good by one person does not diminish the amount available to others (which actually seems closer to jointness of 'consumption' than supply—although to use such terminology would increase the risk of confusion with 'crowding'—see below). Jointness may be exhibited under one of two conditions; first, 'Samuelson jointness' where individuals do

not 'consume' any of the good they merely use it (Milleron, 1972:422–23; Schmid, 1978:78; Hart and Cowhey, 1977), and second, where the supply is infinite and each individual's consumption is finite. These latter are 'free goods' (Snidal, 1979:357) and may be ignored for they do not create supply problems.

Samuelson jointness may result from two conditions, singly or combined. First, it may be caused by the degree of indivisibility and the supply conditions (including current technology and relative labour costs) and demand conditions (specifically the relative wealth of the community). A Samuelson jointly supplied good may be weakly or strongly jointly supplied. It is *weakly jointly supplied* if the good *may* be used by others; it is *strongly jointly supplied* if it *must* be used by others. A public park may be an example of the first; air pollution of the second.[5]

(3) *Degree of discreteness* refers to the difference between 'lumpy' or 'step' goods which are supplied in discrete amounts, while non-step goods are supplied on a continual or continuous basis. However, non-step goods are often supplied at a particular level and so may take on 'lumpy' or discrete features. Hence a better way of making the distinction is between continuous or continual supply and 'once-and-for-all' supply (Kimber, 1981:181).

(4) *Non-excludability* is the condition which creates collective action problems and leads to inefficient market supply. It is technically impossible to exclude people from strongly jointly supplied goods, that is where it is not possible for individuals to choose use levels. Weakly jointly supplied goods are often non-excludable in practice for legal reasons, though it may also be economically infeasible to exclude (Olson, 1971).

(5) *Crowding* occurs where the ratio of individual benefits to total cost declines as the number of people who use the good increases. This condition entails that where goods have jointness two variable properties are distinguished, the physical quantities of the good being used or consumed and the number of people who actually use or consume each unit of the good. Total consumption of a crowdable good depends upon some function which relates the 'total physical quantity available' and 'the number of consumers per unit' (Snidal, 1979:535). Thus there are two marginal costs involved: a marginal cost of production (MC_{prod}) which is the cost of producing an additional unit of the good, and a marginal cost of extension (MC_{ext}) which is the cost of extending a given unit to an additional consumer. For a strongly jointly

supplied good $MC_{ext} = 0$, but for goods which are crowdable MC_{ext} may not be zero as the point of crowding is approached, because here more of the good must be provided (though not more 'units' for each person). For goods which do not become crowded extra provision does not provide more of the good but instead a qualitatively different good (Buchanan, 1968:55). Here MC_{prod} is the cost of providing a better good for all. (With pure private goods every unit produced entails one extra unit of potential consumption, so that the relevant cost of providing the good to an additional consumer is the cost of producing another unit, or $MC_{prod} = MC_{ext}$.)

Under the weak sense of jointness the good can become crowded. Here the good is worth $x_1 + x_2 + x_n = nx$ where n people each evaluate the good at x. If the fall in utility per person multiplied by the number of people is less than the marginal evaluation of the entrant then the total value of the good rises. Another person joining the group devalues the good by m, but there are now $n + 1$ people, so the total value of the good is $(x - m)(n + 1)$. To say that the good is now worth less in total is to say:

$$(n + 1)(x - m) < nx$$
$$nx - nm + x - m < nx$$
$$x < nm + m$$
$$x < m(n + 1)$$
$$m > x/n + 1$$

Under the strong sense of jointness where the good is uncrowdable, $m = 0$, but $x/n+1 > 0$. So the addition of one person must make the total value, as measured by the sum of all individual evaluations, go up.

All divisible goods can become crowded, except the special case of jointly supplied divisible goods with infinite supply but a finite consumption. Those indivisible goods where individuals may choose the amount of the good they use may become crowded, but if individuals cannot choose the amount they use then the good is uncrowdable. The second type is technically non-excludable, but all goods may be legally non-excludable.

The legal category is of paramount importance. New institutional economics recognizes that many of what are considered to be standard 'technical' results are underlain by the institutions which maintain property rights (Bromley, 1989; Eggertsson, 1990). A simple example may help here. We write of 'non-excludability', but of course anyone can be excluded from using any good; you can kill them. However, institutions guaranteeing the sanctity of life (which may be considered a form of property rights), raise the costs of this form of exclusion to the point at which it may be ignored in economic analysis. Whilst it is commonly argued that many markets can operate without being subsidized by the state, in practice markets also depend upon the institutions of the state. The whole notion of 'demand conditions' depends upon this same institutional feature of maintaining property rights.

Applied analyses of collective goods

These are relatively rare in economics, where the collective goods ideal type is tossed around with little if any empirical application. Authors typically remark insouciantly in the following vein: 'Now that we have a definition of public goods, it should quickly be admitted that there is probably no single real-world commodity that satisfies the strict definition of a pure public good' (Stevens, 1993:60). However, less theory-based and more public choice-influenced work translates the array of concepts set out above into more manageable categories with greater empirical specificity, as in Savas' (1987) pro-privatization evangelizing text, where a discussion of the 'Basic Characteristics of Goods and Services' produces the representation shown in ¬igure 3. The two-by-two table focuses on: first, whether goods are excludable or not (easy to deny access here taken by Savas to be equivalent to potentially privately produced, and hard to deny access meaning essentially non-marketable, so produced only by government if by anyone); and second whether goods are consumed by one household or person alone, or whether (once produced) they are consumed jointly by a wider group. Four categories of goods are identified—private goods, toll goods, pool goods, and public goods. Most liberal economists strongly believe that government's role should normatively be restricted to ensuring a supply of genuinely public goods (those which are non-excludable and group-consumed) and perhaps some forms of pool goods.

The joker in the pack is that although this underlying table *should* be decisive for the theoretical reasons discussed above, Savas cheerfully admits that in fact the primary reason why some goods are taken out of market provision and collectively provided

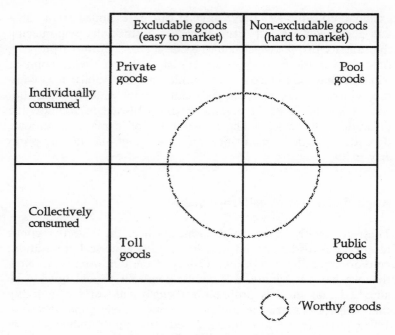

	Excludable goods (easy to market)	Non-excludable goods (hard to market)
Individually consumed	Private goods	Pool goods
Collectively consumed	Toll goods	Public goods

'Worthy' goods

Figure 3 *Savas' Typology of Goods.*

is simply that they are deemed 'worthy goods' by the society in question—that is, a majority of people in the society regard it as essential that these particular goods or services should be distributed either to everyone (as with compulsory education), or made available to those who could not otherwise provide for them. Worthy goods are those which are divisible but are legally jointly supplied for 'moral' or 'political' reasons. For many 'worthy' goods it is perfectly possible to exclude consumers but society has decided to subsidize or regulate these goods because of broader social goals. Neo-classical economists have traditionally neglected the substantive nature of goods, for to do more would involve them in searching for the origins of preferences. The assumption of fixed preferences has been firmly maintained to preserve economics as a set of perfectly generic models, and from a conviction that the division of labour between disciplines legitimates an arbitrary cut-off point. So mainstream economics has no theory to explain *which* goods or services succeed in reaching 'worthy' sta-

56

tus and which do not. This position is unsatisfactory. It reflects the fact that economists have generally focused on the production and the consumption of goods, while leaving on one side issues about paying for the good (disbursement) or the specification or 'organization' of the good. Most of economics ignores these middle elements since the discipline developed by studying simple markets where divisible goods are delivered on payment. In markets disbursement is automatically tied, one to one, with consumption. And the specification of goods is assumed to be controlled by consumers. So there is no need to analyse the central elements.

For modern western societies such as those in western Europe, worthy goods spread almost indiscriminately across Savas' four supposedly fundamental types of goods. In common with many new right authors, at root he sees this situation as explicable only in terms of the vagaries of the political process, an indication of the non-rational or perverse character of politics, and the myopia or misinformation which guides western public opinion to publicly provide for eminently 'private' goods (in terms of Figure 3, such as housing, health care or unemployment insurance). Yet there are no independently specified criteria of a worthy good except the fact that social demands maintain its provision in the public sector, so that Savas' apparent *deus ex machina* for bringing the collective goods approach into touch with reality is in fact no more than a redescription of phenomena which the approach confessedly cannot explain.

NPM policies, especially public utility privatizations and re-regulation, public service contractorization, and the use of 'government by other means' (Salaman and Lund, 1992) have compounded this confusion about 'worthy goods' by creating a strong separation between three different forms of governmental intervention in consumption processes:

- *subsidization* or disbursement, of services provided by private firms, third sector organizations, or state agencies. (Government subsidization is almost exclusively of services, but in addition many western governments subsidize individuals to acquire two specific kinds of goods commodities—private houses, and company cars);
- (external) *regulation* by formal legal codes or discretionary decisions enforced by state regulatory agencies of the conditions under which services (and a few goods) may be consumed. An especially notable feature of public utility

privatizations (such as gas, electricity and water supply) has been the need to re-regulate consumption;

- government *organization* of consumption processes in terms of planning and logistical provision, which usually means that the agencies involved do not operate legally-specified service standards (unlike external regulation) and rely solely or chiefly on bureaucratic supervision (so-called 'internal regulation') for implementation control.

These increasingly differentiated criteria overlap in multiple permutations, shown schematically in Figure 4 as three overlapping Venn diagram shapes spreading across Savas's supposedly foundational categories.

We leave it for interested readers to itemize all 32 possible categories included here, and to think through an appropriate example for each, but it may be helpful to run through the basic permutations in each of Savas's quadrants:

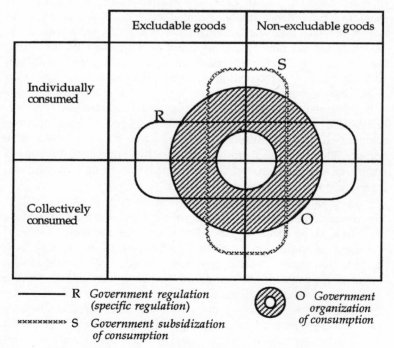

Figure 4 *An extended typology of goods and services.*

- services may be directly organized by government, within a legal regulatory framework and with extensive subsidization or even free provision. Acute hospital care in the UK National Health Service is a good example, although in Savas' terms it would be classified as both excludable and individually consumed;
- services and goods may be completely unregulated, untouched by government provision, and unsubsidized—in which case those which are excludable/individually consumed goods will usually be provided by the market, while those which require to be collectively consumed and are non-excludable will generally not be provided at all, as with clean street air in major UK cities;
- in between these poles there are services and goods subject singly to either regulation, or government organization, or subsidization; and others where the state intervenes in two ways, subsidizing and regulating (without directly organizing), or subsidizing and organizing (without legal regulation), or organizing and regulating (without paying subsidies).

Governments are not alone in deciding to pay for goods on behalf of their citizens. Some capitalist enterprises, such as insurance companies, also intervene between producers and consumers to disburse payments and regulate consumption levels. And here economists have examined extensively the problems of the moral hazard that may develop in the threefold relationship created (Arrow, 1963, 1968, 1974; Barr, 1987; Milgrom and Roberts, 1992). In a private health care market, for example, producers (doctors) have an incentive to provide the most expensive health care (which we will assume is the best), consumers an incentive to receive the most expensive health care (because it is the best and the cost to them is not dependent upon the level of their consumption), while only the insurance companies have an interest in reducing costs. Of course, in such cases, consumers do end up paying more, through higher insurance contributions, just as taxpayers end up paying more if government provides costly goods. But individual consumers do not have (much of) an incentive to reduce the costs of their own consumption. Insurance companies adopt strategies to transfer some of the costs to the consumer so as to avoid moral hazard. Typically patients pay the first $100 or so of treatment, and the insurance company will only reimburse 90 per cent of total costs above a certain figure, as the companies try to ensure that consumers make the marginal calculations which reveal their true preferences for the good.

In recent years 'new institutional economics', which focuses on transactions costs, complex property rights or complex principal/agent relationships (Williamson, 1985; Barzell, 1989; Moe, 1984), has influenced economics and public choice increasingly towards analysing a wide range of institutional 'governance' and insurance mechanisms which have close analogies in both the private and public sectors. Indeed one of the key impacts of NPM approaches has been to try and *create* inside the public sector sets of arrangements which are more directly modelled on private sector disbursement situations—as with the introduction of purchaser/provider distinctions, use of consumer-tagged financing, and efforts to induce greater activism amongst public service consumers. So again the collective goods approach seems vigorous despite the difficulties of theorization, operationalization and application which we have discussed here.

Conclusions: forcing convergence

It should be clear by now that in many ways the collective consumption (or perhaps more generally) 'socialized consumption' approach and the collective goods approach confront very similar problems in adapting to the changing pattern of production and consumption relations of the last fifteen years. There is no fixed boundary for government, its scope of action is still in flux. In many ways the collective goods approach has been quite successful in this or that specific application to explaining, predicting or rationalizing changes away from public organization/regulation or public subsidization and towards privatized solutions. But this apparent grip is dearly bought, for the collective goods approach (as the worthy goods category acknowledges) has no real explanation of why any but a tiny handful of these goods were ever publicly regulated, organized or subsidized in the first place, nor of why public regulation, organization or subsidization should persist in the 'post-reform' new public management world as extensively as it does.

By contrast the socialized consumption approach developed a substantive explanation of the scale and focus of government involvement in consumption, strongly coupling it with the dynamics of economic development. But it has not been very predictive

© The Editorial Board of The Sociological Review 1996

of social and governmental trends. Perhaps exceptions might be made here for the sectoral models, where polarization for party preference-shaping reasons is predicted (Dunleavy, 1991, ch. 4), or the social psychology variant evident in Saunders's later writings on the subject. But this exception is only partial, reflecting these authors' willingness to respond to emergent trends with plausible adaptations. It is by no means comparable with neo-classical economics' and new-right policy analysts' abilities to lay the groundwork for the dominant direction of change many years before their desired trends became immanent. So neither approach has fared all that well.

The question then raised for us is why the two approaches have remained as divorced and separate, as antagonistic and non-communicating, as they have. Behind the superficial similarities of 'collective consumption' and 'collective goods', there seems to us to lie a foundational similarity, and a convergence on quite similar complex categorizations. As we move into a world with dwindling collective consumption, we move also into a world where the 'public goods' category seems to be an overtly empty set, as a result of technological, economic and public service organizational changes. Instead we have a complex world where commodification and state intervention alike focus neither on whole 'goods' but on elusive and intangible characteristics, especially in the service sector (where government involvement is strongest).

The intellectual challenge seems clear—to push and pull the two approaches into some closer alignment, which might offer both a better explanation of where we are (and where we have been), and of where we are going; which might combine the substantive explanation of state intervention in consumption with the formal categorization which seems so applicable to this or that characteristic determining forms of government organization or privatization. Some more general theory of consumption might then emerge, re-energizing and justifying the concerns about the autonomy of consumption processes which haunt economics, public choice and urban sociology alike.

Notes

* During the time this paper was originally written, Keith Dowding was Hallsworth Fellow at Manchester University: he would like to thank the members of the Department of Government for making his stay so enjoyable.

1 Indeed so cheap, that any technologically minded person can illegally produce decoders, which is proving to be something of a problem for satellite TV companies who require the state to enforce their property rights over signals in much the same way that the state enforces licence fees.

2 Some commentators (for example Malkin and Wildavsky, 1991) do not seem to understand that excludability is an 'economic' rather than merely 'technological' phenomenon. The question is, is it economically *worthwhile* to exclude given current technology and demand conditions.

3 These terms are not universally acknowledged and not all authors give the same analysis of each term. Figure 2 and the associated discussion attempts to employ a wide-ranging set of terms to give a fairly comprehensive coverage of the possibilities.

4 Of course a four-room house may be sub-divided into four single-room dwellings and those rooms further sub-divided. But any good is divisible in that sense. A pair of trousers may be cut up and turned into dusting rags. Or sold and the money raised split up. But dusting rags are not a pair of trousers, and four single-room dwellings are not a four-room house.

5 'May' be an example because of the modalities of time and place, that is, current technology and demand conditions.

References

Arrow, K., (1963) 'Uncertainty and the welfare economics of medical care', *American Economic Review* 53, 941–73.

Arrow, K., (1968) 'The economics of moral hazard: further comment', *American Economic Review* 58, 154–8.

Arrow, K., (1974) 'Limited knowledge and economic analysis', *American Economic Review* 64, 1–10.

Barber, B., (1991) 'Democracy and globalization', (Plenary Lecture to the UK Political Studies Association Annual Conference, Lancaster University, 3–5 April).

Barr, N., (1987) *The economics of the welfare state*, London: Weidenfeld & Nicolson.

Barzell, Y., (1989) *Economic analysis of property rights*, Cambridge: Cambridge University Press.

Bell, D., (1974) *The coming of post-industrial society*, London: Heinemann.

Bromley, D. W., (1989) *Economic interests and institutions*, Oxford: Blackwell.

Buchanan, J. M., (1968) *The demand and supply of public goods*, Chicago: Rand McNally.

Castells, M., (1980) *City, class and power*, London: Macmillan.

Castells, M., (1983) *The City and the Grass Roots*, Berkeley: University of California Press.

Castells, M., (1985) *The Informational City*, Berkeley: University of California Press.

Castells, M., Coh, L. and Kwok, R.Y.-W., (1990) *The Shek Kipp Mei syndrome: Economic development and public housing in Hong Kong and Singapore*, London: Pion.

Coase, R. H., (1960) 'The problem of social cost', *Journal of Law and Economics* 3, 1–44.

Coase, R. H., (1974) 'The lighthouse in economics', *Journal of Law and Economics* 17, 357–76.

Cooper, D., (1995) 'Defiance and non-compliance: Religious education and the implementation problem', *Current Legal Problems 1995: Volume 48, Part 2: Collected Papers*, Oxford: Oxford University Press.

Davies, M., (1990) *City of quartz: Excavating the future of Los Angeles*, London: Verso.

Dowding, K., (1992) 'Choice: its increase and its value', *British Journal of Political Science* 22, 301–14.

Dowding, K., (1994) 'Rational mobilization', in P. Dunleavy and J. Stanyer (eds) *Contemporary political studies 1994* Vol. 2, Belfast: The Political Studies Association of the United Kingdom.

Dowding, K., (1995) *The civil service*, London: Routledge.

Dowding, K., John, P. and Biggs, S., (1994) 'Tiebout: a survey of the empirical literature', *Urban Studies* 31, 767–97.

Dunleavy, P., (1986b) 'The growth of sectoral cleavages and the stabilization of state expenditures', *Environment and Planning D: Society and Space* 4, 129–44.

Dunleavy, P., (1989a) 'The end of class politics?', in A. Cochrane and J. Anderson (eds) *Politics in transition: Restructuring Britain*. London: Sage.

Dunleavy, P., (1991) *Democracy, bureaucracy and public choice: Economic explanations in political science*, Hemel Hempstead: Harvester Wheatsheaf,

Dunleavy, P., (1993) 'The state', in R. Goodin and P. Pettit (eds) *Blackwell's companion to contemporary political philosophy*, Oxford: Blackwell.

Dunleavy, P., (1994) 'The globalization of public services production: Can government be "best in world"?', *Public Policy and Administration*, 9.ii, 36–65.

Dunleavy, P. and Hood, C., (1994) 'From old public administration to new public management', *Public Money and Management*, 9–16.

Dunleavy, P. and Margetts, H., (1995) 'The rational basis for belief in the democratic myth', in K. Dowding and D. King (eds) *Preferences, institutions and rational choice*, Oxford: Oxford University Press.

Edgell, S. and Duke, V., (1991) *A measure of Thatcherism: a sociology of Britain*, London: Harper Collins.

Eggertsson, T., (1990) *Economic behavior and institutions*, Cambridge: Cambridge University Press.

Enteman, W. F., (1993) *Managerialism: the emergence of a new ideology*, Madison: Wisconsin, University of Wisconsin Press.

Gambetta, Diego, (1993) *The Sicilian mafia: The business of protection*, Cambridge, Mass.: Harvard University Press.

Gershuny, J., (1978) *After industrial society? The emerging self-service economy*, London: Macmillan.

Gomez-Ibanez, J. A. and Meyer, J. R., (1993) *Going private: the international experience with transport privatization*, Washington DC: Brookings.

Goodin, R. E. and Wilenski, P., (1984) 'Beyond efficiency: the logical underpinnings of administrative principles', *Public Administration Review* 44, 512–17.

Hammer, M. and Champy, J., (1993) *Re-engineering the Corporation*, Australia: Allen and Unwin.

Hart, A. and Cowhey, P. F., (1977) 'Theories of collective goods reexamined', *Western Political Quarterly* 30, 351–62.

Heald, D., (1983) *Public expenditure: Its defence and reform*, London: Martin Robertson.

Hirschman, A. O., (1982) *Shifting involvements*, Oxford: Martin Robertson.

Kaufman, H., (1981) 'Fear of bureaucracy: a raging pandemic', *Public Administration Review* 41, 1–9.

Kimber, R., (1981) 'Collective action and the fallacy of the liberal fallacy', *World Politics* 33, 178–96.

Lancaster, K., (1974) *Introduction to modern microeconomics*, Chicago: Rand McNally.

Lane, R. E., (1983) 'Procedural goods in a democracy: how one is treated versus what one gets', *Social Justice Research* 2, 177–92.

Lane, R. E., (1986) 'Market justice, political justice', *American Political Science Review*, 80: 383–402.

Lane, R. E., (1991) *The market experience*, Cambridge; Cambridge University Press.

Lindblom, C., (1977) *Politics and markets: the world's political-economic systems*, New York: Basic.

Malkin, J. and Wildavsky, A., (1991) 'Why the traditional distinction between public and private goods should be abandoned', *Journal of Theoretical Politics* 3, 355–79.

Margetts, H., (1995) 'The automated state', *Public Policy and Administration*, 10.ii, 88–103.

Marshall, G., (1995) *Concise Dictionary of Sociology*, Oxford: Oxford University Press.

Meyer, J. W. and Rowan, B., (1977) 'Institutionalized organizations: formal structure as myth and ceremony', *American Journal of Sociology* 83, 440–63.

Milleron, J.-C., (1972) 'Theory of value with public goods: a survey article', *Journal of Economic Theory* 5, 419–77.

Olson, M. (1971), *The logic of collective action*, Cambridge, Mass.: Harvard University Press, 2nd edn.

Ostrom, E. and Whitacher, G. P. (1973) 'Does local community control of police make a difference? Some preliminary findings', *American Journal of Political Science* 17, 48–76.

Ostrom, E. and Whitacher, G. P., (1974) 'Community control and governmental responsiveness: the case of police in black neighbourhoods', in Rogers, D. and Hawley, W. (eds) *Improving the quality of urban management*, Beverly Hills: Sage. Urban Affairs Annual Reviews, volume 8.

Ostrom, V., Tiebout, C. M. and Warren, R., (1961) 'The organisation of government in metropolitan areas—a theoretical enquiry', *American Political Science Review* 55: 831–42.

Otnes, P., (1988) 'Housing consumption: collective systems service', in P. Otnes (ed.) *The sociology of consumption*, Oslo: Solum Verlag AS.

Parks, R. B. and Ostrom, E., (1973) 'Suburban police departments: too many and too small?' in L. H. Masotti and J. K. Hadden (eds) *The urbanization of the suburbs*, Beverly Hills: Sage. Urban Affairs Annual Reviews, volume 7.

Parks, R. B. and Ostrom, E., (1981) 'Complex models of urban service systems'. In T. N. Clark (ed.) *Urban policy analysis: directions for future research*, Beverly Hills, Sage.

Pollitt, C., (1992) 'Hospitals'. In R. Maidment and G. Thompson (eds) *Managing the United Kingdom*, London, Sage.

Preteceille, E. and Terrail, J. P. (1985) *Capitalism, consumption and needs*, Oxford: Blackwell.

Quinn, J. B., (1992) *Intelligent enterprise: a new paradigm for a new era*, New York: Free Press.

Ritzer, G., (1993) *The McDonaldization of society: An investigation into the changing character of contemporary social life*, Thousand Oaks, California: Pine Forge.

Rostow, W. W., (1960) *The stages of economic growth: a non-communist manifesto*, Cambridge: Cambridge University Press.

Salamon, L. and Lund, M., (1989) *Beyond Privatization: the tools of Government action*, Washington: Urban Institute.

Samuelson, P. A., (1954) 'The pure theory of public expenditure', *Review of Economics and Statistics* 36: 387–9.

Samuelson, P. A., (1955) 'Diagrammatic exposition of a theory of public expenditure', *Review of Economics and Statistics* 37, 360–6.

Samuelson, P. A., (1958) 'Aspects of public expenditures theories', *Review of Economics and Statistics* 40, 332–7.

Saunders, P., (1980) *Urban politics: a sociological interpretation*, London: Hutchinson.

Saunders, P., (1988) 'The Sociology of Consumption: a new research agenda', in P. Otnes (ed.) *The sociology of consumption*, Oslo: Solum Verlag AS.

Savas, E. S. (1987) *Privatization: the key to better government*, Chatham, NJ: Chatham House.

Schmid, A. A., (1978) *Property, power and public choice*, London: Praeger.

Snidal, D., (1979) 'Public goods, property rights, and political organizations', *International Studies Quarterly* 23, 522–66.

Stevens, J. B., (1993) *The economics of collective choice*, Oxford: Westview.

Tannahill, R., (1975) *Food in history*, St. Albans: Paladin.

Walzer, M., (1985) *Spheres of justice: a defence of pluralism and equality*, Oxford: Blackwell.

Weber, M., (1947) *The theory of social and economic organization*, Edinburgh: William Hodge. Translated by A. R. Henderson and T. Parsons.

Williamson, O., (1975) *Markets and hierarchies: Analysis and antitrust implications*, New York: Free Press.

Williamson, O., (1985) *The economic institutions of capitalism*, New York: Free Press.

Public nightmares and communitarian dreams: the crisis of the social in social welfare

John Clarke

Abstract

This chapter examines the break-up of the welfare state as a process that involved a crisis of representation. In particular, social democratic images of the public and their embodiment in the organizational regimes of welfare bureau-professionalism were dislocated by the New Right's attack on the welfare state. The chapter argues that the attempt to reinvent the public's relationship to social welfare through the couplet of managerialism and consumerism created an impoverished conception of the public realm. Communitarianism has been presented as a response to this impoverishment. However, both lessons from history and the contemporary inflections of community suggest that communitarianism needs to be seen as an attempt to resolve the 'crisis of the social' in social welfare in regressive directions.

This chapter explores some aspects of what has been termed the crisis of the welfare state. It examines the ways in which the break up of several overlaid settlements which supported the construction and expansion of the post-war welfare state in Britain have produced a profound dislocation of representations of the public. It deals with the institutionalization of such representations in the organizational regimes of state welfare and the implosive effects of the break up of the multiple settlements on these organizational regimes. The limits of the attempt to reconstruct these regimes around the couplet of managerialism and consumerism are explored and contrasted with the renewed enthusiasm for 'community' as a figure through which to re-imagine the public realm. The starting point for this analysis is an understanding that the 'welfare state' is itself a political representation not an organizational reality. The welfare functions and activities of the state were embodied in practice in a number of state agencies (departments or ministries) and in different tiers of the state, particularly in the distribution of responsibilities between the central and local state (Cochrane, 1993). As a consequence, attention is focused here on the conditions that supported the representation of the welfare state in the post-war period and the nature of the subsequent crisis as, in part, a crisis of representation.

The settlements of post-war social welfare

Social policy analysts have conventionally treated the development of the British welfare state after 1945 as resting on a double settlement—based in economic and political conditions. The economic settlement was to be found in a managed capitalist economy whose 'natural' oscillations were to be reduced if not removed (thus limiting the dislocatory social costs of economic crises) and whose continued growth would underpin the enlarged public spending necessary to fund the welfare state. This managed economy would be sustained by the bi-partisan political settlement (between Labour and Conservative parties) on the desirability of Keynesian macro-economic policy and (more or less) universalist welfare provision through mainly public institutions. Some have argued that this 'political economy' of welfare also involved a specific form of class compromise or settlement between organized capital and labour, organized around the maintenance of full (male) employment and a 'social wage' (in the form of decommodified benefits and services) provided in state welfare.

Such an analysis is rather skeletal in terms of what the 'social' nature of social welfare represented. An emerging body of work best, but not only, represented in the writings of Fiona Williams (1989; 1992; 1994) has traced what might be called the social settlement associated with the welfare state. Williams has argued that the social character of the welfare state has been articulated around the three dimensions of 'nation, family and work' (1989). This triangle organized formations of national identity ('race'); familial divisions of labour (gender) and work-welfare linkages (class) into an imaginary field of 'naturalized' social relations that constituted the British people as 'citizens'. Such citizens were implicitly 'white', with a racialized distinction between citizens and aliens in terms of access to the rights of social citizenship. They were gendered members of families which provided the

67

informal sub-structure of welfare and care and were (male) workers linked to the state through rights and duties (at least those of financial contribution through taxation and insurance). This triangle produced a unifying imagery of 'the people' which aligned them with the state in mutual defence against 'natural' disruptions to their individual and collective stability (birth, illness, death, etc.) and joined them in collective investment in their future (the promise of social improvement).

This non-antagonistic articulation of the people and the state drew on particular historical representations about class (the failures of old elites); the market (the social consequences of unregulated capitalism); the state (contrasting pre-1940s failures of governance with the enlarged role of the war-time state) within a nationalizing rhetoric of the 'spirit of the British race'. But the limitations and failures of pre-1940s national and local government in the field of social welfare also required a re-imagination of the state's relationship to the people. At the heart of this was a promise to replace old élites, patronage, partiality and the mixture of *laissez-faire*, charity and means-testing that had dominated earlier conceptions of social welfare in Britain. The formation of the 'welfare state' as a distinctive political representation—with its amalgam of Keynesianism and Beveridgean commitments—required an organizational form or regime of the state in which the people could see themselves represented. This points to the fourth settlement associated with the welfare state—the 'organizational' settlement (Clarke, 1995; Clarke and Newman, forthcoming).

The organizational construction of the British welfare state was shaped by a commitment to two principles of coordination: bureaucratic administration and professionalism (for a fuller discussion, see, *inter alia*, Newman and Clarke, 1994; Clarke, 1995 and Hoggett, 1994a). Bureaucratic administration reflected a longer history of reform, primarily in the Civil Service, which aimed at the exclusion of social and individual partiality and patronage through the development of institutionalized practices of rule bound administration. The model of administrative implementation of rules and regulations in the field of social welfare promised that the state could—and would—transcend narrow social interests in the service of the individual citizen. The citizen would be treated according to need as defined by the rules rather than being subject to extraneous social judgements of worth or desert.

Professionalism provided the second mode of coordination in state welfare—the application of specific sets of recognized expertise to dimensions of the 'social problem'. This, too, is not a specific invention of the 1940s. Most agencies of the welfare state drew on more or less established forms of professional knowledge and practice (medicine, teaching, social work, etc.) but nationalized and generalized them in the process. Like bureaucratic administration, though through a different rhetorical register, professionalism represented a commitment to the social neutrality—or impersonality—of the state's welfare activities. Professionalism guaranteed the application of expert knowledge in the service of individual and collective progress without partiality.

The welfare state developed around a dual logic of representation—on the one hand as knowledge (either of rules or specific expertise) in the service of the 'public interest' and on the other as the means of social progress or improvement. Between the late 1940s and the late 1970s, it is possible to see the welfare state as being sustained by a triple social 'neutrality'; first, the bi-partisan political settlement which proclaimed the welfare state (more or less grudgingly) as 'above' party political differences; second, bureaucratic administration which promised social impartiality; and third, professionalism which promised the application of valued knowledge in the service of the public. Much academic discussion of both bureaucracy and professionalism has been addressed to whether such claims are true in practice but what is important here is their 'representational' effect. They supported a particular ideological formation of the relationship between the state and the people in which they served as the organizationally institutionalized guarantors of the pursuit of the public good. 'Public service' was embodied in both the rhetoric and the structure of practices of bureaucracy and professionalism.

The crises of the welfare state

The crisis of the welfare state is conventionally located in the intersection of economics and politics. The underlying weakness of the British economy in the context of both global recession and capital restructuring exposed public spending, particularly on social welfare, to pressures towards retrenchment from the mid-1970s onwards. Such pressures were often articulated through a new economic calculus which treated public spending as a drain

69

on the competitive viability of individuals, corporations and nations. The 'death of Keynesianism'—at least in terms of government policy—marked a shift from a view of public spending as collective or social investment to an emphasis on public spending as unproductive cost. Although different interpretations of the mid-1970s crisis can be offered, the undoubted effect was to dislocate the economic settlement—the commitment to managed growth and full (male) employment—that had formed one the fragile foundations of the expanded welfare state. The place of social welfare in a settlement between labour and capital was equally disrupted, as both national and international capital began to renegotiate the conditions—and even availability—of employment.

The symbolic moment of a Labour government cutting back public spending marked the exhaustion of both British social democracy and the bi-partisan political consensus on the desirability of the welfare state. The dissolution of the forms of representational politics supporting the welfare state played a significant role in enabling the rise of the New Right in Britain to political power. The antipathy of the New Right to the welfare state has been extensively discussed by social policy analysts and others (eg, Loney, 1985; Johnson, 1990; Mishra, 1991). Such accounts capture the ways in which the economic and political 'settlements' associated with the Keynesian Welfare State came apart, but they are often less attentive to the dimensions of crisis in the 'social' and 'organizational' settlements of the welfare state. The social settlement, formed in the intersection of 'family, work and nation' had proved no more stable than its economic and political counterparts. The interplay of social changes—in the make-up of households, workers and the people—and new forms of social, cultural and political movements disturbed the social settlement profoundly.

The imaginary national-popular began to break apart under the strain of the tensions that it attempted to reconcile. In particular, what had been viewed as the 'non-social' dimensions of the composition of 'the people' became socialized by collective action. Where the conception of the nation attempted to cast 'race' out into the realms of biology (and colonial geography), the stumbling attempts at assimilation and multi-culturalism in British social policy pointed to the contradictions encapsulated in trying to sustain a racialized conception of citizenship in the context of a multi-ethnic populace. The 'British people' became an increasingly problematic and contested category. At the same time, the 'Family' emerged as something other than the happy coincidence of God and Nature. Both material shifts in the alignment of family and work and the rise of feminism exposed gendered divisions of labour and power where once only biology had been discerned. Similar challenges were developed in relation to disability and sexuality, again insisting on the *social* character of such identities and refusing the pathologizing statuses attributed by biological or psychological essentialism. In the process, the ideological assumptions of social policy were exposed, challenged and, at points, modified. These 'socializing' challenges also called into question the nature of the welfare state's neutrality as embodied in its bureau-professional organizational regimes (Newman and Williams, 1995).

Such challenges bore particularly on the 'front lines' of state welfare, even though they were also directed at the commanding heights of policy making. Welfare workers, by virtue of the fact that they carried the day-to-day contact between the people and the state, were prone to being captured or coopted by these challenges from the margins and their demands for greater equity or redress (Clarke, ed., 1993). Welfare professionalism as an ideological formation was also vulnerable to socializing definitions of 'social problems', and became one of the sites in which issues about 'discrimination', 'empowerment' and inequalities of different kinds were played out. The results were often limping and uneasy compromises ('matching' black clients with black workers; multi-culturalist policies; bureaucratized equal opportunities statements and so on). Nevertheless, the crisis of the social penetrated deeply into the organizational and occupational worlds of the 'old' welfare state.

Indeed, the crisis of all three external settlements—economic, political and social—imploded into the organizational settlement, making it a central site for the playing out of the multiple problems and conflicts. Enforcing a thoroughly racialized and patriarchal set of norms, embedded in legislation, regulations and professional practice, exposed the claims to neutrality of bureau-professional regimes. It also led to internal tensions as welfare organizations attempted to adapt to or compromise with such challenges—expressed in the search for and struggles over feminist, multi-cultural, anti-racist, anti-homophobic or non-discriminatory forms of welfare practice. Some of these tensions involved splits within the bureau-professional regime itself, as professionals were seen to be vulnerable to excessive 'client-centredness' and in need of tighter organizational regulation and control (see Johnson, 1973, on the characteristic tensions of 'mediating professions'). At the same time, as Hoggett (1994b:42–3) has argued, bureau-professional regimes also proved to be relatively weak institutional arrangements for the exercise of the fiscal discipline thought to be needed after 1976. Attempts to impose such discipline frequently provoked increasing lines of internal fracture, especially between administrators and professionals. I have argued elsewhere (Clarke, 1996) that, although the crisis of the welfare state was forged from a variety of 'organic' conditions in the political, economic and social settlements, it took the 'conjunctural' form of a crisis of the regime. The organizational forms of the state became the distinctive focus of both accounts of the crisis and attempts to create a new settlement—and in both processes the New Right played a central role.

The anti-statism of the New Right has been well documented and one of its central features has been its claim to speak 'for the people' against the overbearing power of the state—and the welfare state in particular. The welfare state has been framed within a number of narrative strands within New Right ideology.[1] The most obvious is the story of costs. Addressing a 'nation of tax-payers', the New Right told of the spiralling demands of taxation required to fund wasteful and inefficient public services. Such demands prevented individuals reaping the rewards of being enterprising and acted as a disincentive to even trying to be enterprising. A parallel story concerned the over generous benefits of welfare, creating 'perverse incentives' to idleness, fecklessness, over-breeding, familial decay and 'dependency'. These stories attempted to split the figure of the citizen into two figures: on the one hand, the tax-payer (the oppressed bearer of social 'obligations'); on the other, the indolent scrounger (the corrupt or corrupted recipient of social 'rights).[2] A third story concerned the relations between the responsible citizen and the state and was articulated around the idea of choice. Through this tale, the binary opposition between the state and the market was realized. The state was monopolistic, denying choice and decision-making to the consumer of welfare services. By contrast, the market was dynamic by virtue of being competitive and 'customer-centred'. The provider monopolies of public services needed, therefore, to be broken up and subjected to the 'real world' disciplines of the market place in order to empower the citizen-as-consumer.

In such narratives, the organizational regimes of the welfare state have—in personified forms—played starring roles, though as villains, of course. There were three evils embodied in the old regime of the welfare state: the politicians, the bureaucrats and the professionals. The politicians were prone to dogma and ideology, which got in the way of clear headed, rational analysis. In particular, they tended to hang on to outmoded beliefs that 'throwing public money at problems' was the way to solve them. Bureaucrats were organizational monopolists, concerned with empire building rather than public service. They hid behind 'petty rules and regulations' to obstruct individuals' needs and wishes. They were ossified and undynamic, committed to maintaining comfort rather than adapting to change. Finally, state welfare professionals were indicted as arrogant and over-bearing, insisting that their expertise meant that they 'knew best' and thereby exercising power over welfare 'consumers'. They were also likely to be the products of '1960s liberalism' or other reforming ideologies ('child-centred' educational philosophies or the 'ologies and isms' of social work) which distorted state welfare practice (Clarke, 1995). Such representations of the organizational regimes of state welfare personified the 'power bloc' which was ranged against the 'people' and which the New Right committed itself to dismantling.

Reconstructing the public realm: managerialism and consumerism

The period of Conservative government in Britain has seen extensive changes both to welfare policy and the organizational or institutional arrangements of social welfare. Processes of privatization, marketization and the construction of a more 'mixed economy of welfare', with the state taking a smaller role as a direct provider of welfare, have appeared as the dominant trends (see, for example, Johnson, 1990, Hill, 1993). However, to treat these as the policy forms taken by the New Right's commitment to 'rolling back the state' misreads them in important ways. As we have argued elsewhere (Clarke, Cochrane and McLaughlin, eds., 1994; Clarke and Newman, forthcoming), such shifts involve reworkings of the nature of state power rather than simply its diminution. State power is now being exercised through a variety of means: the greater centralization of financial control, objective-

John Clarke

setting and evaluation; and the dispersal of 'agency' through sub-contracting and delegated authority. In the process, agencies involved in providing social welfare have been subjected to new disciplining relationships which are both vertical, centralizing and decentralizing, and horizontal through quasi-markets and other forms of 'competitive' relationship (Clarke, forthcoming b).

Managerialism has provided one of the means of accomplishing this reconstruction, both ideologically and practically. Ideologically, managerialism is the representative of those 'good business practices' that the public sector needed to learn from the private sector: how to be dynamic, competitive, efficient and customer centred. Managerialism promises to overcome the problems and limitations of the 'old regime' of bureau-professionalism. In practice, it has provided the means of installing new disciplines in state welfare agencies. It has carried the demands of new pseudo-competitive environments, the shift to purchaser-provider or other contracting relationships, and a greater 'budgetary consciousness'. Managerialism has been used as the 'ideological cement' which holds together the new dispersed form of state welfare, both as a generalized ideological formation and as a set of specific discourses in the practice of intra- and inter-organisational coordination.

The discovery of managerialism by government predated the 'consumerist' turn in social welfare, in that its first incarnation placed a heavy emphasis on the capacity of management to produce cost efficiency (Pollitt, 1993). Since the late 1980s, managerialism and consumerism have appeared as a necessary couplet for the reconstruction of welfare services. The rise of consumerism drew on the New Right critiques of state welfare as insensitive, undynamic and unresponsive and embodied a reconceptualization of the public as an agglomeration of individuated consumers of welfare services. The old regime of state welfare was accused of flattening this diversity of individual needs through bureaucratic routines or professional arrogance. In this process, the New Right attempted to appropriate a diverse set of challenges to state welfare provision (from the left, anti-racist movements, feminists, disabled people's movements and so on) and articulated them around the simplifying axis of 'producer power versus consumer choice'.

One way of reading the complex shifts of centralization and decentralization associated with Conservative welfare reforms is to see them as subjecting the old interstitial institutions of social welfare (particularly in the local state) to a double representation of the public. On the one hand, centralizing tendencies were legitimated by reference to the Conservative party as the people's representatives against the state. On the other, decentralizing tendencies dispersed some forms of power beyond the old institutions to welfare consumers (and their representatives), establishing some types of power, rights and expectations at the 'periphery' of the welfare system. Examples of this process might include the enhanced role for 'parent governors' in the Local Management of Schools; the fund-holding General Practitioner 'proxy' purchasing role for health services; the right to individualized 'needs assessment' (though not necessarily services) in social care, and so on. This form of dispersal was pre-figured in the 'right to buy' legislation for tenants of public housing. At the same time, the old interstitital organizations were simultaneously supplanted (by quangos and agencies) and had their vestigial roles reformed around managerialist principles.

Consumerism in social welfare has been something less than a wholesale transfer of power and choice to welfare users, except perhaps for those who have the money to buy themselves out of public systems. Rather, it has been associated with destabilizing shifts of power within the new regime of social welfare. In particular, it has been the basis for challenging the professional control of 'needs'—a control that was legitimated by the role of expert knowledge in translating and defining lay experiences into the objects of intervention. Consumers or customers have emerged as the focus of organizational micro-politics, competed for by different attempts to 'represent their best interests' (see Walby and Greenwell, 1994). To some extent, this is carried in the different languages of 'demand', 'wants' and 'needs' through which divergent positions are articulated. But it is also present in the different sources and technologies of knowledge through which the 'user' is represented: 'professional experience' contends with 'customer surveys' for the prize of 'capturing the customer' (Clarke, forthcoming). The consumer/customer 'revolution' has, however, changed the balance of forces towards managerialism in these micro-politics in that the language and technologies of 'customer demand' and 'satisfaction' undercut the claims of professional knowledges and laid claim to a more 'transparent' knowledge of what the customer wants.

The result has been a complex and uneven reconfiguration of the 'public', organized around two potentially contradictory tendencies (which themselves are associated with neo-conservative and neo-liberal strands within the New Right). One tendency, allied more closely to neo-liberalism, has driven towards a conception of a 'nation of consumers', wishing to be 'empowered' to exercise choice as individuals. This tendency has been, at least formally, more dominant in welfare policy making. Rather than a wholesale shift to 'marketized' provision, welfare reform has involved a shift towards a rhetoric of 'needs led assessment' (for example, in health and social care) which links the individual consumer to purchaser-provider mechanisms for service provision. In combination with the shift to managerialized coordination of welfare systems, it produces the phenomenon described by Fiona Williams (1996) as 'managed diversity'. In these circumstances, however, the old professional repertoires of needs assessment (embodied in doctors or social workers, for example) have also been managerialized, particularly through the delegation of budgetary responsibilities. In the process, 'needs' and 'resources' have become increasingly compounded as the basis for decision-making at 'front line' sites.

This 'managed diversity' may well include a greater responsiveness to some dimensions of social diversity, both in national policy formulation (eg, the 1989 Children Act's attention to 'race, religion, language and culture') and in more localized sites such as local state anti-racist, anti-discriminatory or anti-poverty strategies. But a second tendency, linked to neo-conservatism, has driven towards an ever narrowing social conception of the 'British people' (the would-be silent majority embedded in 'traditional values') which, in welfare terms, has manifested itself in increasing hostility to 'aliens', 'lone mothers', the 'underclass' and the like. In particular, neo-conservative strands in the New Right have re-invented 'little England' as a cultural identity, which is both racially valorized ('white' versus other, subordinate and alien, cultures) and 'nationalized' (English not British, English not European and so on). At the same time, there has been a constant concern to 'revitalize' traditional morality and its basis in patriarchal familialism—both rhetorically and in the field of social policy. As a result, what counts as *legitimate diversity*—and how it is to be managed—are the continuing focus of different sorts of struggles within and outside the state. They are framed by national tendencies affecting both policy and resources. For example, attempts to expand the 'equal opportunities agenda' to anti-homophobic policies and practices have encountered the limits of legitimacy, whether in policies on local government spending, sex education in schools or on 'homosexuality' in the Armed Forces. Elsewhere, one might point to the tensions between anti-racist welfare policies and practices and the increasing use of welfare systems as a form of surveillance on 'citizenship', directed at rooting out 'illegal aliens' (Walker and Ahmad, 1994; Cohen, 1995).

The impoverishment of the public realm

Making sense of what has become of the 'public' in these processes involves seeing it as the point of reference of a range of dislocatory processes. One of these has certainly been the challenges 'from below' to the mono-cultural conception of citizenship on which the welfare state was founded (Williams, 1994; Newman and Williams, 1995). A second has been the twin strands of New Right populism, appropriating 'the people' to a fragmented and privatized consumerism and to a reinvented mono-culturalism. A third might be identified in the twists and turns of British social democracy since the mid-1970s—unsure about whom it might represent and about the political forms of that representation. Nevertheless, one central issue must be the transformation of the institutional forms through which the 'public interest' was represented and which provided (however imperfectly) points of attachment between the public and the state.

The New Right attack on the welfare state can be seen as involving a particularly sharp understanding of the 'politics of representation' in its hostility to the institutional forms in which social democratic representations the 'public' were materialized and sedimented. The long drawn out attempt to dissolve and replace those institutional sedimentations has had to traverse a complex and contradictory set of forces. Despite recurrent electoral success for the New Right project, other evidence points to the deep persistence of (at least) attitudinal support for the welfare state, especially but not exclusively the National Health Service (Jowell, Witherspoon and Brook, 1989). Particular focal points (such as the symbolism of nurses) have also made clear that widespread hostility to the abandonment of some social-democratic principles and practices exists. Conservative concerns to sustain electoral success have involved complex manoeuvring intended to offer relative protection to forms of welfare that have material significance for middle class constituencies. Finally, popular cultural forms have begun to show signs of hostility to the 'managerialized' form of state welfare, again most dramatically around the health service. Drama series, sitcoms and some popular journalism have effected a re-positioning of managerialism and professionalism—aligning professionalism with 'care' and managerialism with an obsession with 'costs'.[3]

Nevertheless, political representations of the relationship between the 'public' and the state have been dominated by neo-liberal conceptions of an individuated mass of consumers; in the public choice critiques of 'producer monopolies'; in the attacks on excessive 'red tape' and 'regulation'; in the Thatcher claim that 'there is no such thing as society', only individuals and their families, and in her efforts to make the claim come true. Reconstructions of the state form towards more minimalist direct provision of welfare and the 'dispersal' of welfare services to other agencies have been undertaken in the name of this conception of the 'public' (Clarke, forthcoming). These processes of dispersal have broken up the old institutional representations of a social democratic public; diminishing the role of elected local government; creating 'business units' in health and social care; promoting forms of quasi-market in housing, health and education and so on. Such dispersal aims not only to break up the old institutional attachments but also to create new forms of articulation between the citizen-as-consumer and the state. These new articulations centre on the consumer identity and the exercise of 'choice' in relation to a dispersed array of organizational agencies (rather than directly to the state itself).

These changes aimed to dislocate collectivist notions of the public and the public interest, including challenging the legitimacy of any claims (other than those of national government) to be able to speak for the people. Although 'distrust' of such claims was not the invention of the New Right, it has certainly woven them into compelling narratives about the suspect, or even venal, motives of those who make such claims. In their place, the 'legitimate' forms of representing the public are now dominated by the 'mandate' of the national government at the centre and the technologies of customer surveys at the periphery. In place of the presumptions of 'trust' associated with old public service ethics, the relationships of public service have been increasingly formalized through contractual mechanisms, monitoring and both financial and 'performance' audits (Harden, 1992; Power, 1994 and Walsh, 1995).

Paradoxically, this attempt to eviscerate the social democratic conception of the public and narrow it to a nation of consumers has had the effect of opening up representational 'spaces' in which increasing numbers of groups and agencies have attempted to lay claim to being able to speak for the 'public interest'. In the field of social welfare, public sector unions and professional associations have increasingly laid claim to being the real defenders of the public interest by being the protectors of services against both resource constraints and inappropriate organizational changes (for example, the British Medical Association; the Royal College of Nursing; Unison; teachers' unions, etc.). Groups of 'users' and 'victims' of the reorganized services have campaigned against the changes in the name of both their particular interests and a wider conception of the public realm. Often such campaigns are both defensive (of some principles of collective provision) and expansive (aiming to widen the definition of the public by rejecting 'deviant' or 'abnormalizing' statuses). Examples might include disability movements and gay and lesbian campaigns against legalized discrimination. There are other, equally expansive, conceptions of the public interest articulated by environmental campaigners (speaking in the name of future and non-nationalized publics).

It is at this point that the tensions between the neo-liberal and neo-conservative strands of the New Right begin to take on greater significance with an intensification of the oscillation between a nation of consumers and the 'traditional way of life'. Moral authoritarianism has become increasingly visible in pronouncements about the need to defend the 'culture' and 'values' of Britishness or, more accurately, Englishness (Davies, 1986). John Major's 'Back to Basics' campaign may have been an ill-fated venture but its failure should not disguise the widespread neo-conservative concern with rescuing and revitalizing tradition. This concern is most visibly directed at the 'relativism' and 'liberalism' of state provision, attacking educational progressivism' and multi-culturalism or welfare support for lone mothers. This tendency towards trying to reconstitute an imagined 'moral community' is one of the springboards for the contemporary interest in 'communitarianism'.

In search of society

The rediscovery of 'community' has emerged in the impoverishment of the public realm effected by New Right ideology and policy. Community addresses the sense of loss created by the claim that there is 'no such thing as society' and the consequent break-up of collectivist institutional arrangements. Communitarianism presents itself as an answer to the problems created by the failures of the old ('statist') left and the new ('marketizing') right, promising the prospect of a 'third way' between state and market. Community is presented as the force which has been neglected and will 'fill the gap' left by consumerist individualism, revitalizing a *civil* society that can be reduced to neither the nation state nor the market place. Communitarianism suggests that, while both state and market have a role to play, primary attachments, motivations and identities are formed and mobilized *elsewhere*.

Communitarianism has a multi-faceted appeal, drawing on diverse conceptions of community. The first is clearly a nostalgic sense of sturdy and self-reliant 'communities' whose imagery is predominantly drawn from a proletarian past; dense networks of solidaristic and (to some extent) self-regulating locales. This has been most explicitly articulated in the attempt to define a contemporary 'ethical socialism' in the work of Norman Dennis and A.H. Halsey (1988). This has increasingly come to focus on the relationship between the decline of the traditional family and a growing moral disorder (Dennis and Erdos, 1993; Dennis, 1993). In these arguments, the focus is on the capacity of such communities to impose and sustain moral regulation:

> The distinction between the deserving and undeserving poor persisted most strongly in that part of the population, the respectable working class, most adversely affected by (to use their 'punitive' and 'judgemental' language) idleness, fecklessness, slovenliness, brutality, squalor, disorder, insobriety, unreliability, debt, incompetence, dirt, destruction and violence. They were affected directly through, for example, the spread of mice and cockroaches, and the bad example set for their children. Indirectly they were affected through the damage to hard-wrought customs and sanctions when too many people flouted or evaded them. (Dennis and Erdos, 1993:15.)

The rediscovery of this form of community has also restored the Family to centre stage in discussions of moral formation and regulation (Campbell, 1996). In this vision, the family was the institutional form around which such moral regulation revolved and through which it was generationally reproduced:

80

It is not that I see a golden age of traditionalism. Material deprivation, and inequality between the classes and the sexes were integral to British society in the first half of the century. There was no utopia. There was cruelty, incest and child abuse, savage treatment of unmarried mothers, desertions and separations. Nevertheless the traditional family system was a coherent strategy for the ordering of relations in such a way as to equip children for their own eventual adult responsibilities. (Halsey, 1993: xi.)

Although these arguments appear under the sign of 'ethical socialism', their concerns are ones which are more widely shared in the search for the moral community. They are central to Etzioni's communitarian project. They recur in the imagery of 'civic capitalists' in David Green's (1993) pursuit of 'welfare without politics'. They are also the terrain extensively cultivated by Charles Murray in his delineation of the 'underclass'. Indeed, if one substituted Murray's 'respectable poor' for Dennis and Erdos' 'respectable working class', the celebration of moral judgementalism and regulation is the central thesis of Murray's 1984 master work *Losing Ground* which details the demoralizing impact of liberal welfare in the USA. Dennis and Erdos also exploit the same rhetorical contrast between firmly grounded 'common sense' (or what Murray calls 'the popular wisdom') and the bad ideas of the intelligentsia.

The second address of 'communitarianism' is to the field of community action or activism. Community here is identified as a localized mobilizing focus for collective action—in defence of local interests and institutions (schools, roads, hospitals, etc.) and, more expansively, in the creation of new collective resources through self-provisioning. Such conceptions also draw on the increasing visibility of the voluntary sector in shaping a welfare pluralism alongside state and market forms, assisting in welfare provision, sustaining a diversity of needs and playing a role in community regeneration. For example, Stoker and Young talk of 'third force organizations' which are 'independent and outside government like a pressure group' but also 'get involved in implementation and in carrying out projects' (1993:3).

The third form of address in communitarianism is also to an activist conception, but a less spatial one. Here, communities are affective or identity based rather than specified as bounded spatial entities, though they may overlap with places. So, for example, communities can be based in ethnicity or culture—'minority ethnic communities'—or in other forms of socialised identity—the 'gay and lesbian community' (Weeks, 1996). Such images are one way of registering the impact of collective action based on common identities or interests on the realm of the social during the past thirty years, though they may also be referenced as movements (as in 'new social movements') or lobbies (as in the 'disability lobby').

The celebration of such activism in communitarianism overlaps with some of the developments in and around local governance, for example in arguments about the spatial decentralization of public services ('community-based' facilities) and in the reinvention of local government as an 'enabler' rather than a provider (Burns *et al.*, 1994; Cochrane, 1994). The idea of enabling was rooted in New Right views about a minimalist role for local government which would create the conditions for others to engage in service provision (Brooke, 1989). However, as local government has experienced reductions in both its functions and resources, there have been attempts to create more expansive conceptions of 'enabling'. Some of these involve the development of a role in producing the 'strategic vision' that will guide the development of communities, often to be implemented through working in 'partnership' (Mackintosh, 1992). A still more expansive conception has been the community empowerment view developed in the work of John Stewart and others (eg, Stewart, 1989; Ranson and Stewart, 1994). These arguments start from the limitations of both traditional and consumerist models of local governance and aim at constructing participatory democracies alongside representative ones in order to shape both local services and the use of local resources. The resonance of the idea of community for those concerned with questions of local governance is not surprising, given that it draws on a long history of conceptualizing local government as serving spatially particularized publics—the 'local community'. This conception has been central to academic, political and professional views of public services organized and provided at a local level—expressed in organizational or departmental forms and focal concerns such as community services, community safety or Community Health Councils.

Communitarianism both draws on and addresses these varieties of 'community', imagining a civil society populated by a citizenry which is active but particularized (spatially or culturally). Part of the appeal of community as a political idea is the diversity of reference points on which it can draw (Mayo, 1994). Despite this diversity, the dominant tendency appears to be one which stresses the moral agenda of social reconstruction (Campbell, 1996). This has three critical dimensions; first, the centrality of the patriarchal family form to the development of communities; second, the emphasis on duty and responsibility which (supposedly) characterizes well-regulated communities; and thirdly, the issue of how leadership is to be exercised. Each of these, as various commentators have suggested, opens up the possibilities of alliances between communitarianism and the attempted moral closures of neo-conservatism. The crisis of the patriarchal family form finds both communitarians and neo-conservatives identifying similar causal processes; the loss of the male bread winner role; inappropriate encouragement by the state of deviant household formations (whether lone mothers or the 'pretend families' of gay and lesbian households) and so on. The questions of duty and responsibility are intended to redress the over-emphasis on 'rights' associated with both the old left and the new right; the former producing state dependency; the latter pursuing a consumerised individualism. The third—the issue of moral leadership—invokes the demand that those who should 'know better' (typically the professional middle classes) become engaged in processes of moral tutelage, rather than continue their flirtation with moral relativism.

The second time as farce?

Communitarianism presents itself as an idea whose time has come. Its attraction owes much to the way in which New Right policies, especially in their neo-liberal forms, have systematically denigrated ideas of the public realm and undermined their institutional representations. However, a more historical perspective would suggest that it is, in fact, an idea whose time has come again and again—not always with happy results. We have been here before and ought to know the issues that are repressed in these visions of communities (see, for example, Pahl, 1995). However, given the contemporary predisposition to historical amnesia and the obsession with the New, it is perhaps worth restating some of the more mundane observations about 'community' as a motif in political and social action.

Perhaps the most important 'history lesson' ought to be the ill-fated Community Development Project of the 1970s which demonstrated both the possibilities and limits of community action. The limits reflected the unequal relationship between localized power and the wider structures of both capital and the state. Even if not all formations of capital are becoming 'globalized', there are clearly increasing distances between critical centres of decision-making and those of local communities by comparison with the already depressing gaps visible in the 1970s. Indeed, one might suggest that in such contexts of globalizing networks of capital and continued public spending restraint, community activism now finds itself identified as a 'value added' process. What communities can do is to produce resources to fill gaps in collective provision and enhance the stock of 'social capital'. However, the dominant conceptions of social capital are those features that enhance the 'quality of life' and thereby make communities attractive to inward investment and neo-corporatist partnerships (Cochrane, 1993, 1994).

The celebration of 'traditional communities' needs to be tempered by a recognition of their tendency to be resolutely mono-cultural, both in terms of their ethnic composition and in terms of their limited tolerance for other forms of social diversity. Their moral orders were often highly repressive, exclusionary, hierarchical and intensely regulatory of the patterns of public and private social interactions. Mutual solidarity also went hand in hand with intense hostility to those defined as 'beyond the pale' (whether by ethnicity, sexuality or disability). Equally, such communities were often bound up by webs of patriarchal relations with strict demarcations of male and female 'spheres'. Such tendencies are, of course, not exactly bad news to the revisionists, since their imaginings of a restored moral order hinge around precisely such simplifying conceptions of morality.

Some signs of what such a revival of community might mean are visible in recent efforts to equate community with cultural tradition. In both Britain and the USA there have been examples of attempts to break 'multi-cultural' schooling by the invocation of a white, majoritarian 'cultural tradition' to which subsequent generations have a right to access. This appropriates the discourse of 'culture' from multi-culturalism as a legitimation for forms of resegregation based on essentialist notions of cultural tradition and identity. Paradoxically, this comes at the same time as black scholars and activists are rejecting such cultural essentialism as a shaky foundation for black politics and identity formation (Gilroy, 1987, 1993; Lewis, forthcoming). In such contexts, even limited forms of 'community empowerment' may have some dele-terious effects. For example, school exclusions by 'empowered' parent governors or the practical definitions of what 'community safety' means in local forms of policing may be the bearers of socially and culturally regressive formations of what community embodies.

Communitarianism is characterized by both a celebration of 'activism' and a concern to establish the limits of what good citi-zens do. In part, this is driven by the centrality of morality or ethics to the conception of community that is articulated here. The active citizenry busies itself with good works: a volunteer labour force supplementing policing, health and social care provi-sion, or the maintenance of housing and other public facilities. There are two problems with this vision. One concerns the elastic-ity of supply of this labour force. Rhetorically, it may be pre-sented as an untapped and potentially bottomless well. Practically, it is constrained by the increasing demand for its time and energy. Such limits are visible in the growing literature on 'primary caring' in the health and social care fields where the pressures of multi-generational caring, allied to either paid employment or limited state support for carers, places an increas-ing stress on those who feel 'responsible' (Ungerson, 1993).

'Being responsible' also signals a further problem about the activism of communities, since not all forms of being active are seen as desirable. Breaches of the criminal law (trespass, unlawful assembly, etc.) may define some of the parameters of 'responsibil-ity' since not all activism is law-abiding. Equally, those forms of activism whose purpose is to insist that *others* do something threaten the self-provisioning and self-regulating logic of commu-nitarianism. Much recent activism has been directed less at self-sufficiency than at demanding that other agencies (the state in particular) take responsibility for redressing social inequalities and social problems. Demands for social reparation or the removal of discriminatory or disabling institutional arrangements fit less comfortably into the communitarian imagination, even though they may be potent source of its legitimation.

The final and most recent history lesson can be derived from the experiences associated with implementing 'community care' in Britain, following the 1990 NHS and Community Care Act. Community care draws on something of the same diversity of sources of support that is visible for communitarianism. It too has drawn on the attractions of de-institutionalization, self-sufficiency, independence, being responsive to individual and communal wishes and the promises of being enabled and empowered. Its introduction has been dominated by the central imposition of tight budgetary constraints in the expectation that the combination of competition and informal care will 'take up the slack' (Langan and Clarke, 1994). The problems of resource management have driven the boundary disputes between the NHS and local authorities about who 'owns' some types of care needs, particularly those of the elderly (Vickridge, 1995). Informal care has fallen as a burden of obligation on families, and particularly on women within families (Brown and Smith, 1993). Their labour has been increasingly planned into the 'packages of care' assembled by social services departments as a key element in promoting non-institutional forms of care. At the same time, formal recognition of 'diversity' has tended to be under-supported in practice and limited in its effects—often throwing 'responsibility' onto minority ethnic communities without resources (Walker and Ahmad, 1994).

The revival of interest in community as a focus of political ideology and action can be located in the impoverishment of the public realm effected by New Right ideas and policies. It is sustained by the diverse forms and reference points on which communitarian ideas can draw. But this revival of community should not be de-historicized. There are historical lessons about the limitations, contradictions and tendencies of community that suggest where new formulations might lead, although whether to 'farce' or to further 'tragedies' remains to be seen.

Such history lessons indicate the elementary forms of what might emerge from communitarian dreams. The dispersal of state power through a range of delegated agencies organized around the contradictory principles of partnership and competition and sharply constrained by the principles of public spending control creates a new network of nodal points of state power within civil society (Clarke, forthcoming, b). Alongside the dispersal of power is the dispersal of responsibility. This, of course, is one of the objectives of 'entrepreneurial' governance (Osborne and Gaebler, 1992) in which everyone is encouraged to define 'what business they are in' and how they contribute to its success. The process of dispersal and the identification of each organization's 'core business' is associated with the reduction of the state's role in the direct provision of services.

At the level of state institutions, the emphasis is now on identifying and managing the 'strategic issues'—concentrating attention on what Osborne and Gaebler call 'steering not rowing'. Images of the community are essential to such processes because someone still has to do the rowing. A 'volunteer' labour force offers the possibility of a resource which fills the gaps left by limited public provision. However, if we take the 'steering not rowing' metaphor seriously, do we end up with a community of galley slaves? While communitarianism offers itself as a way of reinventing the public realm, its central assumptions point towards the formation of 'managed communities'—encouraged, or even required, to row in the directions identified by the 'steering' strategists. Communities in practice are likely to turn out to be both more and less than this vision contains. They are likely to be more in the sense that forms of collective action may either challenge the 'direction' or even insist that a bit more 'rowing' is needed from public sources. They are likely to be less in the sense that neither local areas nor identity groupings are the source of an infinitely elastic supply of labour ready to do their duty for the 'public good'.

Although communitarianism addresses a wide variety of potential sources of support for its way of filling the impoverished conceptions of the public created by the managerialist-consumerist couplet, there are some problems attaching to how 'community' becomes specified in more detail. 'Community' is a polysemic representation, deployed in a variety of different meanings and uses and therefore contested in the politics of representation around how the social and the public are conceived. Nevertheless, identifying such diversity is only part of understanding the playing out of a conjunctural politics of representation. Attention also needs to be given to what uses are emerging as the dominant inflections and articulations—and the sorts of closures of meaning that they attempt to impose. The signs are that communitarianism moves to increasingly 'regressive' closures of how communities and their empowerment are to be understood. Its centring on methodological familialism has the effect of repressing tensions and conflicts around gender and sexuality. Its concern with moral order attempts to create a closure which denies the significance of cultural difference and diversity. It represses the consequences of trying to define 'morality' in mono-cultural forms. Its concern with 'responsibility' attempts to both abrogate it (at the level of the state) and enforce it with its attendant costs on those below. Communitarianism may represent itself as a 'kinder, gentler'

John Clarke

managerialism (in opposition to is individualist and consumerist incarnation) capable of revivifying civil society but it threatens to resolve the 'crisis of the social' in social welfare in regressive directions.

Acknowledgements

This chapter is part of a programme of work developing the arguments about managerialism and social welfare advanced in Clarke, Cochrane and McLaughlin (eds) *Managing Social Policy* (1994) towards a book being written with Janet Newman. Its development owes much to conversations with Allan Cochrane, Gordon Hughes, Gail Lewis, Eugene McLaughlin and Janet Newman.

Notes

1 By and large, ideologues of the New Right have not been converts to post-modernism and demonstrate a charmingly nostalgic belief in the power of narrative. This is true at both the level of meta-narratives (for example, about the state) and in their use of micro-narratives and 'moral tales' through which the deadening or corrupting influence of the state can be exemplified. Charles Murray's work on welfare policy (1984; 1990) reveals both varieties at work.
2 The 'scrounger' has appeared in a variety of guises: the work-shy, the lone mother, the underclass, etc. This figure is one of the places where the neo-liberal strand of New Right ideology (with its concern for the economic calculus of incentives) meets the neo-conservative strand (with its concern for 'de-moralization'). The 'splitting' of the citizen is discussed at more length in Clarke, forthcoming a.
3 I am thinking of series such as 'Cardiac arrest' and 'Health and Efficiency' on TV which have articulated of populist critique of the inappropriateness of managerial governance for the NHS. More widely, there has been an interesting set of crises about whether 'costs' or 'needs' determine the availability of care and treatment and a complex set of images about whether welfare services are being run by 'managers' or 'bureaucrats'.

References

Brooke, R., (1989) *Managing the enabling authority*, London: Longman.
Brown, H. and Smith, H., (1993) 'Women caring for people: the mismatch between rhetoric and women's reality?' *Policy and Politics*, Vol. 23(3), pp. 185–93.
Burns, D., Hambleton, R., and Hoggett, P., (1994) *The Politics of Decentralisation: Revitalising Local Democracy*, London and Basingstoke: Macmillan.

© The Editorial Board of The Sociological Review 1996

Campbell, B., (1996) 'Old Fogeys and Angry Young Men: A critique of communitarianism.' *Soundings*, Issue 1 (Autumn), pp. 47–64.

Clarke, J., ed. (1993) *A Crisis in Care?* London: Sage.

Clarke, J., (1995) 'Doing the Right Thing? Managerialism and Social Welfare.' Paper presented to ESRC seminar 'Professionals in late Modernity', Imperial College, June.

Clarke, J., (1996) 'After Social Work?' in N. Parton, ed., *Social Change, Social Theory and Social Work*, London: Routledge.

Clarke, J., (forthcoming, a) 'Capturing the Customer: consumerism and social welfare.' *Self and Agency*, Vol. 1.

Clarke, J., (forthcoming, b) 'The problem of the state after the welfare state', in E. Brunsdon and M. May (eds) *Social Policy Review 8*, Canterbury: Social Policy Association.

Clarke, J., Cochrane, A. and McLaughlin, E., (eds) (1994) *Managing Social Policy*, London: Sage.

Clarke, J. and Newman, J., (forthcoming) *The Managerial State: power, politics and ideology in the remaking of social welfare*, London: Sage.

Cochrane, A., (1993) *Whatever happened to Local Government?* Buckingham: Open University Press.

Cochrane, A., (1994) 'Managing change in local government,' in J. Clarke, A. Cochrane and E. McLaughlin, eds, *op. cit.*

Cohen, S., (1995) 'The mighty state of immigration controls,' in J. Baldock and M. May (eds) *Social Policy Review 7*, Canterbury: Social Policy Association.

Davies, S., (1986) 'Towards the remoralization of society,' in M. Loney *et al.*, eds, *The State or the Market?* London: Sage.

Dennis, N., (1993) *Rising Crime and the Dismembered Family*, London: IEA Health and Welfare Unit.

Dennis, N. and Erdos, G., (1993) *Families without Fatherhood*, London: IEA Health and Welfare Unit (second edition).

Dennis, N. and Halsey, A.H., (1988) *English Ethical Socialism*, Oxford: Oxford University Press.

Green, D., (1993) *Reinventing Civil Society: The Rediscovery of Welfare Without Politics*, London: IEA Health and Welfare Unit.

Gilroy, P., (1987) *There Ain't No Black in the Union Jack*, London: Hutchinson.

Gilroy, P., (1993) *The Black Atlantic: Modernity and Double Consciousness*, London: Verso.

Halsey, A.H., (1993) 'Foreword' to N. Dennis and G. Erdos, *Families without Fatherhood*, London: IEA Health and Welfare Unit (second edition).

Harden, I., (1992) *The Contracting State*, Buckingham: Open University Press.

Hill, M., (1993) *The Welfare State in Britain: a political history since 1945*, London: Edward Elgar.

Hoggett, P., (1994a) 'New modes of control.' Paper presented to Employment Research Unit conference on 'The Contract State', University of Cardiff, September.

Hoggett, P., (1994b) 'The politics of the modernisation of the UK welfare state,' in R. Burrows and B. Loader, eds, *Towards a post-Fordist Welfare State?* London: Routledge.

Johnson, N., (1990) *Reconstructing the Welfare State; A Decade of Change, 1980–1990*, Hemel Hempstead: Harvester Wheatsheaf.

Johnson, T., (1973) *Professions and Power*, London: Macmillan.

Jowell, R., Witherspoon, S. and Brook, L., eds, (1989) *British Social Attitudes: Special International Report*, Aldershot: Gower Publishing.

Langan, M. and Clarke, J., (1994) 'Managing in the mixed economy of care,' in J. Clarke, A. Cochrane and E. McLaughlin, eds, *Managing Social Policy*, London: Sage.

Lewis, G., (forthcoming) 'Difference, what difference? Ethnicity, Social Work and Ethnic Absolutism,' in F. Williams, ed., *Social Policy: A Critical Reader*, Cambridge: Polity Press.

Loney, M., (1985) *The Politics of Greed*, London: Pluto Press.

Mackintosh, M., (1992) 'Partnerships: Issues of Policy and Negotiation.' *Local Economy*, 3, pp. 210–224.

Mayo, M., (1994) *Communities and Caring: the mixed economy of welfare*, Basingstoke, Macmillan.

Mishra, R., (1991) *The Welfare State in Capitalist Society*, Hemel Hempstead: Harvester Wheatsheaf.

Murray, C., (1984) *Losing Ground: American Social Policy 1950–1980*, New York: Basic Books.

Murray, C., (1990) *The Emerging British Underclass*, London: IEA Health and Welfare Unit.

Newman, J. and Clarke, J., (1994) 'Going about our business? The managerialization of public services,' in J. Clarke, A. Cochrane and E. McLaughlin, eds, *Managing Social Policy*, London, Sage.

Newman, J. and Williams, F., (1995) 'The dynamics of change: gender, welfare and organizational relations,' in C. Itzin and J. Newman, eds, *Gender, Culture and Organizational Change*, London: Routledge.

Osborne, D. and Gaebler, T., (1992) *Reinventing Government: How the entrepreneurial spirit is transforming the public sector*, Reading, Mass.: Addison-Wesley.

Pahl, R., (1995) 'Friendly Society.' *New Statesman and Society*, 10.3.1995, pp. 20–22.

Pollitt, C., (1993) *Managerialism and the Public Services*, Oxford: Basil Blackwell (second edition).

Power, M., (1994) *The Audit Explosion*, London: Demos.

Ranson, S. and Stewart, J., (1994) *Management for the Public Domain: Enabling the Learning Society*. Basingstoke: Macmillan.

Stewart, J., (1989) 'A Future for Local Authorities as Community Government,' in J. Stewart and G. Stoker, eds, *The Future of Local Government*, Basingstoke: Macmillan.

Stoker, G. and Young, S., (1993) *Cities in the 1990s*, London: Longman.

Ungerson, C. (1993) 'Payment for caring—mapping a territory,' in N. Deakin and R. Page, eds, *The Costs of Welfare*, Aldershot, Avebury.

Vickridge, R., (1995) 'NHS reforms and community care—means tested health care masquerading as consumer choice?' *Critical Social Policy*, Vol. 43, pp. 76–84.

Walby, S. and Greenwell, J., (1994) 'Managing the National Health Service,' in J. Clarke, A. Cochrane and E. McLaughlin (eds), *Managing Social Policy*, London: Sage.

Walker, R. and Ahmad, W., (1994) 'Windows of Opportunity in Rotting Frames? Care providers' perspectives on community care and black communities. *Critical Social Policy*, 40, pp. 46–69.

Walsh, K., (1995) *Public Services and Market Mechanisms*, Basingstoke: Macmillan.

Weeks, J., (1996) 'The Idea of a Sexual Community.' *Soundings*, Issue 2 (Spring), pp. 71–84.

Williams, F., (1989) *Social Policy: A Critical Introduction*, Cambridge: Polity Press.

Williams, F., (1992) 'Somewhere over the Rainbow: Universality and Diversity in Social Policy,' in N. Manning and R. Page, eds, *Social Policy review 4*, Canterbury: Social Policy Association.

Williams, F., (1994) 'Social relations, welfare and the post-Fordism debate,' in Burrows and Loader, eds, *Towards a post-Fordist Welfare State?* London: Routledge.

Williams, F., (1996) 'Postmodernism, feminism and the question of difference,' in N. Parton (ed.) *Social Theory, Social Change and Social Work*, London: Routledge.

Producing consumption: women and the making of credit markets

Janet Ford and Karen Rowlingson

Abstract

The importance of credit to low-income households is widely recognized, providing a mechanism for managing poverty. In such households women are generally the money-managers, and as such they are significant consumers of credit. Much less attention has been paid, however, to the role that women play in creating and maintaining some credit markets, thereby becoming central to a key means of consumption. Using data from two recent qualitative studies, one on moneylending and one concerned with mail order (both forms of credit widely used in low-income communities), the paper will explore processes whereby access to credit comes to be largely in the hands on women and the continuing importance of gender in the recruitment of customers and maintenance of credit markets. The paper will suggest that the role of credit provider is a consequence of women's economic vulnerability and domestic responsibilities but that the structure and process of credit provision has the potential to reinforce the providers' economic hardship and financial distress. Central to these outcomes is the need to both 'risk and trust' in order to develop and maintain the market and thereby earn. The paper will examine how risking and trusting are undertaken and the consequences of a failure of trust for credit providers.

Introduction

Historically, the use of regulated and unregulated credit to manage poverty has played a central role in the economic life of low-income households (Tebbutt 1983). Although the institutional forms of **regulated** credit traditionally provided in low-income communities have changed and evolved (for example, the decline of pawnbroking and the rise of mail order, hire purchase, the

Social Fund and, to a much lesser extent credit unions), research shows that low-income households still use these forms of credit to manage poverty (Daly and Walsh, 1988; Bradshaw and Holmes, 1989; Kempson *et al.*, 1994). The use of **unregulated credit** is much more difficult to document, and in particular quantify, not least because of the illegality of some transactions (for example, the 'loan shark' trade) and the informality of others (for example, loans between friends or family members). Nevertheless, the use of both these forms of unregulated credit is long standing (Tebbutt, 1983) and continuing (Bolchever *et al.*, 1990; Ford, 1992) in low-income communities.

Women are the principal users of both regulated and unregulated credit in low-income households, stemming from their role as the main money managers (Pahl, 1989; Parker, 1987; Ford, 1991). Credit may be used to purchase basic goods, to manage critical social occasions (such as Christmas) that require extra expenditure (Oppenheim and McEvaddy, 1987), to pay household bills and to manage debts, and may be necessitated by inadequate household income *per se*, or by an unequal distribution of resources within the household (Parker, 1987).

In contrast to the view of women as consumers of credit, the role of women in the provision of credit is much less frequently discussed. However, with respect to the unregulated, informal sector, there is both historical and contemporary evidence of women lending money, typically to women, with mothers lending to daughters and female friends to each other (Kempson *et al.*, 1994). With regard to the regulated sector, women's involvement also has a long history. Jordan (1993) documents the existence of female creditors in pre-industrial society where they provided credit partly for investment but, more commonly, for consumption purposes. Vesselitsky and Bulkley (1917) noted the role women played as informal and formal money lenders during World War One, while Tebbutt's historical review of working class credit provision quotes Booth's observation of one London area at the end of the 19th century where 'every street has its lender, often a woman'. Further, for example, 1,000 of the 1,380 registered money lenders in Liverpool and Birkenhead in 1924 were women (Tebbutt, 1983).

In contrast to this historical data, the contemporary involvement of women in the production of regulated credit provision has attracted relatively little interest, certainly outside some consideration of equal opportunity issues typically discussed in relation to the large, mainstream bank and building society creditor organizations (Crompton and Sanderson, 1990). Here, the conclusions have emphasized women's historical under-representation, particularly in managerial positions. And despite some reduction in the extent of verticle occupational segregation, at the time of writing, there is in England still an under-representation of women in senior positions in the credit industry and no bank or building society female chief executive.

This chapter suggests that, in practice, women's involvement in regulated credit provision in low-income communities has continued and remains significant. This is particularly so with respect to two forms of widely used credit; mail order and regulated money lending. In general, these forms of credit have received relatively little attention, in part, as has been argued elsewhere, because they are assumed to be relatively insignificant (particularly money lending), a view reinforced by the 'invisibility' of such credit organizations. Typically they lack a high street presence and conduct the majority of their transactions (both granting credit and collecting payments) within the privacy of the customer's home (Ford and Rowlingson, 1996).

Two recent qualitative studies, one of mail order (Ford and Piper, 1990) and the other concerned with regulated money lending (Rowlingson, 1994), are used in this chapter to explore the extent and form of women's involvement in credit provision, and more centrally, the ways in which gender is utilized to create and maintain a credit market.[1] This discussion is prefaced by some contextual material on money lending and mail order.

The extent of money lending and mail order activity

Loans from money lenders and mail order credit are still used widely by people, usually women, in low-income households. The most recent estimate, which is drawn from industry sources, indicates that regulated money lending (often referred to as weekly collected credit), involves approximately 1,200 licensed companies in the UK, employing around 27,000 collectors who lend money and collect repayments from about 3 million customers. Thus, access to and use of money lenders is roughly six times greater than previously reported in household surveys (Public Attitudes Surveys, 1987; Berthoud and Kempson, 1992). Money lenders make loans to households to enable them to buy goods or pay bills. They also sell shopping vouchers, usually with a cash value up to £100, which can be exchanged for goods, while the voucher is repaid weekly. Money lenders are regulated and must be licensed by the Office of Fair Trading. As the doorstep selling of money loans is prohibited, the response of many companies is to use doorstep canvassers to sell goods, with canvassers letting it be known that the goods can be paid for by taking a loan from a money lender who will call in due course.

Most of the 27,000 money lending collectors work as agents for large companies, such as Provident Financial Services plc, Shopacheck plc and Morses Ltd. The Provident alone employed 8,000 agents in 1994, most of whom were women. A best estimate suggests that there were between 15–20,000 women collectors in 1994, who dealt with between 1.5 and 2 million customers. There was little evidence that women were employed as managers in the medium and large companies nor that many of the 400 sole trading companies were run by women. The role played by women as providers of weekly collected credit was therefore confined to the role of an agent for a large, often very profitable, money lending company. For example, in 1993, Provident Financial Services plc had a turnover of £249 million from its weekly collected credit arm and made £55 million in pre-tax profits.

The mail order industry had an annual turnover of £5 billion in the early 1990s (Business Monitor, 1991). The incidence of mail order use is higher in middle than lower income households, but mail order is the main form of credit used by low income households. About half of households with weekly income under £100 use it (Berthoud and Kempson, 1992). Some mail order companies sell their products directly through catalogues, while others employ agents to sell either through catalogues and/or demonstration products (eg, Avon, Tupperware or Betterware). Not all companies offer credit, but many do, providing up to 52 weeks 'interest free' credit. Although the total number of agents is unknown, one of the largest cosmetics companies had in excess of 100,000 agents in 1989, practically all of them women. Another company has indicated that agency generated business counted for 80 per cent of its sales, although in a proportion of cases agents sell only to members of their own household and for the industry as a whole, research suggests that the number of customers per agent is falling.

The centrality of women in these forms of credit provision can only be understood as the outcome of a range of influences. One is the nature of the market(s). These are often highly localized, primarily confined to household goods, clothes and accessories or money for household related bills, and typically involve home-based transactions. In the main, the customers are women. A second influence is the particular selling structures and processes adopted by money lending and mail order organizations which rely primarily on social rather than bureaucratic processes to develop and control economic transactions. These influences mesh with the characteristics and circumstances of many women in low-income areas. Many are poor and so economically vulnerable. Often they are in relationships of economic dependency and these factors increase the likelihood that they will look at opportunities to obtain extra resources. However, the range of employment opportunities open to them may be limited, part-time and poorly paid while the lack of adequate child care provision may make it difficult to take even poorly paid work.

The impact of these influences and the ways in which they come together to encourage women to become credit agents will be explored below, starting with a consideration of the nature of the credit relationship in general, and its form in money lending and mail order in particular. This is followed by a consideration of the process of recruitment, and finally a discussion of making, maintaining and extending these credit markets. Finally, the chapter examines the risks that characterize money lending and mail order, and the ways in which, through the casualization of the employment relationship, these are devolved from the credit organizations to credit agents and therefore to women.

All the data presented below come from the two qualitative studies of money lending and mail order referred to above, unless indicated otherwise. It is, however, important to recognize that the two studies do not necessarily address every issue raised equally, and that despite overwhelming similarities in the organization of the two forms of credit lending, there are some differences. For example, as will be discussed in more detail later, while both money lending and mail order agents are casualized, the process is more pronounced in mail order than money lending. Further, mail order agents are part-time workers, while money lenders work longer hours, and more often regard their work as a 'real' job than do mail order agents.

Creating and maintaining a credit market

Credit relationships

The essence of the credit relationship has been summed up as follows.

'Credit is the exchange of two deferred promises: I will do something for you, you will pay me later.' (Braudel, 1973).

From the point of view of the creditor, any credit relationship therefore involves both 'trusting' and 'risking'. All creditors have to trust that people will pay for what they have received (a money loan, clothes via mail order, a holiday 'on Access') and as a consequence they seek ways of reducing the risks of trusting via assessment and management procedures. These vary from formalized credit scoring systems (for example, as used in retail credit), to taking security via a 'charge' on property (as in a mortgage) or via a guarantor (often where the loan is to a young or unemployed person), to promoting credit insurance, to reliance on social processes and 'knowing' the customer.

Money lending and mail order rely heavily on this last means, seeking to establish an economic relationship on social relationships and social processes. These are central processes whereby the market is developed and extended, but also controlled in order to minimize the extent of payments' default. Notions of friendship, loyalty, and favours, but also notions of obligation and coercion, underpin the agents' ability to secure business, earn commission for themselves and thereby profit for the organization.

The use of informal, social relationships in ostensibly 'formal' and certainly contractual transactions and processes is quite widespread. Examples can be found in studies of labour market recruitment where word of mouth recruitment is used by employers not only to reduce costs, but principally to ensure the recruitment of workers who are both 'acceptable' and 'compliant', a result of their 'indebtedness' to the person who introduced them (Jenkins, 1983), but also within direct selling (Taylor, 1978). In each case, there is the use of ascription to achieve the desired goal. Considering the direct selling of Tupperware, Taylor (1978) concluded that:

'The success of the whole enterprise (a sale) depends on its ability to exploit the pre-existing relations between a hostess and her guests'

Credit based selling mirrors this process but adds a further dimension to the social interaction, critically importing the additional need to trust and so risk. This is a process of shifting the balance from the use of ascription to secure an initial transaction (a sale) towards ascription to control a continuing collection process in order to enhance the certainty that payment agreements will be maintained.

Identifying and drawing upon or establishing an appropriate set of social relationships between the borrower and lender is therefore central to the success of these forms of low-income credit. Creditor organizations such as mail order and money lending rely heavily on women to achieve this for them, particularly in low-income communities where the customer base is predominately female. A number of assumptions and stereotypes inform this strategy centred around some perceived differences between men and women with respect to their social skills, and so, implicitly, the nature of their friendships, and their preferences. For example, one manager explained:

'Well, I think (money lending) is a woman's world . . . and I think it's a woman's job, the majority of women have the credit for one, right, (and) if they've got a problem they'd rather talk to a woman, the man frightens them'.

Others argued that it was women rather than men that possessed the necessary social skills. It was argued that women found it easier than men to get on with people and that the predominantly female customer base ensured an immediately common ground. Shared experiences of managing household budgets and so, of using credit, contributed to co-identification, and this was reinforced by the insistence in some companies that agents must have first been customers. In some cases, credit organizations insisted that agents continue as a customer of the company, even if only buying one item a year.

The emphasis on a 'woman to woman relationship' was in part due to the belief that it was also more likely to be an informal one. As a consequence, the sense of hierarchy and power that were an inevitable aspect of the trading/lending relationship were able to be minimized or even disguised. Women were also likely to find it easier to gain entry to the customers' home than men. All of these credit 'advantages' were reinforced where customers and agents lived locally and shared other connections through mutual acquaintances and shared leisure activities. Thus agents (particularly mail order agents) were encouraged to think of their friends, neighbours or work colleagues as potential customers. But the research on money lenders also provided examples of 'extra-trading' links between agents and customers. For example, an instance where the daughter of a customer regularly baby-sat for the agent, and where agents and customers went to the same bingo hall, church or shops.

The evidence from the studies is that the presumptions held by credit organizations were largely fulfilled, particularly amongst money lenders. Agents were welcomed into customers' homes, often calling at tea-time when collectors knew they would be likely to find them in, particularly those with small children just home from school. Collectors were invited into the kitchen or kitchen-diner and the informality of place encouraged an informality in the relationships. Women collectors were very relaxed with their customers, skillful in their interactions, and in the space of a minute or two would find out the latest news on someone's marriage troubles or illness. Common topics of conversation included personal relationships, children, health and work situations. The success of the women agents in establishing relationships with their customers emanated from their willingness to divulge details about themselves and their families. Customers too clearly valued the social relationships, and older customers who were housebound often positively looked forward to the agent's visit. One customer interviewed drew an interesting comparison between two different collectors, one male and one female, from who she had loans. The fact that the man made longer calls and had more time to chat, whereas the woman was always in a hurry was not the significant issue for her, rather it was the nature of the relationship.

> 'She's normally in too much of a hurry . . . hers is just more like a part-time job for her, whereas (John), its his living. She just calls of an evening . . . I mean she comes in and I know all her family and she knows all my family and that, you know because we lived quite close'

Recruitment of money lending and mail order agents

The importance of social relationships in the forms of credit selling considered here, along with the perception that women are particularly adept at establishing such relationships, have important implications for the process of recruiting agents. Companies in these sectors have therefore established a number of forms of recruitment, all designed to reproduce the gendered nature of their current agent workforce.

Money lending and mail order organizations both recruited from their pool of existing customers who were principally women. Managers believed that agents should identify with their customers, although not to the extent that it jeopardized their ability to manage customers, particularly those with payment problems. Existing agents in both mail order and money lending companies often receive financial rewards for persuading existing customers to become agents. In one fairly typical case, an agent in her late 30s and married to a manual worker was recruited. She had previously worked in various part-time jobs in the service sector. Her daughter was 17, had just left school and was starting out as a hairdresser. She had been a customer of the company at one time and then was good friends with another agent who introduced her to the work. The bonus for introducing new agents could reach £25.

Both industries also recruited agents by advertising in newspapers, attracting well motivated recruits. In addition, the mail order company engaged in what they referred to as 'swooping'. Here, area managers combined together to have a day targetting a residential area or town centre area, door knocking or approaching women with small children out shopping, and asking them to become agents. They could be signed up straight away or an arrangement made for a follow up home visit. 'Swoops' produce recruits with variable degrees of motivation and are essentially about existing agents meeting targets for new agents (and so extra earnings) by pointing out to potential recruits the social and economic benefits of becoming an agent.

'A woman came round, up and down the street . . . and I sat there and thought about it and then, and thought—yes I would do it'

'She was talking to me for ages at the door and I said I don't want to do it. She said it's great you know and I said oh well, come in and that's how I got to do it'

Irrespective of the recruitment process, new agents in money lending and mail order were often sympathetic to the range of potential advantages outlined to them by the recruiters; social contact, economic rewards, a job that could be combined with childcare and undertaken at their convenience. Two money lending agents said:

'When I started this . . (it) fitted perfectly because I could go up here to take our children to school. I didn't actually ever bring them to work with me but if I'd needed to I could have done' and 'You're a bit of a social worker and everything in this game. Everybody tells you their problems . . . I would say that 90 per cent of the people you deal with are very nice'

While two mail order agents said:

'I thought it would be a little break, get to meet a few people,' and 'She said if you got a good round . . . you can earn up to £25 a week, so I thought I'd give it a go'

One important consideration to the mail order agents was that selling in this way was not really a job but rather 'just something I do', 'a hobby'. Because of this, becoming a mail order agent was attractive to those on benefit who believed that their earnings would not affect their benefit entitlement however successful they were, and in any case they might take their commission in the form of products.

Agents were recruited to employment that was, to varying degrees, casualized. Most money lending agents were self-employed and paid commission, ranging from 7 per cent to 10 per cent of money collected. The amount collected during a week varied from about £2,000 to just over £3,500 leading to weekly earnings of between £140 and £300 before tax. Along with the basic commission there were several bonuses which, depending on the company, agents could earn. For example, as noted above, in one company there was a £25 bonus for recommending a new agent, and in several, a bonus of £5 for each new customer. There were also regular sales drives among companies, and performance bonuses.

Mail order agents were also casualized; nominally self employed, commission based workers, but typically they earned much lower sums in commission than did money lending agents. In the company studied, earnings were considered per campaign; a three week selling, delivery of goods and money collecting cycle. New recruits were advised that net earnings per campaign averaged £25–30 but only a minority of those interviewed ever reached that figure. There was also a minimum selling threshold before any commission was payable. Both groups of agents had to meet their own work related travel costs, mail order agents also had to pay for brochures, demonstration products and delivery bags. Money lenders were responsible for any pension provision they wished to make (typically of most interest to the small number of male agents for whom money lending might be a full-time job), and for tax, insurance and had to cover their own holiday periods. Most of these latter concerns were of little relevance to mail order agents because of the very part-time nature of their work. There was, however, considerable disaffection amongst agents with some aspects of this casualization, in particular, amongst mail order agents the system of deductions for consumables was regarded as unfair. One mail order agent spoke for several when she noted that:

> 'No it wasn't explained . . . She says (the manager) that you get five brochures and so many bags (for delivery) for your customers. She didn't say whether you'd got to pay for them or not, but I found out on the bill! They were a ridiculous price'

The patterns of recruitment adopted were therefore tailored to the objective of recruiting women. However, as suggested above, it is not a sufficient explanation to argue that women were recruited because they were 'available'. Men too are often without work in many low-income areas, and they are increasingly willing to consider part-time employment and low-paid work, even at incomes below that available through benefit (Ford *et al.*, 1996). As important were the structures and processes that characterized the selling and credit granting process and the characteristics of the consumers. All of these factors led the companies to seek women agents.

Making, maintaining and extending credit markets

If social relationships are seen as central to the development and maintenance of money lending and mail order, it is important to examine the ways in which these relationships are utilized to secure economic ends. This is done most clearly by first considering agents' management of their current portfolio of customers and secondly their attempts to develop new customers.

To establish their commission based livelihoods, agents needed to establish a network of customers and so a flow of lending or sale of goods. As noted earlier, this was most frequently done by turning to those with whom there was a pre-existing relationship, although in the case of money lenders, new agents sometimes took over someone else's 'round' and so inherited a set of customers. A further implication of the commission based system was that increased earnings were dependent on increasing the amount borrowed by existing customers or by recruiting new customers. One of agents' major concerns was therefore to encourage existing customers to take new loans or re-order goods as their current agreements drew to a close.

Agents drew on their social relationships with and knowledge of customers to encourage further credit use, adopting a range of approaches. These can be characterized as persuasive marketing, conveying dependence and the use of sanctions.

Because agents had access to their customers' homes they had access to information and observations about some of their needs. This could form the basis for marketing further credit. For example, an agent might suggest a loan for a new settee, or that a loan might be the way the customer could meet their wish to redecorate etc. On customer explained her collector's more generalized marketing 'technique':

'[The collector] says, "do you fancy anything? Bedclothes, hairdrier, anything like that?" I say, "What you got?" when I know my bill's gone down and I'll say, "How much does it cost me more a week if I pay for the one whatever I've had before that?" and [the collector will] say, "well, it'll only cost you an extra quid or something like that." So I don't mind that.'

In another instance a different collector tried to persuade a customer as follows:

'she kept on for quite some time before, when [my son's loan] was coming towards the end, kept asking if he was interested in having another and we kept saying "no". Then he finished it and the same went for me and when my husband came towards the end, it was the last one and we did actually have another one with her in my husband's name. But I turned round joking and I said to her, "Are you happy now that you've had another one?" And she says, "Well, not really, no, because you haven't had one".'

Another approach observed was that of making explicit the dependence between lender and borrower. One collector in particular played this in the form of mutual dependence. She made a point of telling customers that collectors received a bonus when a customer took out a loan. Over the weeks and years, the collector 'conditioned' customers by praising them when they took out a loan, remarking that they were 'doing her (the collector) a good turn'. If people were thinking of taking out a loan, the collector would convey her dependence on the borrower (as opposed to their mutual dependence) and encourage them by saying that she had not arranged many loans that week and that she would not reach her target unless someone helped out by taking a loan. The collector tried to identify with her customers by saying that she needed the money and that the managers would not be happy if she did not meet her target. This was the most manipulative way of encouraging people to borrow. It 'used' the friendship built up with customers in order to increase business. One customer admitted that she had taken out loans from a previous collector because she was,

> 'soft-hearted. I liked to help her out. . . . I did it for custom for the girl'

Clearly, collectors varied in the extent to which they tried to manipulate their customers. One customer compared two collectors that she had used,

> '[Pat] was very loud. I mean she was really nice, very nice. But she was a bit pushy, whereas [Lesley], if I say, "no, thanks," away goes the papers. With [Pat], it was, "go on, go on, because you're helping me out," and then that makes you feel guilty, you know. But with [Lesley], you know, she don't give a damn about her commission. If you don't want the stuff, then don't have it, you know, she is really good.'

Yet another way of encouraging business was through the use of sanctions, to threaten, albeit in a subtle way, that if someone stopped using the company, they might not be able to use them again in the future. One customer said that she always renewed loans with one of her money lending companies, precisely because she did not want to risk the loss of a line of credit. As she explained:

'with [one of the companies] I've got down to where I'm only paying, say £10 a week and I've only got five or six weeks left to pay and [the collector] starts panicking, you know, "you've got to have another loan," you know. And she really panics because she thinks I'm going to finish with her, which I never do. I mean I get right down low and then I might want £500 for something, you know . . . she just says, like, "do you realise you've only got five or six weeks?" "yes," and then I might take out a loan for about £100 to keep it going until a time when I do want a large loan. Because their policy was—she says it doesn't really apply to me—but it always frightens me a bit: if you are a new customer and you went to [the company], you can't get a large loan right in the beginning, you have to build up to it . . . So I tend to keep it going.'

This last quote also clearly illustrates the complexity of money lending; the mutual dependence between the collector and the customer; the collector's need to retain customers and the customer's need to retain a line of credit, yet the suggestion by the agent that their relationship is such that it will protect the customer from disadvantageous aspects of the company's lending policy. It is unlikely that the customer would have lost her credit-rating if she had taken a break because while it is true that companies only lend small amounts to most new customers, they are often willing to take a risk if they have some previous knowledge about the customer. There is, however, no advantage to the collector in making this known. The advantage lies in encouraging the client's dependence and anxiety about retaining access to an important source of credit.

Many agents used one or more of the tactics outlined above. However, the processes had to be managed skillfully. As one customer said of another collector she had used in the past:

'She was a very abrupt woman and she used to come in here sometimes and she used to make really sarcastic remarks, "Isn't it about time you decorated?" or "Isn't it about time . . ." you know. And that was another reason why I stopped using that company.'

Equally, the research showed that it would be wrong to characterize money lending as wholly, if subtley, predatory. The social basis that allowed lenders to exert a pressure to purchase in some cases also led agents to draw back. Many customers said that they liked their current collector precisely because they did not try to push anything on to them. As one agent said:

> 'I never push anything on any customer at all because (although) it's great to be able to push things on to people, but it's no good if they can't pay for it.'

A mail order agent commented that she knew her customers well enough to know that if they said 'no' this was best accepted because to disregard their views was to take an unnecessary and substantial risk.

> 'I was talking to my friend, and she says 'I can't afford any so don't give me the book.' If she can't afford it she won't take a book off me, but if she can she will.'

These qualitative data above show how social relationships underpin the management of lending, typically, but not always, activated to obtain repeat lending, if possible at a higher level. These processes work most effectively where agent and client are well acquainted, but agents are also under pressure to extend their customer base, both from their managers who also work to targets, but as noted before, to keep up their own commission-based earnings. Socially embedded customers may already have loans up to or past a manageable level (indeed, some loans may have been taken out to clear default on earlier loans), and existing networks can become 'saturated'. Extending their customer base may therefore only be possible by accepting as customers people agents know little or nothing about and with whom they have no pre-existing social ties. In these circumstances, the trust that is a central component of the credit transaction has to be given in the absence of any social supports which reduce the risks of trusting.

An earlier paper (Ford and Rowlingson, 1996) discussed this last issue in detail, and showed the ways in which agents sought to protect themselves over the initial period while clients 'proved' themselves and agents developed the appropriate social relationships, which then increased their control. In particular, agents looked to existing customers to recommend new customers, either explicitly or implicitly regarding the introducer as the 'guarantor' of the new client, a process that parallels that found in informal, word of mouth recruitment in the labour market (Jenkins *et al.*, 1983). Other 'safety' mechanisms included a reduced level of lending for the initial loan, attempting to restrict sales to those in employment and an exchange of information between agents, identifying problem households.

However, despite the attempt to exercise safeguards, the pressure for sales was strong and agents sometimes had to trust in the absence of anything to offset the risk. One mail order agent indicated the dilemmas and potential consequences associated with trusting and risking in the absence of an adequate social infrastructure. Speaking about customers she had picked up by door knocking she said:

> 'If you can't have a bit of trust in your customers, they aren't going to be interested . . . but . . . it was like this . . . it was my third order, they'd paid before, so when they asked me to leave the goods I had to trust them. They said they'd pay if I called back. I tried five or six times to get the money.'

Equally, the competitive nature of money lending and mail order may encourage inappropriate trusting, bringing it close to gambling. One manager explained the conflicts when business was not going too well and an agent or company feared losing customers to rival companies:

> 'You have to be careful not to over-indebt people, but it's very difficult because there are other firms going round as well.'

Another agent highlighted a case of extreme pressure from the company to expand sales which led her to leave the company after three months:

> 'I was ready to go out of my mind. Every week it was, "you're going out with this fella on his van" and I'm afraid I'm not the type to want to go and sit in a great big van with a fella, pull up outside somebody's house and expect people to come outside and do it in the street . . . it was just a case of "it doesn't matter what they've got, just put more, more in there". That's how it seemed to me and I couldn't cope with that.'

Trusting and risking: the risk to women?

The credit granting and credit management process, as it applies to money lending and mail order was, and is, a transaction of considerable danger. This is despite attempts to institute social control by embedding it in the ebb and flow of social life and seeking to make selling and paying 'episodes in continuous social relations' (Taylor, 1978). This final section examines the range of dangers involved. Because the overwhelming majority of agents are women, these are dangers most typically experienced by women, who also bear the consequences. The dangers were both financial and physical and could lead to agents losing or giving up their employment.

One implication of the casualized nature of the employment relationship that characterizes money lending and mail order agents (discussed above) is that it results in a situation where typically, the agents are responsible for any transactions that go wrong. In the mail order company, the legal position was that the agents had bought the goods themselves, which they then sold on in an entirely independent capacity. In effect, mail order agents were doubly casualized in the sense that the mail order company transfered two sets of responsibilities to the agent; once in the form of payment for the customers' goods and a second time in relation to the collection of credit. The company would therefore take agents to court for non-payment of the goods, not the final consumers. Despite this, in some cases, where customers missed payments, the area manager would visit the agent's customer to try and obtain payment, but ultimately, the agents either had to make up the payment or face court action for the recovery of the money and/or the loss of their agency. Agents were highly unlikely to be insured against their customers' default (unlike many companies who might insure against their agents' default), and could only make up the shortfalls by paying it out of their earnings. The mail order company never 'wrote off' customers' debts for agents, but this did sometimes happen amongst money lending companies where the legal relationships were rather different.

These sanctions reinforced the agents' need to have confidence that people would pay and increased the risk of trusting in the absence of some social leverage. But trust was necessary to have any chance of earning. However, even where there were pre-existing social relationships, problems could arise particularly in the poorest households where financial pressures could mean that even if customers had every intention of paying when they ordered the goods, other demands might have intervened and taken priority. One agent noted:

'There is no doubt about it, they do want it (the goods). I mean they don't order it to say they've ordered something, they genuinely want it and then of course when the bill comes in they have got to pay another bill rather than mine . . . I mean, when all's said and done, these things are not necessities are they?'

The studies were not able to identify the scale of default, nor the distribution of outcomes for agents. Certainly in mail order, where the turnover of agents is quite high, issues of customer default play a key role in agents either giving up or not being allowed to continue.

However, there was a further aspect of default that contributed to agents losing their agencies. Earlier, it was noted that a proportion of agents accepted the work because of their own precarious financial position. This was particularly so for mail order agents operating in low-income areas, a number of whom were Income Support claimants. Those agents who were not in work could only sell around where they lived or to their friends and relatives and typically, their customers were people in similar circumstances to themselves. This was an inevitable outcome of the policy in many companies that agents should be allocated a local selling 'territory' and have some identification with those to whom they are selling, if only a geographical one. As a result, in areas of severe financial deprivation, the same poverty that led some customers to default, and led some women to take up agency work, in turn led some agents to default on their payments to the credit organization. Money gathered in as credit payments was on occasion 'borrowed' to meet pressing bills, rather than sent on to the company.

'I feel rotten if you know what I mean, but I needed the money at the time cos no one had any. I thought I'd put it back but I just haven't been able to.'

In addition to the risks associated with default, agents faced other problems. Money lending agents in particular faced personal physical risks stemming from the fact that a 'collection round' meant that they were carrying large sums of money at the same time of the week in the same places. They were therefore a fairly easy target for theft and they took precautions to try and avoid this eventuality. Agents were careful about where they put the money that they collected. They also tried to avoid the money being visible in the street but this was not always easy where some customers preferred to deal with the agent on the doorstep. A more drastic step was to refuse to deal with people living in estates or areas perceived as particularly dangerous.

Two of the money lending agents had had their bags stolen, in one case by a man in the street with his face covered. The agent was very shaken by the experience and did not work for a short time, losing income as a result. When she resumed work, she only did so because her husband drove her round to all her calls and waited while she went inside. Another agent got into her car to drive off only to find that a stranger was in the back of the car and was demanding her money.

In contrast to money lenders, mail order agents rarely carried sizeable sums of money, and so, for them, the risks of theft were less, but they reported instances of abusive behaviour from potential customers and sometimes found the areas in which they were calling difficult and even threatening, not least in areas with high rise flats. Despite the recruiters' claims that this was a job that could be combined with child care responsibilities, the reality was that broken lifts, deck access flats and stairs made the work very difficult if accompanied by small children. Evening calls, sometimes required to catch customers in, could also be threatening:

'My sister used to come with me because it was that dark. I was a bit scared to be honest. You just never know who you are going to meet, you hear that much nowadays, it just isn't worth the risk.'

Conclusions

As key money managers, women consume credit. But this chapter has also presented evidence to show that women are also central to the production of credit consumption in low-income communities, at least with respect to money lending and mail order credit. While they neither own the credit resources, nor occupy key managerial roles in the credit organizations, they are central to the development and maintenance of these credit markets. Their centrality stems from the structure and organization of these forms of credit, that bases the selection and regulation of credit users on social rather than bureaucratic processes. By

110

virtue of the nature of the customer base and the home-based transaction, women are deemed the most appropriate agents and the work, in principle, fits with the needs of many women in low income areas who face financial uncertainty and limited alternative options for employment.

These structural and organizational processes however, create significant pressures for agents. In particular the commission-based employment relationship creates a situation in which they may have to 'lean' on existing customers calling on notions of loyalty, friendship and utilizing knowledge of their personal circumstances and needs to increase sales. The same pressures may lead them to risk transactions before the social means of control are in place. A wide range of consequences may follow, from physical assault to economic loss, all of which fall on agents, the majority of whom are women. Thus, whatever personal gains accrue to women from involvement as producers of credit (and the gains can be substantial in some cases), the structure of the system often means that they are earned at a considerable 'price'.

Acknowledgements

1 The study of money lenders was funded by the Joseph Rowntree Foundation and the study of mail order agents by a large mail order company. The support of both organizations is gratefully acknowledged.

References

Berthoud, R. and Kempson, E., (1992) *Credit and Debt: The PSI Report*, PSI.

Bolchever, S., Stewart, S. and Clyde, G. (1990) 'Consumer credit: investigating the loan sharks', *Trading Standards Review*, Vol. 98, no. 1.

Bradshaw, J. and Holmes, H., (1989) *Living on the Edge*, Tyneside: CPAG.

Braudel, F., (1973) *Capitalism and material life 1400–1800*, London: Fontana/Collins.

Business Monitor, (1991), April, HMSO.

Crompton, R. and Sanderson, K., (1990) *Gendered Jobs and Social Change*, London: Routledge.

Daly, M. and Walsh, J., (1988) *Money Lending and Low Income Families*, Dublin Combat Poverty Agency.

Ford, J., (1991) *Consuming Credit: Debt and Poverty in the UK*, CPAG Ltd.

Ford, J., (1992) 'Young adults use of credit', *Youth and Policy*, No. 37, pp. 22–32.

Ford, J. and Piper, J., (1990) *Representatives in Debt*, Department of Social Sciences, Loughborough University.

111

Janet Ford and Karen Rowlingson

Ford, J. and Rowlingson, K., (1996) 'Low-income households and credit: exclusion, preference and inclusion', *Environment and Planning* Vol. 28, pp. 1345–60.

Ford, J., Kempson, E. and England, J., (1996) *Into work? The impact of housing costs and the benefit system on people's decision to work*, Joseph Rowntree Foundation.

Jenkins, R. *et al.*, (1983) 'Information in the labour market', *Sociology*, Vol. 12 No. 2: 260–7.

Jordan, W., (1993) *Women and credit in pre-industrial and developing societies*, Philadelphia: University of Pennsylvania Press.

Kempson, E., Bryson, A. and Rowlingson, K., (1994) *Hard Times?* PSI.

Oppenheim, C. and McEvaddy, S., (1987) *Christmas on the Breadline*, CPAG Ltd.

Pahl, J., (1989) *Money and Marriage*, London: Macmillan.

Parker, G., (1987) 'Making Ends Meet: Women, Credit and Debt' in C. Glendenning and J. Millar, *Women and Poverty in Britain*, Hemel Hempstead: Wheatsheaf.

Public Attitudes Surveys (1987) *The Consumers' Use of Credit*, London: PAG.

Rowlingson, K., (1994) *Money Lenders and their Customers*, Policy Studies Institute.

Taylor, R., (1978), 'Marilyn's friends and Rita's customers: a study of party-selling as play and as work' *Sociological Review*, Vol. 28(2): 573–94.

Tebbutt, M., (1983) *Making Ends Meet. Pawnbroking and Working Class Credit*, Leicester University Press.

Vesselitsky, V. and Bulkley, M., (1917) 'Money-lending among the London poor', *Sociological Review*, Vol. IX pp. 129–38.

Consumption and class analysis

Rosemary Crompton

Abstract

The growing significance of 'consumption' is one of the factors which has contributed to sociological debates relating to the 'end of class'. In this chapter, the different strands of consumption-related critiques are identified, and their implications explored. It is argued that one of the most prominent disputes in the field—Saunders on 'consumption classes'—in fact engaged with but one strand of 'class analysis', the 'employment-aggregate' approach. Subsequently, the chapter explores discussions relating to the impact of consumption growth and developments on class *processes*, particularly those arguments concerning the significance of the experience of employment for the development of ('class') identities. It is suggested that recent changes in the structuring and organization of employment might, indeed, have significant consequences for the shaping of identities.

Introduction

Although public interest in the topic of social class shows no sign of going away,[1] recent debates within sociology have suggested that 'class' is no longer a central or significant sociological concept (Bauman, 1982; Pahl, 1989; Clark and Lipset, 1991). In these critiques, the issue of consumption has assumed a central role. In brief, some sociologists have argued that, in contemporary societies, 'consumption processes' are in the process of becoming, or have become, *more* important than production (or 'class') processes in shaping social identities and explaining social behaviour, and that as a consequence the consumer has become a more suitable case for sociological treatment than the producer. Not all sociologists would agree that class has lost its significance.

However, even amongst those more sympathetic to the continuing sociological significance of 'class', it is often argued that what is required is a new approach to—even a complete rethinking of—the concept (Lee, 1994; Scott, 1994).

This chapter will focus upon current consumption-related changes in labour markets and employment, and their implications for theories of 'class' identity and consciousness. As we shall see, these are considerable, and 'new approaches' may indeed eventually be required. However, it will be argued that for the moment it would seem preferable to rest with an explicit plurality of approaches to 'class analysis', rather than to reject existing strategies in favour of new ones. As has been discussed elsewhere, much of the sociological debate relating to the 'end of class' is in fact a reflection of the fragmentation of different approaches to 'class analysis' within the discipline, as a result of which misunderstandings have been rife. Indeed, one feature of the 'pseudo-debates' which followed these misunderstandings was a marked lack of progress in the field of 'class analysis' as a whole (Crompton, 1993, 1996). Here it will be argued that this line of argument is nowhere more appropriate than in respect of the topic of class and consumption. It will be suggested that one of the sociological disputes with the highest profile—Saunders (1987) on 'consumption classes'—is an important example here. Nevertheless, the view will be taken that lack of progress as a consequence of pseudo-debate does not necessarily render the concepts in question irrelevant or unhelpful. In this chapter, therefore, we will examine another major topic of the 'consumption and class' debate—that is, that which focuses upon the significance of 'class' (by which is usually meant employment and/or occupation) for the formation and development of social and individual identities.

Employment Aggregates versus Consumption Aggregates

'Class analysis' is cross-cut by a number of different distinctions. For the sake of brevity, we will here focus on only two, one a broadly theoretical, the other a broadly empirical, axis. First, we may identify the distinction between 'Marxist' and 'Weberian' class theoretical approaches, particularly in respect of their discussions of class *consciousness*. both theorists saw 'classes' as groups of economic actors in the broadest sense. However, for Marx, 'classes' were also major historical actors ('all history is the history of class consciousness'), and thus the development of class consciousness and identity was regarded as (almost) inevitable (Marx and Engels, 1962). Weber, in contrast, regarded the development of class consciousness as essentially contingent, depending upon particular circumstances such as the increasing transparency of class inequalities (Weber, 1948).

Second, we may make a distinction between two broad empirical approaches to class analysis: (i) the employment-aggregate approach, which rests upon the macro-level analysis of large data sets, grouped (most usually by job or occupational status) into aggregates which are described as 'classes', and (ii) the study of the *processes* of class formation and action, which is here being used as a shorthand to describe case study work which has explored the particular circumstances through and contexts in which 'classes' have developed as social categories and potential social forces.

The empirical work of British proponents of the employment aggregate approach (in particular, Goldthorpe, 1987, and Marshall *et al.*, 1988), has tended to emphasize above all the persistence and *stability* of 'class' effects. Changes in the employment structure (for example, the relative decline of the manual working class) are not denied, but they are given less prominence than the *persistence* of the relationship between class differences and a number of indicators including relative mobility changes, educational opportunity and political preferences. Indeed, the persistence of the empirical association between employment aggregate classes and levels of social mobility, educational attainment, etc., has been one of the major planks in their arguments as to the continuing significance of 'class' in contemporary societies (Erikson and Goldthorpe, 1992; Goldthorpe and Marshall, 1992).

In contrast, case studies of class processes (including studies of labour markets, organizations, professional and occupational groups and so on), have tended to emphasize the *changing* nature of the class/employment structure. This includes developments such as the increasing participation of women in paid employment, changes in work associated with technological change and flexibilization, the increase in long-term unemployment, etc. The constant flux of the occupational structure seems to belie the employment aggregate practitioners' emphasis upon stability and lack of change. However, in the British case at any rate, employment aggregate practitioners have explicitly rejected the utility of historical or case study evidence, and have accepted as legitimate *only* arguments and empirical evidence deriving from large data sets—that is, arguments couched within the methodological framework of their 'research programme' (Goldthorpe, 1991)[2]. This insistence has decisively shaped one of the more heated debates that arose in the arena of class and consumption— Saunders on 'consumption classes'. We will, therefore, discuss this aspect of the consumption and class debate before examining how the question of consumption has been approached within the processual, case study, approach.

Saunders (1987) was concerned to demonstrate that consumption had replaced production (or 'class') as a—if not the—major axis of differentiation in contemporary societies. As we have seen, within class analysis the convention had been established whereby employment aggregates could be taken as proxies for 'classes'. Saunders' empirical strategy, therefore, was isomorphic—that is, he sought to match employment aggregates with consumption aggregates (such as 'housing classes', as represented by different kinds of housing tenure). The consumption aggregates (or classes) so identified were correlated with the same kinds of attitudinal variables (for example, political preferences) as the employment aggregates (or classes), and the 'winner' declared on the strength of the association. Saunders' approach has been extensively criticised. With the collapse of the housing market bubble and the growth of negative equity, consumption indicators such as housing have proved to be extremely unstable as empirical measures. However, perhaps the most important criticism is the fact that in any case, the statistical association between employment 'classes' and social indicators such as political preference has proved to be closer than that of consumption 'classes'—that is, the argument has been falsified empirically (Hamnett, 1989).

It would seem, therefore, that this particular aspect of the 'consumption classes' debate has been brought to a conclusion and that little would be gained from pursuing the matter further. However, although his empirical work on consumption classes engaged largely with the 'employment aggregate' tradition of class analysis, it is important to recognize that Saunders was also taking part in *theoretical* debates about class—in particular, those concerning the origin and nature of 'class'—or other—identities and consciousness. As we have seen, these kinds of issues were central to the 'Marx *vs* Weber' debates. Saunders argued that consumption, particularly housing, *meant* more to people than their job—the phrase he uses is the 'ontological security' deriving from home ownership. As we have seen, the empirical strategy followed by Saunders, which mirrored the employment aggregate approach, meant that his claims could be falsified in respect of attitudinal variables such as political preferences. Nevertheless, the broader question of identity and meaning, which is raised by Saunders' work, remains of central interest to sociologists. To put the matter crudely, in class analysis meaning or consciousness has commonly provided the elusive link between location in a social ('class') structure and action/institutional outcomes.

In the 1970s, Saunders (1978) was engaging with 'conventional marxist orthodoxy' within urban sociology, which argued that tenurial divisions contributed to the 'false consciousness' of the working class. In contrast, Saunders argued that these were real divisions which could not be reduced to the level of relations in production. In the broadest terms, he was arguing that interests and identities in relation to consumption were independent of the interests and identities developed in relation to employment. As we have seen, in class analysis, employment is widely used as a proxy for production relationships. There is an established tradition in British industrial sociology, closely associated with class analysis, which has argued that employment/work situations have been an important source of (class) identity (see Newby, 1977; Brown and Brannen, 1970).[3] This kind of work has focused upon the processes of class formation and the acquisition of class identities, and empirically, has incorporated case studies of particular occupations or 'classes'.[4] Besides his debates with the 'employment aggregate' approach, Saunders' emphasis upon the independent significance of consumption can be seen as engaging with this tradition, which has viewed work as employment as a primary source of identity. In the rest of this chapter, therefore, we will examine the class/consumption debate in relation to the second broad area of class analysis identified above—that is, the study of class processes.

Consumption and Class Processes

Here there are two major areas where consumption-related trends have been identified as relevant to class analysis. First, there are the linkages between consumption practices and class formation. Second, there is the question of the extent to which the shift to the service sector and consumption related employment has transformed employment relationships and the experience of work, and the consequences of this for potential 'class' identity and consciousness.

The suggestion that social classes are in part constituted through cultural practices, including patterns of consumption, is not a new one (Veblen, 1934).[5] Bourdieu's work (1984), although by now somewhat out-of-date, remains the most comprehensive sociological treatment of the topic, although there have been recent empirical studies of the 'middle classes' which have also explored in some depth the way in which consumption practices or 'lifestyles' have served to differentiate between social groupings (Savage et al., 1992). Given the importance of the links between social class position and consumption (purchasing) practices, the connections between economic/occupational ('class') position and patterns of consumption have been constantly investigated and reinvestigated by market researchers.

Thus we may agree that in the broadest sense, consumption practices serve to reinforce and reproduce social hierarchies. Whether or not such practices have become *more* important than they once were is difficult to judge, and in any case, the answer would be likely to vary considerably depending on the social group in question. In addition, the simple point that the maintenance of consumption practices is heavily dependent upon economic class position should not be forgotten. However, our subsequent discussion will focus largely on the second area identified—the experience of employment.

The experience of employment, class consciousness and identity

Two further divisions characterize consumption-related changes in employment: (i) developments in the labour market and (ii) changes in work practices. In order to explore these factors, it is first necessary to demonstrate the linkages between the sociology of work and employment and the study of class processes. Here the work of Lockwood and Braverman has been crucial.

In British sociology, the 'work' and 'market' situations of employees were taken to be the most significant elements contributing to class situation in employment. Lockwood (1958) argued that (i) although clerical workers were, like manual workers, propertyless employees, nevertheless such 'white-collar' workers could not be said to share the same 'class situation' as manual

workers because of their different employment circumstances—
including more employment security, better opportunities for
upward mobility, and less oppressive working conditions.
Furthermore, (ii) similar variations existed *within* the clerical category, which served to explain variations in levels of trade union-
ism amongst clerical workers. Thus the work and employment
circumstances of clerical workers were used as indicators in order
to locate these occupations within the 'class structure' as represented in employment. These insights were carried over into the
'Affluent Worker' (Goldthorpe *et al.*, 1969) study, which similarly
examined the 'work situation' of 'affluent workers' in researching
their 'class situation'.

Braverman's arguments relating to the links between the labour
process and processes of class formation has many parallels with
Lockwood's work. Like Lockwood, Braverman (1974) argued
that the nature of the labour (work) process directly affected the
class location of employees—although unlike Lockwood, he
argued that clerical workers were undergoing a process of 'de-
skilling' and should more properly be allocated to the 'proletarian' class category. A further difference is that Braverman's
analytical framework was decisively influenced by a Marxist
approach, whereas Lockwood (1988) has been highly critical of
aspects of Marx's work.

Another very influential contribution made by Lockwood was
his (1966) article on 'Sources of variation in working class images
of society'. On the basis of case study evidence, he suggested that
three different types of working class imagery could be identified;
traditional proletarian, traditional deferential, and privatized.
These different world views were linked to variations in work (ie
employment) and locality situations. Here Lockwood may be seen
as attempting to describe the empirical link between location in
the social (class) structure and propensity for action—or at least,
consciousness—of a class kind.

Despite the theoretical differences between Lockwood and
Braverman, their work may be seen to have some important similarities of approach. Both held that the labour market was a
major source of social structuring, which generated particular
kinds of interest groupings and particular forms of social consciousness—and both regarded class concepts (in the most general
sense) as central to the analysis of these processes.[6] However,
over the past fifteen years or so, it has increasingly been argued
that, at the end of the twentieth century, changes in the labour

market, and in the nature of employment have been so profound that the previous links that have been made between employment, interests, and social consciousness no longer apply. As a consequence, it is argued that we have reached a point beyond which 'class' is a useful concept for the analysis of contemporary societies.

It has been argued that the labour market has been progressively fragmented, as a result of which there has been a growth of flexible and non standard employment such as part-time work, short-term contracts, and self-employment (see Beatson, 1995; Gregg and Wadsworth, 1995). These developments have been associated with increasing insecurity of employment and the decline of the long-term career. In Britain, Conservative Government policy has encouraged corporate and organizational restructuring associated with 'downsizing' and job loss, and popular management magazines (such as 'Business Age'[7]) have chronicled the subsequent travails of middle management. According to Beck (1992), these kinds of changes have resulted in the development of an 'individualized society of employees' in a '. . . risk-fraught system of flexible, pluralized, decentralized underemployment' (143). In these 'new forms' of employment (which include homeworking, casual work, and so on), the boundaries between work and non-work are becoming increasingly fluid. 'Work' in the sense of an occupation once provided a focus for the development of class-based identities in industrial societies, but as a consequence of increasing insecurity and 'flexibility' in the labour market, Beck argues, both 'class' and 'status' are losing their significance.

A further set of arguments relates to changes in the nature of work itself, particularly those associated with the expansion of service work and the growth and application of Information Technology. Authors such as Offe (1985), and Lash and Urry (1994), have argued that the growth and development of consumption-related employment, particularly in services, has radically transformed the *meaning* of work for employees, and that as a consequence employment no longer has the capacity to generate 'class' related consciousness and action. Thus Offe has suggested that 'work' is no longer a 'key sociological concept': 'work', he argues, no longer has '. . . a relatively privileged power to determine social consciousness and action' (1985:133). Furthermore, Lash and Urry (1994) have argued that with the development of Information Technology, production systems have themselves become expert systems, and that 'reflexive modernities' are increasingly becoming 'economies of signs and space'. Indeed, they suggest an inversion of the Marxist thesis in relation to consciousness, rather than structure (ie classes) shaping consciousness, '... in informationalized and reflexive modernity it is consciousness or reflexivity which is determinant of class structure' (319). These kinds of arguments will be explored in the discussion that follows.

Has the expansion of consumption-related employment in services, and service practices in organizations and production, dissolved the link between experiences in employment and class consciousness and action?

That the increase in service employment is a marked feature of recent labour market developments can hardly be contested. In the UK, for example, service employment increased from 53 per cent to 73 per cent between 1973 and 1993, and a similar trend is to be found in other countries (Frenkel *et al.*, 1995). Service employment encompasses a heterogeneous range of occupations amongst which it is not difficult to find examples of work as routine and 'de-skilled' as is any to be found in manufacturing industry (Gabriel, 1988). Routine and de-skilled work in services is still widespread. However, it is important to move on from the 'de-skilling' debate to focus on changes in the organization and management of paid employment which have been developed over the last one-and-a-half decades. Many of these are associated with the growth of *interactive* service work (retail and other sales including telephone sales and servicing, the leisure industry, and so on), which is the fastest-growing sector of service employment. Besides this growth, 'marketization' and changes in legislation such as the deregulation of the finance sector in the 1980s has also resulted in the transformation of work in other sectors such as finance into *de facto* sales employment.

Two particular consumption-related features of contemporary service work have been identified in making the case that the links between employment and class identity are disappearing: (i) that the boundary between 'work' and 'non-work' is more problematic in contemporary service employment than in other types of work, and (ii) that recent developments in the organization and control of service employment have transformed the work relationship, which is in consequence less oppositional and less likely to generate collective 'class' identities. These kinds of managerial techniques, it is argued, are also being applied to non-service employment, with a corresponding decline in the salience of 'class' (ie employment) identities.

The 'work'—'non-work' boundary

Here, it has been argued that the development of service work has led to a blurring of the boundary between producers and consumers as individuals. In respect of employment in retail, Du Gay, for example, has argued that:

> In contemporary British retailing there is no longer any room for the base/superstructure dichotomy. As the 'economic' folds seamlessly into the 'cultural', distinctions between 'production', 'consumption' and 'everyday' life become less clear cut (1993:582–3).

It is being suggested here that the dissolving of the production/ consumption boundary means that it is not possible anymore to identify specifically 'class' practices and/or identities in 'reflective modernity' or 'post-modernism', given that the 'producer' (ie class) cannot be independently specified (the parallels with Lash and Urry (1994) are evident here).

The observation that particular kinds of employment actively incorporate the personal commitment—indeed, the personality— of the employee is not a new one. This is particularly likely to be the case in respect of interactive service employment, which frequently draws upon roles developed in a non-market context—for example, the work of caring is widely regarded as 'women's work'. In such cases, the employer is not purchasing an undifferentiated capacity to 'labour', but is able to draw upon skills and capacities not usually associated with 'work' as employment. It is often a feature of such work situations that despite the fact that they may be materially 'exploited', the employees in question gain considerable satisfactions from their work (Crompton and Sanderson, 1990).

It does not follow, however, that this blurring of work and non-work identities means that the producer/consumer boundary has thereby been erased. It is well established in economic anthropology and sociology (Davis, 1985) that *social* categories are intrinsically bound up with the operation of (supposedly) rational (or asocial) markets. Indeed, it might be suggested that this fundamental argument constitutes the major point of differentiation between sociology and economics, (Ingham, 1996). That is, 'the producer' is socially constructed by and in both the context of employment as well as by employment itself. In short, it is being argued here that the fuzzy and problematic boundary identified by Du Gay has long been recognized in respect of an extensive range of 'work'—indeed, of 'work' in general—and the case remains to be established whether contemporary developments have led to significant changes in this respect.

Work Organization and Control

The second feature of service work that has been argued to result in the erosion of the links between employment and class identity and action relates to strategies of work organization and control. Here we will focus on recent changes in the nature of employment organization following from the development of sophisticated technological and behavioural techniques. Recent commentaries have suggested that the 'carrying over' of the self into employment discussed briefly above has been consciously ratcheted upwards, as increasingly, employees are trained or persuaded to transform themselves in order to carry out their jobs. With the expansion of mass service provision and the increasing importance of 'emotional labour' (Hochschild, 1983), complex scripts governing interpersonal interactions have to be acquired. This kind of training extends along the full range of the occupational hierarchy, as even the lowest level of employee in the Macdonalds hamburger chain is instructed in how to 'treat every customer as an individual in sixty seconds or less' (Leidner, 1993). Such employment is increasingly incorporating a level of *self*-involvement on the part of the employee which would seem to cut directly across the kinds of conflictual and repressive work relationships implied by Braverman and much of the 'labour process' school.

As in the case of the transferable nature of employment and non-employment roles which we have just discussed, it may also be suggested that the observation that contemporary management techniques directly incorporate the identity of the employee is of long standing. In 1951, Mills identified the 'personality market' in respect of sales, and at the same time Riesman (1961:264) wrote of 'false personalization'—the 'spurious and effortful glad hand'

—as a major barrier to autonomy in the sphere of work. Both of these writers were critical of the manipulation of identities within employment, which they saw as an essentially bogus exercise. These kinds of analyses may be made in respect of today's managerial strategies, and we will be returning to these points in our concluding discussion. However, it has also been suggested that the kinds of personality adjustments required of sales and interactive service workers also being developed and applied to *non-service* employees.

The quality of personal interaction has become increasingly important in all areas of work, including manufacturing, with the emphasis on positive customer relations as one of the ways to organizational success, and the improvements in production that may be gained through workforce 'empowerment', Total Quality Management (TQM), and so on. Firms compete via their services to customers, teams within firms compete via their services to other teams as the service relationship becomes generalized through the process of production itself. 'Performance' is becoming central to the work process, and increasingly, performance monitoring (made more effective as a consequence of IT developments) is becoming a major form of control over the workforce. Empirical investigations such as the Workplace Industrial Relations Survey have recorded these developments through such factors as the increase in Performance Related Pay.[8] In the language of the '70s debates on the labour process, therefore, many commentators would seem to agree that there has been a growth in the conscious development of 'responsible autonomy', rather than 'direct control', as a means of controlling the labour process. Frenkel *et al.*, (1995:774) have described this as 'info-normative' control, that is 'control based on data objectification (performance indicators) and employee accommodation or commitment to performance standards'.

In summary, it may be argued that the shift to people-centred work as a consequence of the expansion of service employment, together with recent developments in the workplace relating to the organization and control of employees, are making it increasingly less likely that the experience of work will generate the consciousness of solidarity and cohesion with other employees which has been conventionally described as the identity of 'class'. It may be objected that workers will not find it difficult to see through these cynical attempts at manipulation, and that in essence, the purchase of a worker's personality is no different from the purchase of their labour or skills. However, as Leidner (1993) has emphasized, far from experiencing their scripts as manipulation and thus a source of resentment, interactive service workers find them very useful on the job. Similarly, it may also be objected that TQM is in essence a sham, a screen for the intensification of effort and 'downsizing' rather than a genuine attempt to improve the quality of service provision and workplace relationships (Webb, 1996). However, surveys of employees suggest that most workers *do* believe that their work has become more skilled and demanding (Gallie and White, 1993).[9]

In the contemporary employment situation, therefore, the shift towards service and related employment has been accompanied by increasing employment insecurity together with developments in technological monitoring and managerial strategy in which material rewards are becoming increasingly dependent upon individual performance. Even if employees do develop oppositional attitudes to managerial control strategies such as HRM and TQM, developments in the labour market might reduce the likelihood of a collective response. Here the increase in 'non-standard' work, increasing employment insecurity and declining establishment size, all mean that employment has become increasingly likely to generate individualistic, rather than collectivist, sentiments.

Summary and Conclusions

'Unpacking' the complexities of the relations between consumption and class analysis has been a laborious business—not least because both 'class analysis', and the purported ways in which 'consumption' has been held to be significant to it, have themselves proved to be many-stranded. Figure 1 summarizes the trajectory of the argument so far (see over).

Following from our identification of the two broad empirical approaches to class analysis and their consumption-related critiques, our exploration of their connections has apparently revealed a paradox. On the one hand, as we have noted in previous sections of this paper, employment aggregate practitioners have been able to demonstrate that, despite the very real changes in the structure and patterning of paid work, 'class' schemes deriving from the job structure still provide a useful indicator of 'life chances' and opportunities, and that these 'class' schemes have *not* yet been superseded by consumption-based indicators. Indeed, as inequalities in the area of paid work intensify (Rowntree,

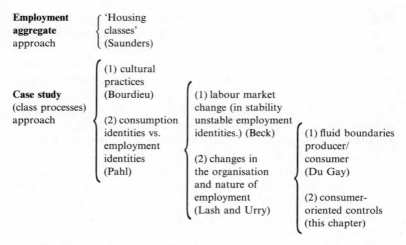

Figure 1 *Different approaches to 'class analysis' and the trajectory of 'consumption' related critiques.*

1995) it is likely that, in the broadest terms, this association will persist. On the other hand, our exploration of changes in the realm of work and employment, and the identities and attitudes associated with these experiences, suggests that work as employment might be becoming *less* significant as a source of what have been by convention in sociology described as collective or 'class' identities and consciousness. These developments are closely associated with the growth of consumption, both as a source of employment, and as a focus of new customer-oriented management practices.

These conclusions may appear to be contradictory, but both are empirically valid. At a gross level of aggregation, the employment structure is associated with established continuities of advantage and disadvantage, which are, to varying degrees, passed on from generation to generation. At the level of production itself, it is evident that the circumstances and experiences of employment are changing rapidly. There is no need, therefore, to resolve the paradox as such.

However, the kinds of changes in the 'work situation' described in previous sections might have rather disturbing consequences. It has been suggested that recent developments in the organization and control of work might make overt conflict at the workplace less likely, but this does not mean that there is a total absence of conflict and contradiction in employment.[10] Indeed, both can be identified, deriving from the nature of 'people-centred' work as

126

well as the 'new management' practices associated with the increasing 'marketization' of employment. As Leidner argues, routinized interactive service work affronts the individuality of both service worker and service recipient, and may generate a 'defensive unwillingness to enter into the spirit of interaction' (1993:228). TQM and other such management practices may give workers control over their own capacities for self-exploitation, but do not carry with them the power to directly influence strategic management decisions. Thus the threat of unemployment, or radical restructuring, will be likely to increase individual feelings of cynicism and insecurity.

These dangers have been classically expressed by Mills (1951):

The personality market . . . underlies the all-pervasive distrust and self-alienation so characteristic of metropolitan people. Without common values and mutual trust, the cash nexus that links one man to another . . . has been made subtle in a dozen ways . . . Men are estranged from one another as each secretly tries to make an instrument of the other, and in time a full circle is made: one makes an instrument of himself, and is estranged from It also (187–8).

This leads to the question of the implications of the arguments reviewed in this paper for 'class analysis' in general. As noted in the Introduction, a common reaction to the recent disputes which have characterized the field of class analysis has been to suggest that we develop a 'new' approach to the topic as a whole. For example, Lee's (1994) arguments extend the sociological critique of the 'economic' to argue for a Durkheimian-inspired perspective on 'class' as a 'social fact', and Scott (1994) has argued for a revived Weberian perspective. It may be suggested, however, that rather than attempting to develop a new, comprehensive theory, we should learn to co-exist with a range of approaches to 'class analysis', as all have particular strengths. For example, it is significant that 'classes' located within the major contours of the employment structure continue to shape attitudes and 'life-chances', as is demonstrated by the 'employment aggregate' approach, but at the same time, we also need to continue to carry out in-depth case studies of major areas of change in the class structure—such as the spatial concentration of the 'underclass' (Morris 1995).

Nevertheless, it is still necessary to try to answer the important questions raised by the problematic of 'consumption'. At the end of the twentieth century, have consumer-identified groups become more important than production or 'class' groupings in mapping the contours of social inequalities and explaining social behaviour? The arguments and empirical evidence of 'employment aggregate' approaches, together with the theoretical discussions of authors such as Warde (1994)—suggests that this is not, in fact, the case. However, much of the debate relating to consumption has focused upon the question of whether individual identities are shaped by 'consumption' or 'employment-related' (class) practices. One strand of argument examined in this paper focuses on the import- ant developments that seem to be taking place in the 'work situa- tions' of many employees, and the implications of this for 'class' consciousness and identity. Has the link between experiences in employment, and class consciousness and action, been dissolved?

Some have argued that the kinds of changes in work organiza- tion discussed in this paper are having a fundamental impact on the meaning of 'work' and its implications for class formation. Lash and Urry's description of 'post-Fordist' production—and the 'post-Fordist' worker—under conditions of 'reflexive accumu- lation' may be taken as an example: 'This sort of reflexive eco- nomic actor is no longer to such a great extent circumscribed by the constraints of 'structure', subject to the rules and resources of the shopfloor. Instead, he/she operates at some distance from these rules and resources; and he/she finally is responsible for the continuous transformation of both shopfloor rules and (in process and product) resources' (1994:122). This description is somewhat fanciful. Although it might be appropriate as far as a minority of highly-skilled, high-tech, occupations are concerned, these condi- tions clearly do not apply to the average MacDonalds' employee, or the four-hour shift, on call-salesperson in a modern shopping mall. It may be argued that, nothwithstanding the development of more sophisticated, consumer-oriented management techniques such as TQM, worker resistance remains a persisting feature of organizational life (Thompson and Ackroyd, 1995). However, such resistance may be individual rather than collective, and it is not too difficult to argue that, in contemporary workplaces, the circumstances of collective resistance might be being eroded. Collective advantages and disadvantages may be very real, but they are, increasingly, experienced at the individual level only.

This whilst capitalist societies continue to be fundamentally structured by the class relations of ownership, production and market (that is, they are still 'class' societies), the experience of employment itself might increasingly have the effect of masking rather than revealing, these relations. In consequence, it might be argued, feelings of class and collective identities are being eroded. These arguments have been made before—as in the 60s and 70s theories of 'mass society' which asserted that 'alienating' employment circumstances left the working class open to *culturally* hegemonic domination. It would be ironic if, at the end of the twentieth century, the causal basis of the 'mass society' had extended into the nature of employment itself. On the other hand, it may be suggested that the causal factor of last resort is in fact chronic economic insecurity. If this is indeed the case, then the return of full employment and job security (if it ever happens) might transform current sociological debates relating to class— and consumption.

Acknowledgements

This chapter has been given as a paper at the ESRC consumption seminar and the University of Essex. I would like to thank both sets of participants for their advice and comments.

Notes

1 At the time of writing (April 1996) in recent weeks: Prince Edward has declared the class system 'dead', John Prescott has caused a minor furore by publicly asserting his 'middle classness', the Duchess of York's lack of class has been held responsible for the break up of her marriage, and the topic has been the focus of a three-week television series and a radio 'phone-in programme.

2 In actuality, the class/employment structure is characterized by both continuity *and* change, and these perspectives are not, therefore, incompatible. However, the differences between different sociological approaches to 'class analysis' have been clarified only recently, and the rather confused situation which prevailed, particularly during the 1980s when the employment aggregate approach achieved considerable prominence, may attributed in part to this. As others have noted, the Nuffield 'research programme' has been finally made explicit some two or more decades after its inception—a fact which has no doubt contributed to persisting confusion. See Scott and Morris 1996.

3 Goldthorpe's early work (see Goldthorpe *et al.*, 1969) was closely associated with this tradition, a fact which made its contribution to the confusion noted above (Note 2).

4 It should be noted that case studies of class processes incorporate quantitative, as well as qualitative, research methods (see Savage *et al.*, 1992; Crompton and

Jones 1984), and that the distinction between the 'employment aggregate' and the 'process' approach should not be thought of as primarily a methodological distinction.

5 There are also a range of relevant non-consumption practices which act not only as social markers, but also have material consequences. See, for example Scott (1991) on the social practices of the upper classes.

6 The best-known sociologist to have incorporated Braverman's Marxist account of the labour process within his framework of class analysis is Wright (1989).

7 For example, the current issue (May 1996) includes a leading article entitled 'Revenge of the middle manager—job insecurity: make it work for you'.

8 See Millward *et al.*, 1992. The semantic shift in the labelling of individualized pay systems—from 'piece rates' to 'performance related pay' is a revealing one, 'piece' referring to the product, whereas 'performance' relates to the individual.

9 The debate on 'skill' as such is not one that is being addressed directly in this paper. One feature which makes it highly problematic is an absence of universally-agreed definitions or measures of 'skill'. For example, a recent research interview established that in successive years, 28 per cent and 31 per cent of the employees of a major clearing bank had been downgraded as a consequence of reorganization (their pay would be frozen, rather than reduced, in consequence). However, they were simultaneously being exhorted to acquire selling skills.

10 I have not discussed in this chapter the systematic political attacks on collective representation, particularly the Trade Union movement, which have taken place over the last fifteen years. This does not mean that I am not aware of their significance. However, in this chapter I have focused upon the broader trends transforming employment and work relationships, which it may be argued are (relatively) independent of direct political intervention. See Crompton *et al.* (eds), 1996.

Bibliography

Bauman, Z., (1982) *Memories of Class*, London: Routledge.

Beatson, M., (1995 'Progress towards a flexible labour market', *Employment Gazette* February 55–66.

Beck, U., (1992) *Risk Society*, London: Sage.

Braverman, H., (1974) *Labor and Monopoly Capital*, New York: Monthly Review Press.

Brown, R. and Brannen, P., (1970) 'Social relations and social perspectives among shipbuilding workers' *Sociology* 4(1): 71–84; 197–211.

Bourdieu, P., (1984) *Distinction: A Social critique of the Judgement of Taste*, London/New York: Routledge.

Clark, T. and Lipset, S.M., (1991) 'Are Social Classes Dying?' *International Sociology* Vol. 6(4) 397–410.

Crompton, R. and Jones, R., (1984) *White-Collar Proletariat: Deskilling and Gender in the Clerical Labour Process*, London: Macmillan.

Crompton, R., and Sanderson, K., (1990) *Gendered Jobs and Social Change*, London: Unwin Hyman.

Crompton, R., Gallie, D. and Purcell, K., (eds), (1996) *Changing Forms of Employment*, London: Routledge.

Crompton, (1993) *Class and Stratification*, Cambridge: Polity.

Crompton, R., (1996) 'The Fragmentation of Class Analysis', *British Journal of Sociology*.

Davis, J., (1985) 'Rules not laws: outline of an ethnographic approach to economics' in Roberts, B., Gallie, D. and Finnegan, R. (eds), *New Approaches to Economic Life*, Manchester: Manchester University Press.

Du Gay, P., (1993) 'Numbers and souls: retailing and the de-differentiation of economy and culture', *British Journal of Sociology* 44: 563–87.

Erikson, R. and Goldthorpe, J.H., (1992) *The Constant Flux*, Oxford: Clarendon Press.

Frenkel, S., Korczynski, M., Donoghue, L., and Shire, K., (1995) 'Re-constituting work: trends towards knowledge work and info-normative control', *Work, Employment and Society* 9(4) 774–796.

Gabriel, Y., (1988) *Working Lives in Catering*, London: Routledge.

Gallie, D. and White, P., (1993) *Employee commitment and the skills revolution*, London: Policy Studies Institute.

Goldthorpe, J.H., Lockwood, D., Bechhofer, F., and Plat, J., (1969) *The Affluent Worker in the Class Structure*, Cambridge: Cambridge University Press.

Goldthorpe, J.H. and Marshall, G., (1992) 'The Promising Future of Class Analysis' *Sociology*, Vol. 26(3): 381–400.

Goldthorpe, J.H., (1987) *Social Mobility and Class Structure in Modern Britain*, Oxford: Clarendon Press.

Goldthorpe, J.H., (1991) 'The uses of history in sociology: reflections on some recent tendencies', *British Journal of Sociology* 42(2): 211–30.

Gregg, P. and Wadsworth, J., (1995) 'A short history of labour turnover, job security and job tenure: 1975–94', *Oxford Review of Economic Policy* II, 1, 73–90.

Hamnett, C., (1989) 'Consumption and class in contemporary Britain' in Hamnett, C., McDowell, L. and Sarre, P. (eds), *Restructuring Britain: the Changing Social Structure*, London: Sage.

Hochschild, A., (1983) *The managed heart*, Berkeley: University of California Press.

Ingham, G.K., (1996) 'Some recent changes in the relationship between economics and sociology', *Cambridge Journal of Economics* vol. 20: 243–75.

Lash, S. and Urry, J., (1994) *Economics of Signs and Space*, London: Sage.

Lee, D.J., (1994) 'Class as a social fact' *Sociology* 28(2): 397–415.

Leidner, R., (1993) *Fast food fast talk*, Los Angeles: University of California Press.

Lockwood, D., (1958, 1989) *The Black Coated Worker*, London: Allen and Unwin, Oxford: OUP.

Lockwood, D., (1966) 'Sources of variation in working-class images of society' *Sociological Review* 14(3): 244–67.

Lockwood, D., (1988) 'The Weakest Link in the Chain' in D. Rose (ed.) *Social Stratification and Economic Change*, London: Unwin Hyman.

Marshall, G., Newby, H., Rose, D. and Vogler, C., (1988) *Social Class in Modern Britain*, London: Unwin Hyman.

Marx, K. and Engels, F., (1962) *Manifesto of the Communist Party in Selected Works* Vol. 1, Moscow: Foreign Languages Publishing House.

Mills, C.W., (1951) *White Collar*, New York: Oxford.

Millward, N. *et al.*, (1992) *Workplace Industrial Relations in Transition*, Aldershot: Dartmouth.

Morris, L., (1995) *Social Divisions*, London: UCL Press.

Newby, H., (1977) *The Deferential Worker*, London: Allen Lane.

Offe, C., (1985) 'Work—a central sociological category?' in C. Offe (ed.) *Disorganized Capitalism*, Cambridge: Polity.

Pahl, R.E., (1989) 'Is the Emperor Naked?' *International Journal of Urban and Regional Research*, Vol. 13(4) 711–20.

Riesman, D., (1961) *The Lonely Crowd*, New Haven Connecticut: Yale University Press.

Joseph Rowntree Foundation (1995) *Inquiry into Income and Wealth*, York.

Saunders, P., (1978) 'Domestic Property and Social Class' *International Journal of Urban and Regional Research* 2:233–51.

Saunders, P., (1987) *Social Theory and the Urban Question*, London: Unwin Hyman.

Savage, M., Barlow, J., Dickens, A., and Fielding, T., (1992) *Property, Bureaucracy, and Culture*, London: Routledge.

Scott, J., (1991) *Who Rules Britain?* Cambridge: Polity.

Scott, J., (1994) 'Class Analysis: Back to the future' *Sociology* 28(4): 933–942.

Scott, J. and Morris, L., (1996) 'The Attenuation of Class Analysis' *British Journal of Sociology* Vol. 47:45–55.

Thompson, P. and Ackroyd, S., (1995) 'All quiet on the workplace front?' *Sociology* 29(4): 615–633.

Veblen, T., (1934) *The theory of the leisure class*, London: Modern Library.

Warde, A., (1994) 'Consumption, Identity Formation and Uncertainty' *Sociology* 28(4): 877–898.

Webb, J., (1996) 'Vocabularies of motive and the 'New' Management', *Work, Employment and Society*, Vol. 10(2): 351–71.

Weber, (1948) 'Class, Status and Party' in H. Gerth and C.W. Mills (eds) *From Max Weber*, London: Routledge.

Wright, E., (ed.), (1989) *The Debate on Classes*, London: Verso.

Part II
The Experience of Consumption

The enigma of Christmas: symbolic violence, compliant subjects and the flow of English kinship

Pnina Werbner

Abstract

Adopting a structural position, this chapter argues against the view of Christmas as an orgy of self-indulgent, hedonistic personal consumption. Instead, drawing on the myths and traditions of Father Christmas, the Nativity and Christmas Pantomime enacted in England[1] every Christmas, it elaborates the notion of a hierarchical gift economy in which the directionality of Christmas gifting coincides with the flows of obligation, nurture and sentiment animating English kinship. Such unilateral gifting—from old to young and from rich to poor—serves to legitimize hierarchical structures of power by converting them into 'soft' domination through symbolic violence, thus creating compliant subjects—individuals who, as members of families, corporate organizations and the 'family' of the nation, are dialogically made through the imaginings of significant others. The simultaneity of millions of acts of consumptive giving each Christmas reproduces the imagined community of the nation, while excluding ethnic and religious minorities who, in effect, redefine themselves as internal stranger-citizens by their non-participation in this annual sacrificial potlatch.

Introduction: hierarchical gift economies

The current postmodernist stress on consumption as a semiotics of everyday life marks a major sociological shift away from an earlier privileging of the work place and of political economic theories of class and nation. By contrast to those earlier theories, consumption theory interrogates the place of goods in identity formation, the emergence of new subjectivities and the aestheticization of everyday life in post-industrial societies (Featherstone,

1991). Yet this refocusing on signifying cultural practices as constitutive of new subcultures of resistance or of self-fashioned lifestyles has often tended, in Campbell's words, to 'foreground the isolated individual, juggling with assorted signs and symbols in a never-ending attempt to construct and maintain identity in a fragmented and ever-changing environment' (Campbell, 1995:101).

Baudrillard's pessimistic scenario of postmodern consumption is of an almost helpless passivity in the face of the infinitely expanding production of cultural signs. As these spiral out of control, all modern subjects come to inhabit a space of hyperreality which renders political economic discussions of class or the reproduction of hierarchy and inequality essentially meaningless. The only remaining meaningful opposition, according to Baudrillard, is that between the future-orientedness of America and the past-orientedness of Europe, with the latter desperately attempting to catch up with the New World (see, for example, Baudrillard, 1988:23).

Such a recasting of consumption as the site of hyperreality, individual reflexivity and unique subjectivity has obscured the original attempt by Pierre Bourdieu in *Distinction* (Bourdieu, 1984) to formulate a theory of taste which might explain the perpetuation of class and stratification in modern societies, *despite* the apparently homogenizing and/or individuating impact of the culture industries. The superficial inventiveness of these industries is subordinated, Bourdieu has argued, to a hierarchy of taste which maps a more fixed semiotics of differential consumption. Social distinction is, accordingly, maintained and reproduced through the differential access of subjects to economic, cultural and symbolic capital. In this respect, the experience of choice generated by the culture industry in capitalist societies is an illusion, since consumers are ultimately restricted by their habitus—the cultural and economic constraints and dispositions they occupy by birth, education or wealth.

But that illusion of choice is important because it creates what I want to call here compliant subjects; free agents who ultimately accept their 'place' in society, who 'fit in' and submit to bureaucratic and corporatist modes of authority and social control, while nevertheless retaining the sense of being 'individuals', that is, self-conscious decision-making agents.

Against a view of consumption as symbolic display of infinite difference, the present chapter attempts to formulate a structural, semiotic theory of exchange and consumption which explains the reproduction of compliant subjects as the outcome of unilateral, unidirectional flows of giving on ritual occasions. I thus hope to expose the primitive roots of the present postmodernist consumerism. My model draws on several sources; Bourdieu's notion of 'symbolic violence' in *Outline of a Theory of Practice* (Bourdieu, 1977), Levi-Strauss's contrast between generalized (or unilateral) and reciprocal modes of exchange as developed by Dumont (1970), Veblen's (1950) notion of 'vicarious consumption', and Mauss's (1966) theory of the gift and of sacrificial offerings. My central claim will be that class-based consumer societies resemble earlier hierarchical societies in sustaining what I propose to call a 'hierarchical gift economy'. Such economies are typified by the symbolic predominance of unilateral (as against reciprocal) ritual giving by superiors to inferiors on occasions framed as sacred and ceremonial. Unilateral giving is a form of generalized exchange characterized by downward flows without expectation of direct return (a gives to b who gives to c; a will not accept gifts from either b or c). This pattern of symbolic exchanges is typical of stratified societies where the normal direction of labour exploitation is reversed by symbolic gifting on key ritual occasions. Symbolic gifting of this type thus serves to embody authority as a form of 'soft domination' (Bourdieu, 1990:128). Through giving, subjects come to be situated in chains of symbolic subordination and authority which are both reproduced and legitimized as 'natural'.

In capitalist, commodified societies, hierarchical gift economies are characterized by an initial conversion of commodities (purchased in the consumer market) into personalized and sacrilized gifts. Rather than simply signalling sentiments of love and intimacy, however, hierarchical gift economies continue to be grounded in pre-capitalist religious ideas about sacrifice, expiation, and the meritorious accumulation of virtue, which animate religious giving not only in Christianity but in other great religions such as Islam, Judaism and Hinduism as well. In all these religions giving as sacrifice paradoxically serves to reproduce inequality and compliance, and thus to revitalize and perpetuate social subordination through acts not merely of anti-consumption, but of vicarious consumption.

The volume of expenditure, the endless shopping, the hyper-advertising, the novelty of the products purchased, the choice of goods meant for personal adornment (clothes, jewelry, cosmetics) for entertainment and aesthetic-cum-intellectual gratification (records, books, videos, toys, computer games), the sheer volume of expensive food, alcohol and sweets feasted upon, the hours of television consumed, the leisure time enjoyed—all these make Christmas the festival of postmodern consumption *par excellence*. Yet Christmas does a lot more than merely celebrate Dionysos, the God of hedonistic pleasure; the cosmology of Christmas and the symbolic complex of performance and giving it enacts, makes it not only a festival of regeneration and revitalization but one which, I shall argue, reproduces compliant subjects within the family, workplace, localized class and nation. Through unilateral giving it also, *ipso facto*, reproduces the nation as a moral community. Paradoxically, however, such acts of mass generosity also draw cultural boundaries within the nation-state, creating by default a class of stranger-citizens. The reasons for this will be discussed more fully below.

The Christmas potlatch

In his analysis of Christmas in Middletown, Caplow, following Antony Heath, rejects the idea that Christmas is a gigantic pot-latch, as suggested by Levi-Strauss in *The Elementary Structures of Kinship* (Levi-Strauss, 1969:56). According to Heath: 'There is simply no room for competitive giving [in industrialized societies] to determine status as it may (or may not) have done among the Kwakiutl Indians' (cited by Caplow, 1982:390). Similarly, David Cheal, in his study of the gift economy in a Canadian town, claims that Levi-Strauss must be wrong in defining Christmas as a potlatch because of the '*diversity* of objects transferred, especially at Christmas' (Cheal, 1988:77, my emphasis). Cheal objects also to Veblen's theory of conspicuous consumption which regards a gift as a 'challenge that must be answered'. The agonistic giving of potlatch is quite different, he argues, from the small-scale giving at Christmas. Such gifting serves not as a mode of status competition but as a way of creating 'small worlds of intimacy' in a larger world of anonymous relations. Hence, too, Cheal objects to theories that attempt to relate the gift economy to the wider political economy.

In rejecting the idea that Christmas is a form of potlatching, what is misrecognized by both Heath and Cheal is the nature of potlatch which is, above all, a sacrifice, a destruction of goods in the sight of the gods which fellow-men witness (Mauss, 1966). Unlike reciprocal giving which, over time, comes to be balanced, such destructive sacrificial giving is made with no expectation of return. The ability to match the destruction is a game of status which is arguably secondary to the expiatory meaning of the destruction itself. Christmas, I shall argue here, is a potlatch to the extent that it is a giant sacrificial act of destruction. In alienating wealth objects to dependents, givers are essentially destroying them in a magnanamous gesture of annual revitalization.

Veblen's theory of consumption illuminates this process. As I argued in my earlier theorizing of hierarchical gift economies (Werbner 1990a and 1990b), while Veblen does not appear to have a theory of exchange, an implicit recognition of the *pattern* such exchanges might assume in stratified societies is provided by him in his notion of 'vicarious consumption'. He argues that in order to display waste conspicuously an individual requires a circle of others around him to consume this excess (Veblen, 1950:117). A man's wife, his children, his servants, his slaves and even his competitors are all, according to Veblen, mere vehicles through whom he displays his prodigious wastefulness (1950:199, 124).

The key feature of hierarchical gift economies is the free alienation of goods given as gifts which cannot, should not, be reciprocated. Studies of Christmas, and there is a veritable industry of such academic studies, repeatedly show that gifting at Christmas flows hierarchically downwards from rich to poor, from male to female and from old to young. The metaphor of 'flow' is critical here, as we shall see. In Britain today, charitable giving has itself become a giant media event in which members of the public 'phone in their donations while being entertained by artists who give freely of their services for the sake of humanitarian causes. As a result, millions of pounds are raised for charity at Christmas time. The BBC's Save the Children fund-raising campaign is timed to allow for charitable distribution to handicapped and underprivileged children at Christmas. Band Aid, the record following the concert which raised funds for Ethiopia, was released at Christmas. The Father Christmases who wander through England's cathedrals of consumption, its shopping malls and village shopping centres, invariably rattle charity collection boxes, suitably decorated in red and white. In pubs, fund-raising rounds for charity are a common feature of the festive spirit of pre-Christmas conviviality. Workers in firms and factories not only receive Christmas bonuses from their bosses, they themselves often club together to raise money for charity. Giant cheques from factory or firm employees, the fruits of sponsored walks, runs, swims and so forth, are beamed on television screens into English living rooms as Christmas draws near. The purchase of charity cards is also *de rigeur* nowadays for the English middle classes (Searle-Chatterjee, 1993).

In a recent anthropological collected volume on Christmas (Miller, 1993), many of the contributors stress these hierarchical features of gift giving and examine some of the symbolic and mythological motifs underlying Christmas as a ritual complex (see especially the contributions by Carrier, Kuper, Belk and Searle-Chatterjee). They fail, however, to situate this patter of gifting within a broader structural analysis of unequal subjects. Instead, these acts are seen as a minor attempt to deny the hedonistic self-indulgence which is the hallmark of Christmas consumerism.

A disciplinary disjunction is evident here between contemporary approaches to exchange and current theories of consumption. The anthropological volume on Christmas makes no mention of Bourdieu and contains only a passing mention to Baudrillard's theory of signs, despite its stress on the tension between the 'consumerism' or 'materialism' of Christmas and the attitudes of love and generosity implied by gift-giving. Consumption is taken in these texts to have a transparent monolithic meaning, whereas recent theories of consumption stress its complex aesthetic and differentiating aspects.

The need is thus to link theories of exchange and consumption in order to interrogate how Christmas creates compliant subjects, 'docile bodies', to use Foucault's expression. To illuminate this process, I want to situate my discussion in a comparative framework by considering the nature of sacrifice as an act which embodies metonymically relations of both equality and inequality.

Sacrifice

Pakistani immigrants in Britain, like other Muslims throughout the world, celebrate the feast of the Hajj with a sacrifice known in Urdu as *qurbani*, the *eid* sacrifice (see Werbner, 1990a, Chapter 4). There are clear rules regarding the division and distribution of the sacrificial animal on *eid*: the beast should be divided into three parts with a third given to members of the family, who consume it in a joint feast on the day of *eid*; a third should go to friends and here the meat is divided into two-pounds parcels which are distributed during a round of brief visits to friends' homes; the final third of the animal is supposed to be given away to the poor. It is highly significant that the sacrifice distributed to family and friends is understood to be freely offered with no expectation of return. Unlike other types of Pakistani gifting, recipients are under no obligation to reciprocate at a later date. Indeed, consuming a share of the sacrifice is a service performed by recipients for the sake of the sacrificer. The sacrifice is a gift to God in which consumers act as mediators, conduits of the good intentions of the sacrificer and his or her family.

In Pakistan, a third of the *eid* sacrifice is given away to orphanages, to beggars around saints' tombs or to the servants of a household. In Britain, however, settlers face a peculiar dilemma because, as they told me, 'there are no poor people here'. The problem is that without giving to the poor, a sacrifice cannot be regarded as a sacrifice; it is in danger of being redefined as an excuse for personal or familial gluttony, for the staging of an event of selfish consumption. In Islam, the poor are the mediators *par excellence* with God. This means, in effect (and this is equally true of Christianity or modern Judaism), that built into the central ritual practices of these religions are presuppositions of social inequality; the ability to make an offering to God depends on the existence of a category of persons defined as destitute, dependent or needy. In its threefold division, the sacrificial animal objectifies two communicative acts: expiation before God for possible sins; and commensality, the sharing of substance in the sight of God, with family and friends.

In the face of the peculiar predicament Pakistanis in England encounter—namely, that there are no poor people in England, or at least no one willing to define themselves as poor—Pakistani immigrants have begun to donate vast sums to transnational Islamic charities which distribute their donations to the needy in countries such as Bosnia, Albania or Palestine. In effect, this uni-directional flow of goods has created an international hierarchy of givers and recipients which is also a hierarchy of privilege and symbolic capital. Pakistani immigrants to Britain are more privileged than their Muslim brethren elsewhere. This hierarchy is reproduced annually during the celebration of *eid*.

This same threefold division of a metaphorical sacrificial beast is replicated, as we shall see below, in Christmas giving. Each

flow of gifts (to kin, friends, 'the poor') substantiates different
types of relationships metonymically within a matrix of equality
and inequality. In order to recognize why this is so we need, however, to examine first the mythological narratives and notions
about English kinship which together form the cosmological complex of symbolic beliefs animating Christmas giving as a signifying act of consumptive regeneration.

The myths of Christmas

The three central myths of Christmas I want to discuss here are
the myth of Father Christmas, the myth of the nativity and the
fairy tales fabulated in Christmas Pantomimes. The three myths
refract also upon a fourth, more contemporary, myth—that of
the First Family of the Nation.

Much has been written by anthropologists and others about the
magical figure of Santa Claus and his reinvention on a massive
scale during the past century. Levi-Strauss's insightful analysis of
the figure in France is worth citing:

> Father Christmas is dressed in scarlet and he is a king. His
> white beard, his furs and his boots, the sleigh in which he
> travels evoke winter. He is called 'Father' and he is an old
> man, thus he incarnates the benevolent form of the authority of
> the ancients (Levi Strauss, 1993:43).

How old is Father Christmas? We cannot be quite sure but he is
certainly very old, his beard is snow-white. Despite his age, however, he is extremely robust and, indeed, physically powerful as he
travels great distances through the night in his sleigh, driving his
reindeer and carrying vast numbers of gifts. Why do we need
Father Christmas? Who is he? We need Father Christmas, I want
to suggest, to carry out gifts for us, to disguise their source. To
put the matter differently, Father Christmas acts as the sacrilizer
of gifts, the mediater who transforms gifts into sacrifices. The illusion of his reality must be sustained because the gifts given by
parents to children are supposed to be freely given without any
expectation of return. Father Christmas effects that transformation by disguising the parental origins of the gift. He is, we said,
very old, perhaps older than any living being, and he is, of
course, infinitely generous. Yet despite his antiquity he is the

bringer of heat and life. His mythical figure generates a series of symbolic oppositions: between hot and cold, light and dark, laughter and sadness, inside and outside, consumption and fasting, fertility and barrenness. The colour of his robe and cheeks, red, contrasts with the cold white of the snow which touches only his beard and the trims of his red gown and shawl. Father Christmas and his reindeers—alive and thus hot—live in the North Pole, the extremity of coldness. He enters the (cold) chimney, perhaps the channel of birth, and descending into the soon-to-be-hot mythological hearth where a log fire will burn, he is offered a hot brandy in exchange for the gifts he brings. The gifts are thus hot because of their association with him; they are revitalizing conduits of life. The Christmas tree, brought into the warm home from the dark, bare cold outside, is lit with hot lights. Christmas, as many have noted, is the time of the winter solstice when the days are at their darkest and the earth cold and bare. In this respect Christmas has often been interpreted as a pagan agricultural festival of revitalization.

But the myth of Father Christmas makes no sense without the complementary myth, that of the nativity, which is enacted in primary schools throughout England every Christmas. The hero of this myth is 'baby Jesus', the child marked out as the miraculous recipient of gifts from the three wise men of the East, a hot place, who have travelled great distances to honour the birth of the new God. They enter the cold manger bearing (hot?) gifts for the newborn child. If we mesh the symbolism of the two Christmas myths, both of which are performed annually in England, it becomes clear that gifts to children via Father Christmas are in fact gifts to God. Young children are ambiguous representations of the newborn king and of weak subjects; they are pure mediators, since children are believed to be incapable of evil. But at the same time, the moment of gifting is a moment of familial incorporation in which the parental and grandparental generations of givers assume moral responsibility and authority over the family and the younger generation. In other words, children and other junior, inferior or impoverished recipients of Christmas gifts are reconstituted through unreciprocated authoritative giving as compliant subjects.

Cheal says of Christmas that it constitutes a 'cult of the individual'. To push his point further one might argue that recipients of gifts at Christmas are reconstructed through the semiotic specificities of gifting as complex subjects. This would fit in with a postmodernist stress on subjective style and choice. However, by contrast to ordinary, everyday consumption in which consumers are individual agents and bricoleurs who create personal styles and selves, at Christmas their 'consumption' of gifts constitutes their passivity as embodiers of externally imposed definitions; a recipient's identity is the product of his or her imaginary constructions by valued others; each giver interprets the recipient from a unique perspective, and thus imposes upon him or her an image or personal quality which is salient to their relationship. A subject is constructed through such multiple personifications. From this perspective, Christmas is a moment not for the reflexive discovery of identity and subjectivity but for the interactive emergence of partible subjects as defined and constituted through external relationships. In this respect all recipients of gifts— whether dependents or friends—become the compliant subjects of givers' imaginative projections. One may talk, perhaps, of modern gifting as an act of dialogical reflexivity, a conscious attempt to define the other's distinctiveness. Christmas can then be construed not merely as a potlatch but as a *postmodern* potlatch; a ritual of conspicuous consumption in which fractable identities are imposed dialogically, and the meaning of objects consumed is externally determined by significant others.

We need to remember that Father Christmas is not simply benevolent—he is a jolly old fellow who loves his glass of brandy. The corporeality and hedonism of Christmas as a ritual of fertility and reproduction, the renewal of the year, is best understood through the third myth of the English Christmas, embodied in the performative narratives of the Christmas pantomime. The Christmas pantomime is a fairy tale of love and marriage in which androgynous or transvestite figures personify sexual lust, license and transgression. Usually pantomimes contain satirical comments about Christmas shopping and contemporary department stores; the protagonists mock the royal family in a Bakhtinian ritual of rebellion in which hierarchy is denied and inverted. The poor in pantomimes triumph over the rich and the powerful. But the final outcome of the pantomime is a wedding, usually a royal wedding, at the very least a gloriously sumptuous wedding. In the end, hierarchy is reconstituted as legitimate and virtuous. Hence the pantomime completes the generational narrative by celebrating sexually active youth. A wedding is, of course, the occasion of consumptive reproduction *par excellence*, and once again, most of the gifting is from the older to the younger generation. As in Christmas, weddings too are potlatch events in which parents give generously, beyond their means, as a sacrificial offering to the success of the new union.

The Christmas pantomime evokes another, more contemporary, collective myth, now shattered, perhaps, irrevocably (a sign of times?). I refer, of course, to the fable of the Royal Family. The Royal Family in its exemplary, iconic perfection duplicates the Jesus myth; the Queen, like the Virgin Mary, is the key protagonist in this myth; she cares for and nurtures her children, the nation and even the Commonwealth. Appropriately, she makes her speech to her subjects on Christmas Day. But if the moral decline of the Royal Family reflects the decline of Empire and nation, and the realities of seduction, physical desire, blood, flesh and (selfish) passion, signify the end of selfless duty and *noblesse oblige*, then the Jesus myth—detached from real time—can be relied upon to embody eternal verities of selflessness and giving, of nurture and protection for the young and helpless.

Blood and the flow of English kinship

The organizing metaphor of Christmas, crystalized in the Father Christmas and Baby Jesus myths, is also that of English kinship, encapsulated in the symbolic image of a 'flow': the flow of blood, love, service, obligation, gifts. In a book on family obligations, Janet Finch speaks of 'support flows' (1989:14,15,36 *passim*), 'flows of money' (*ibid*:15), flows of giving (*ibid*:22), 'linear flows' (*ibid*:39,55) which are often:

... one way, and where apparently this is regarded as quite proper. Parents give to the children and their grandchildren and they continue to give ... One way flows are tolerated here, perhaps expected (Finch, 1989:55).

In similar vein, Strathern speaks of the 'flow of obligation and emotion' as being 'downward' (Strathern, 1992:49,15).

Yet a focus on this image, of flowing, goes against the view that kinship is constituted by a symbolic duality; on the one, of relations of fixed 'substance', and, on the other, of an (equally fixed) 'code of conduct' (Schneider 1980). American ideas about kinship, according to Schneider, define relations of immutable substance as those between 'blood' relatives who share the same 'genetic material'. Codes of conduct, by contrast, apply to relations with affines as well, and are regulated by contract or the law. The opposition is between two fixed givens; nature and the law. Uniting them is 'love'—a (spiritual) union of flesh and blood (conjugal, fraternal, parental, filial) (Schneider, 1980:49). Love defines 'enduring, diffuse, solidarity' which, Schneider indicates, can be expressed and affirmed through many different kinds of acts and gestures (*ibid*:50,51).

One of the problems of glossing 'blood' as 'biogenetic material' as Schneider does (*ibid*:23) is that while this captures the *fixity* of kin relations, it misses the crucial dimension of continuous *movement* implied by the symbol of blood—the fact that blood flows. Strathern recognizes the power of the image of flowing without drawing out its full implications:

> Substance may be metaphorized as blood, and the connections created by the transmission of substance metaphorized as flow. However, the blood that flows between English relatives is imagined as always flowing in one direction (downwards in irreversible time), so that *what comes to rest in any individual no longer moves*. It will only be reactivated when he or she comes to procreate . . . (Strathern, 1992:80, emphasis added).

But does this flow really stop at the moment of conception? British opinions on the rights of surrogate mothers reveal that this may not be so; that biological notions of 'blood' are not simply synonomous with 'biogenetic material' but encompass notions of long-term, continuous nurturing as well. The blood of blood relations may implicitly refer not only to fixed genetic substance but to the flow of blood from the placenta through the umbilical cord. Thus, according to Edwards, 'certain characteristics of children are said to develop through their experience in the womb', so that the shared substance mediated by the placenta *does not require a genetic link* (Edwards, 1993:48). The variability between persons, her English informants suggested, is at least partly produced by gestation and 'primary feeding relations' (*ibid*:58). One woman speculated that a child born of an artificial womb would have 'no feelings because no feelings are going through it' (*ibid*:59). Feelings are produced by nurture and the tie between gestating mother and child was thus seen as more 'real' and compelling even than that produced by the genetic material of the fertilised egg (*ibid*:49). The rights of the surrogate mother to keep the baby were regarded thus as 'natural'.

In a later work Schneider recognizes that the construction of kinship includes 'a notion of something like an instinct of motherhood' having a formative nurturing role. But such a notion assumes, he argues, a pre-existing natural bond (Schneider, 1984:170). It is this putative popular identification which Edwards' work on New Reproductive Technologies throws in doubt. If one wishes to search for 'key symbols' of British kinship these must surely link love as copulation (reciprocal exchange) and as nurture (unilateral giving), through the image of flowing; the semen flows/feeds/fertilizes the womb whose blood flows/feeds the foetus, the product of both reciprocal (conjugal) and unilateral (parental) giving—the person produced by these flows—continues to be nourished *after* birth through flows of giving by both parents.

A deconstruction of the multivocal meanings of 'blood'—fixed genetic stuff and flowing nurture/feelings—has thus become possible in the light of real conundrums raised by the New Reproductive Technologies. In the USA, surrogate mothers have won cases against 'genetic' 'fathers' on appeal to higher courts (Strathern, 1996). In a sense, what has been decoupled by the new technological interventions are the demotic meanings contained by the idea of 'nature'—ideologically, it can now be seen that such ideas about natural procreation refer to process as well as fixity; indeed, the immutable, 'natural' status of parent depends upon continuous nurture and not simply on the pre-existence of shared genetic substance.

But my dissatisfaction with the 'relations of substance'–'code of conduct' distinction does not stem simply from any straightforward denial of the immutability ascribed to so-called 'blood' relations or the negotiability regarded as inherent in legal and normative ideas about the rightful conduct of marital and familial relations. My objection is to the further elaboration of this distinction which implies that the creation of substance *precedes* socialization, which is then glossed as an insubstantial process constituted by 'sentiments' of 'love' and 'spirituality' (Schneider, 1980:49), as though 'pure intimacy' (Giddens, 1991) were a real possibility. The implication is that whereas kinship codes of conduct, like other contractual relations in the society (involving 'work', 'money' or 'commodities') prescribe *material* transactions, the relations between blood relatives are understood, paradoxically, as 'spiritual' and non-substantial precisely because they are seen to be pregiven and thus immutable. Such paradoxes, as

Evans-Pritchard demonstrated in *Azande Witchcraft* (Evans-Pritchard, 1937), are the product of attempts to elicit theoretical constructions from persons who live their kinship in embodied practices, in response to the realities of everyday life, without feeling the need to integrate their partial understandings into a coherent 'theory'; for whom 'nature' is that which seems natural in the present circumstances. Such ideological inventions go against the obvious truth that family relations are materially and emotionally constituted in practice. In performance, the divide between substance and code is blurred so that relations of substance are as much the product of legal claims as are familial codes of conduct, and *vice versa*—codes of conduct may come to be regarded as natural and binding, a 'unity of flesh and blood'. In practice what orders relations of code-substance and endows them with meaning is the directionality of flows. Familial 'solidarity' is not simply 'diffuse' but indexically ordered between generations and collaterals in ways which generate meanings such as 'love' and 'spirituality'.

My critique echoes the contrast drawn by Marriott between Indian and Western ideas of the person. In India, 'code and substance cannot have separate existences' writes Marriott (1976:110). Hence, 'those who transact as well as what and how they transact are thought to be inseparably "code-substance" or "substance-code"' (*ibid.*). Indians are thus 'dividuals' by contrast to Western 'Individuals'; they are the product of directional flows of goods and ideas, or of exclusions and avoidances which create persons as heterogeneous and constantly shifting beings.

That this contrast is, at best, only partially true is indicated by English ideas about kinship. These too accord value to combinatorial mixings, including the mixing of 'blood' in marriage, as creating unique, autonomous *individuals* (Strathern, 1992:19,29). To think of these combinatorial mixings as finalized at the moment of conception (or even birth), however, is surely to negate all the activities of nurturing, clothing, adornment and intellectual stimulation that create the (post)modern individual in her/his uniqueness. Moreover, as Bourdieu in particular has shown, substantive flows of cultural capital in western industrial societies are aesthetically coded, graded and ranked by taste and distinction, embodied in extreme avoidance by elites of what is perceived to be aesthetically facile, vulgar or disgusting (Bourdieu, 1984:486 *passim*). Who you are as an adult is the product of such aesthetic flows. As in India, inherited cultural capital in the West is expressed in bodily and facial dispositions and civilisational manners. Taste, the product of socialization and cultural inheritance, is thus substantially *embodied* (*ibid*:190 *passim*).

I do not wish to push the parallels between South Asian and European 'hierarchical gift economies' too far but, as Ursula Sharma has recently argued: 'There is surely some space between a thorough-going cultural particularism and a naive universalism for provocative illustrations which are more than mere illustrations of difference' (Sharma, 1994:73). We can study 'other' cultures (in the present case, 'the English') because 'they are not totally incommensurate with our own culture' (*ibid*: 88). And importantly, it is by focusing on process rather than ideological content that we are able to draw provocatively insightful comparisons. Thus, against Dumont's (1970:239–60) stress on the uniqueness of the Indian caste system, Sharma argues that comparisons between Western stratificatory systems and caste 'are instructive in that they encourage us to think about general interactional processes through which domination is achieved and resistance expressed' (*ibid*:73).

Unlike commodity exchange, unilateral giving and reciprocal gift exchanges create identity (Carrier, 1995:35). But the need is to recognize further that in the industrial West, such created and recreated identities are positioned in a network of legitimate power and compliance. The identities created are those of compliant individuals. If this seems a contradiction in terms, it is one endorsed by modern Western psychological theories which see the 'well adjusted', well-behaved and cooperative child as the product of loving parental care. What has changed since the Victorian era is a shift in the mode of domination; from strict duty, coercively enforced, to voluntaristic compliance, lovingly elicited. The compliant subject is both an active agent with her/his own subjectivity, *and* the willing subject of legitimate authority.

But if flows of objects individuate, this can only be achieved in capitalist societies against and despite the market. Once objects are not the direct product of one's own labour or that of known others, a tension arises between 'the need to have the object express the giver's identity, and the fact that the objects that are available for giving are impersonal mass commodities' (Carrier, 1995:146). Carrier thus identifies two distinctively modern dilemmas; the tension between gifts and commodities, and the tension between freedom and obligation, between the 'desire to be self-reliant and independent' (*ibid*.) and the compelling nature of sociality. According to Carrier, the perfect gift, freely given without expectation of reciprocity, is a concrete embodiment of the value modernity places on individual autonomy. Yet this gloss on modernity misrecognizes Mauss's fundamental insight, developed by Bourdieu in his notion of symbolic violence, that freely given gifts generate not equality but a 'gentle' domination. This is why the recipients of freely given gifts nevertheless feel compelled to reciprocate if their relation with the donor is understood to be one of equality.

Scales of Giving

A commonsense assumption of modern sociology is that within capitalism, the family remains a haven of tradition set apart from work relations and the market. Within the family transactions are unspecified and uncalculated, 'freely given'. Giddens identifies the family as the 'protective cocoon' which endows individuals with their sense of self and secure reality (Giddens, 1991:40 *passim*). Modernity, he argues, allows for the development of 'pure' relations of intimacy, unencumbered by calculated materialism (*ibid*:88 *passim*). In a well-known passage, Schneider contrasts the construction of 'love and money in American culture'; money creates transitory, impersonal relations of power and calculated value; love is 'spiritual' and based on personal considerations in relations between 'persons' that endure (Schneider, 1980:48–49).

It is this oppositional duality that my own work, like that of Carrier's, has sought to question, interrogating the way gift economies operate within capitalist societies in relations of intimacy, work and in major events of conspicuous consumption. Pakistani settlers in Manchester manage commodity and gift relations simultaneously with family members (Werbner, 1990a), and although such management is fraught with potential conflict, some of the largest industrial and trading firms in the world today are (or started off as) family firms. Politicians and top executives or diplomats' wives fulfil key roles in their husbands' careers. Above all, however, it is major events of social reproduction—weddings and other rites of passage and, indeed, Christmas—which by their very nature blur the distinctions between (individual) consumption, (commodity) production and (familial) reproduction.

If for South Asians large scale consumption events reproduce caste and family hierarchies, it is, I believe, the corporate, administrative nature of the modern state and its economic institutions which Christmas in England images. Benedict Anderson argues that,

> . . . regardless of the actual inequality and exploitation that may prevail in each, the nation is always conceived as a deep, horizontal comradeship. Ultimately it is this fraternity that makes it possible, over the last two centuries, for so many millions of people, not so much to kill, as willingly to die for such limited imaginings (Anderson, 1983:7).

But this 'fraternity', this 'horizontal comradeship', is premised, as Floya Anthias and Nira Yuval-Davis have stressed, on a further gendered and generational imagining of the nation which is often symbolised as a woman who constitutes, along with 'her' children, the ultimate objects of male self-sacrifice (Yuval Davis, forthcoming). The 'family' of the nation (Balibar, 1991:100) thus establishes a division of labour and hierarchy between active male and passive female citizens. As in the family, men emerge as net givers (in their selfless work for the national community and their willingness ultimately to sacrifice their lives), while the task of women is to reproduce the nation biologically and preserve its culture.

Christmas is a moment in which this moral economy of the nation is enacted so that the imagined community reconstitutes itself as a hierarchical moral community. It is significant, however, that this is not an explicit, state-directed nationalist agenda of cultural 'homogenization' but the product of a multiplicity of small-scale voluntary gestures of giving and consuming at different scales of inclusion; the family, the national community, the international community. Nor are the boundaries that are drawn exclusively British. It is notable that the Christmas myths all focus upon strangers and foreigners—Father Christmas, Baby Jesus and the Pantomime heroes and heroines are all characters originating from beyond the English nation. Symbolic mediators are ritual boundary figures who revitalize and purify the community (R. Werbner, 1989, Chapter 3). Father Christmas respects no national boundaries, visiting, as my daughter aptly put it, 'everywhere he's wanted.' His symbolic role is thus that of the unconditional giver.

A recent development in consumption studies is the growing interest in the way national boundaries are constituted through everyday shared consumption practices (see, for example, the contributions to Foster, 1995). In the case of Christmas an additional element is crucially implied; Christmas is a giant sacrificial potlatch in which the imagined community is reconstituted as a moral community, the dialogic product of unilateral gifting.

Christmas involves everyone who celebrates it, even against their better judgement. It is an agonistic holiday in a sense that it involves potlatch-like expenditure beyond what can be afforded. The round of Christmas parties held by friends and workmates around Christmas time demands reciprocity in the long run. Relativities of symbolic capital are embodied in gifting and visiting (some people have more friends and relatives, others have none). Moreover, Christmas compels people who regard themselves as having more-or-less similar incomes to buy their respective children more-or-less the same expensive novelty toys—Nintendos one year, mountain bikes the next, depending on the current fashion of a particular Christmas season. Christmas gifts must be new and what could be more new than a new fashion? The sum total spent by middle-income individuals and families can thus be quite crushing, well beyond their means, even if each item purchased is not very expensive. People are compelled to buy and spend 'irrationally' insofar as they perceive themselves to be members of a particular class which sets yardsticks of expenditure. The imperative to give what is beyond the affordable defines the ineffable value of the relationships which the Christmas gifts personify. In this sense—in terms of the consumption items chosen by parental givers as gifts—Christmas defines relations of agonistic or competitive equality and solidarity between adults belonging to a single class, community and neighbourhood, while being an occasion for the accumulation of personal symbolic capital.

Moreover, Christmas donations to international relief agencies and charities such as Oxfam or UNICEF expand national citizens' ideas about the frontiers of humanity, to use Levi-Strauss's apt term (Levi-Strauss, 1966:166). The paradox is, of course, that by defining themselves as net givers, Westerners also symbolise the prevailing global hierarchical relations between the North and the South. What is exported with western humanism is also western hegemony in its 'gentler' form. Similarly, within Britain, charitable collections for the handicapped and other disadvantaged groups reveal the internal inequalities within the society and the contradictions which capitalism generates for those of its members who have somehow escaped the familial safety net.

Christmas humanitarian giving is thus an act of expiation in the context of apparently selfish and family-centred mundane consumption. The frenzy of shopping and donations which all this entails, and the elaborate ways in which commodities are converted into personal sacred gifts through their wrapping and placement under the magical Christmas tree, are very specifically English, Christian, Western customs. It is their sacrificial beast which is symbolically divided in these gestures of giving; to the family, the community and 'the poor'.

Stranger-citizens

The simultaneous celebration of this complex of ceremonial and ritual acts, culminating in the Christmas feast held co-temporaneously in hundreds of thousands of English homes, recreates the imagined community of the nation in its simultaneous co-presence, in the same way that the morning ritual reading of the daily newspaper does (Anderson, 1983). But equally important is the fact that the nation so imagined is a humane, moral community of givers with co-responsibility for the misfortunes of its members, for the needy, the unfortunate and the destitute in its midst and even beyond its national boundaries. British Jews, Muslims and other minority groups who are neither givers nor recipients at Christmas are necessarily excluded from this imaginary collectivity. The nation-state as a state of equal citizens thus redefines itself at Christmas by contrast to the stranger-citizens in its midst. For these strangers Christmas is a period of limbo, a no-man's land, a kind of embarrassing realization of their otherness. This, despite the fact that both Jews and Muslims have traditions of philanthropy and hierarchical giving which parallel those of Christians. In England, the start of the Christmas vacation invariably witnesses a veritable exodus of English Jews on holidays to Israel, to Switzerland or to some other far away destination. This negative tourism is a way of avoiding the reality of Christmas. Those who do celebrate Christmas do it in a half-hearted way, they never fully enter into the spirit of Christmas dictated by the whole symbolic complex.

Having a Christmas tree (as some Jews and Hindus do) is not quite the same as celebrating Christmas. The Christmas tree, as I have attempted to demonstrate here, is merely a single item in a whole cosmology of giving and belief. It is embedded in a highly elaborate ritual festival through which persons are defined as willing and compliant subjects of their extended families, their classes and their nation. To a Jew or a Muslim in England, nothing defines their externality, the fact that they are stranger-subjects in their English homeland, more than Christmas.

This means that those who exclude themselves from giving or consuming at Christmas time, for whatever reasons, are also implicitly and unintentionally excluded from the moral community. During Christmas, the position of all non-Christians as internal citizen-strangers of the nation is rendered highly ambiguous. In Germany, for example, Turkish parents find difficulty explaining to their children why they should not celebrate Christmas with fireworks as is the local custom. 'I *know* there's no such thing in our religion,' one Turkish migrant explained to anthropologist Lale Yalcin-Heckman, 'but we don't have the ability to explain this to a 7-year-old child!' (Yalcin-Heckman, 1994:184).

It goes without saying that modern nation-states contain within them several ethnic diasporas who form, in Bauman's words (1992:76), discrete aesthetic communities, each associated with its own gift economy and modes of sacrificial giving (on these see Werbner, 1990a and Bhachu, 1985). The critical role played by immigrants in disrupting unitary myths of the nation has been noted (Bhabha, 1990). By analogy, the culturally distinct gift economies and consumption patterns of migrants, immigrants and strangers are interperlated into the moral economy of the nation. This is the reverse side of the movement towards globalized mass consumption—the Coca-Colazation or Macdonaldization of the world—which a contemporary anthropology of consumption needs to address. Yet a recent review of the anthropology of consumption (Miller, 1995) makes no reference to migrant consumption patterns, thus ignoring the central importance of migration and diaspora for anthropological (as well as sociological) theories of postmodernity.

A focus on ethnic consumption and the reproduction of ethnic collective identities indicates where the *limits* of mass national and global consumption are to be found. These limits are set, it must be stressed, not by the daily consumption of mundane, everyday goods, but by the festive consumption of luxury goods, aesthetically defined within diasporas of taste, convened for the sake of reproduction. After all, only Muslims in Britain buy massive numbers of whole lambs for sacrificial purposes on *eid*, just as only Jews buy thousands of boxes of unleavened bread on

Passover. The sacrificial lambs slaughtered on *eid* are consumed in parallel feasting events convened by British Muslims through-out the whole of Britain. At the very same moment, hundreds of thousands of animals are slaughtered and consumed in the valley of Mina in Saudi Arabia as the culmination of the annual pil-grimage to Mecca, and in parallel rituals throughout the Muslim world. It is on these occasions that ethnic and diasporic subjects are constituted and it is precisely these occasions which also define collective hierarchies and exclusions.

This leads to a more general theoretical question as to how morality is created and reproduced both globally and in the modern nation-state. Within the family extreme asymmetrical gift-ing at Christmas arguably marks a key phase in the socialization of pre-school children into the wider community. It thus reflects a problematic shift in relations of authority between young children and adults, from unconditional to conditional gratification. It is noteworthy that in some *middle* class families, attempts are made to stress intra-familial reciprocity rather than downward flows. Such families are often ill-at-ease with the potlatch dimensions of Christmas, interpreting this profligate giving as waste rather than generosity. Yet it is in such families that global giving to humani-tarian causes is most stressed. They too are ultimately caught up in redemptive notions of giving. Gifts ease the pain of inequality for givers as well as receivers, they soften relations of domination. Because children are willing recipients of adult largesse they fulfil the ritual role of symbolic mediators who can objectify the social imperative to give and share. Thus Bauman, citing Levinas, argues:

> . . . morality is the encounter with the Other as Face. Moral
> stance begets an essentially *unequal* relationship; this inequality,
> non-equity, this not-asking-for-reciprocation, this disinterest in
> mutuality, this indifference to the 'balancing up' of gains or
> rewards—in short, this organically 'unbalanced' and hence non-
> reversible character of the 'I versus the Other' relationship is
> what makes the encounter a moral event (Bauman, 1993:48–9).

Children and the poor enable adults to be moral human beings at Christmas.

Yet all this presupposes that society is 'moral' in some sense. In reality, English bourgeois notions of *nobless oblige*, of self-sacrifice and selfless service by the privileged for the sake of the

Pnina Werbner

wider community (Williams, 1990:329), of the 'one nation', no longer seem to apply; leaders of the nation raid the public purse with impunity to line their own pockets. New Right policies attempt to deny the responsibility of the nation-state for its underprivileged or vulnerable citizens by invoking the 'family' as the final port of responsibility (Finch, 1989:7–12). The Right thus rejects the central trope of nationalism, of the nation as a single family, while at the same time it incongruously makes appeals to 'Englishness'. Moreover, interrogating the moral and mythological narratives of Christmas in contemporary England fails perhaps also to interrogate the changing nature of English kinship as well as of English society more generally. It has been argued, for example, that the very ground of nature upon which kinship has hitherto been 'constructed' has been lost, and with it also the possibility of making individuals 'out of' nature. Instead, we have an endless multiplication of 'diversity without individuality' (Strathern, 1992:193). In such times, is Christmas merely an anachronism, a mystification or a postmodern orgy of simulated 'individual' consumption reflecting this selfishness at the top? Or is it, perhaps, a carnivalesque form of resistance to a new world order?

Conclusion: The enigma of Christmas—symbolic violence and the making of compliant subjects

We have seen that the organizing metaphor of English kinship is that of flowing—the directional flow of blood, sentiment, nurture, care and obligation. I have also proposed that gifts are made dialogically, with an eye to the special individuality or identity of the recipient. In the light of these two propositions, perhaps one might argue that Christmas gifts do not so much personify the giver or objectify the relationship between giver recipient, as they do in most pre-industrial gift economies; what English Christmas gifts do is *to substantialize the flow of substance* after the originary flow of blood has 'stopped'. Trying to unravel this flow of giving highlights, however, the enigma of Christmas.

The enigma of Christmas is perhaps that of all altruistic giving. Janet Finch lists (and at least partially rejects) several established theories of altruism; the least persuasive, by sociobiologists, argues that 'hard core altruism', serves to perpetuate a person's 'genetic material' (Finch, 1989:18); Becker sees investment in children as a rational, long-term economic investment in human capital (*ibid*:222–23); feminists theorize the concept as legitimising women's domestic self-sacrifice (*ibid*:223); psychologists such as Pincus see it as a way of transmitting feelings about family relationships between generations (*ibid*:226). Seen from this perspective, the 'secret' of Father Christmas which children uncover is not that 'Father Christmas doesn't exist' but that he is really the combined figure of parents, aunts, uncles and grandparents. It is this 'secret' which is transmitted between generations. Talcott Parsons is perhaps the intellectual source of the view that modern societies separate 'particularistic' and 'universalistic' relations, the former centred on the family/home, the latter on work and the public sphere (*ibid*:229–30); like Parsons, Meyer Fortes's notion of 'prescriptive altruism' defines the morality of kinship as distinct in being non-instrumental (*ibid*:230–231).

A further option which Finch only hints at, but is the one proposed here, is to grasp altruism as a dialectical process which legitimizes a 'soft' domination in contexts where overt shows of power are not tolerated. This is what Bourdieu calls 'symbolic violence':[2]

> . . . when domination can only be exercised in its *elementary form*, i.e. directly, between one person and another, it cannot take place overtly and must be disguised under the veil of enchanted relationships . . . it is present both in the debt and in the gift which, in spite of their apparent opposition, have in common the power of founding either dependence (and even slavery) or solidarity, depending on the strategies within which they are deployed. . . . symbolic violence, the gentle, invisible form of violence, which is never recognised as such, and is not so much undergone as chosen, the violence of credit, confidence, obligation, personal loyalty, hospitality, gifts, gratitude, piety—in short, all the virtues honoured by the code of honour—cannot fail to be seen as the most economical mode of domination. The gift, generosity, conspicuous distribution—the extreme case of which is the potlatch—are operations of social alchemy which may be observed whenever the direct application of overt physical or economic violence is negatively sanctioned, and which tend to bring about the transmutation of economic capital into symbolic capital. Wastage of money, energy, time and ingenuity is the very essence of the social alchemy through which an interested relationship is transmuted into . . . *legitimate authority*. (Bourdieu, 1977:191–92).[1]

At Christmas time, this enchanted alchemy of giving creates docile subjects not only within the family but also within the nation. Christmas is a liminal period in which the consumption of goods received signals love and solidarity while simultaneously reproducing legitimate inequalities within a single moral community.

Modes of domination are, of course, historically determined. As we have already seen, contemporary Christmas giving creates postmodern subjects, each with his or her own 'unique' combinatorial identity. Bourdieu believes that the institutionalization of inequalities has made the paternalism inherent in the code of honour redundant, since inequalities are now upheld by state law (*ibid*:196). Yet the law remains in tension with current ideas about legitimacy and honour. Even within capitalism or modernity, each era constructs what is legitimate by disguising the naked brutality of power, and does so somewhat differently. This is illustrated by the transformation of another Christmas myth, *A Christmas Carol* by Charles Dickens.

In its original version Scrooge was the Victorian money lender and slum landlord who threatens to evict his poor tenants into the snow on Christmas eve. The spirit of Christmas plagues him and ultimately, confronted by premonitions of hell and damnation, he succumbs to it, exhibiting generosity, goodwill and fellowship beyond the logic of capitalist accumulation and profit. The impact of the book in America was, apparently, quite dramatic (see Carrier, 1995:184). Yet it could be argued that the concern it reflected with the iniquities of class has now been displaced, as Christmas has increasingly come to be focused on the family (*ibid*:185).

Not so, I believe. Inequality remains intrinsic to Western societies, but in the late twentieth century, relations of hierarchy are objectified in a different form—that of the big corporation and the vast state bureaucracy within which each worker is expected to know his or her place and to kowtow to immediate superiors.

This transformation in the form hierarchical relations assume is reflected in the modern-day version of Dickens's novel. The film 'Scrooged' stars Bill Murry as the media corporate mogul who shows his employees no mercy, is indifferent to their personal predicaments and even demands that they work on Christmas eve. The plot is set in a violent Manhatten where homeless people are left to fend for themselves and the corporation determines people's fate. Our postmodern Scrooge sells violence as a formula for media advertising success, while denying his own personal and familial commitments. As in the original, he is increasingly plagued by ghosts and the spirit of Christmas, and is compelled finally to succumb, becoming the good, caring employer who joins his staff and the wider 'family' of TV viewers in celebration, making an emotional appeal to love and mutual care. Indeed, he celebrates the recovery of his own conjugal love on the screen, in front of millions of viewers.

What, then, is the spirit of Christmas? As ritual and mythology it occupies a space of carnevalesque liminality in which excessive consumption and role reversals make children sacred kings and queens of the day; in which superiors are compelled not only to give but to mingle as equals with inferiors; where gifts, wine and love flow from the powerful to the vulnerable and the needy, creating bonds of substance across social divisions. Like other such rituals, the meaning and political message of the ritual is not, however, predetermined or historically fixed. It may simply mask relations of domination, perhaps a feature of the present historical moment; it may be an excuse for hedonistic enjoyment and postmodern self-indulgence; it may be a time when family relations have to be endured. But whatever else, Christmas both endorses hierarchical domination while it also preserves a potentially revolutionary anti-capitalist and anti-corporatist message. The dialectic between legitimate domination, selfish self-indulgence, compliance and the demand for personal recognition which Taylor has argued is the hallmark of modernity (Taylor, 1992) is embodied, yet remains unresolved, in the ritual of Christmas, as indeed it does in late twentieth century English society.

Acknowledgements

This chapter was first presented to the ESRC Consumption seminar which took place at Salford University in June, 1995. I would like to thank Steve Edgell and Kevin Hetherington for their patience and trust in the final product and David Morgan and Ursula Sharma for their very helpful comments during the seminar. The chapter is based on twenty-five years of participant observation in England and I owe a special debt to one of my key informants, Donna Werbner, for her penetrating and acutely perceptive comments and observations.

Notes

1 In using the term 'English' I follow the conventions of the literature on the subject; but what is said would apply equally to Scotland, Ireland and Wales.
2 In *Distinction*, Bourdieu uses the notion of symbolic violence to refer to the imposition by dominant classes of their own life-styles and taste on the masses. 'Cultural capital' thus substitutes for the 'symbolic capital' accumulated through displays of generosity (1984:511). This seems to me to collapse two distinct concepts and to subvert Bourdieu's own important insight into the dialectical nature of ma/paternalistic generosity, substituting for it a simple theory of mystification. This is doubly unsatisfactory since, in late capitalist societies, the ability of élites to control the 'tastes' of youth or the masses is in reality minimal.

References

Anderson, B. (1983), *Imagined. Communities: Reflections on the Origin and Spread of Nationalism*, London: Verso.
Balibar, E., (1991), 'The Nation Form: History and Ideology', pp. 86–106, in E. Balibar and I. Wallerstein, *Race, Nation and Class: Ambiguous Identities*, London: Verso.
Bauman, Z., (1992), *Intimations of Postmodernity*, London: Routledge.
Bauman, Z., (1993), *Postmodern Ethics*, Oxford: Blackwells.
Baudrillard, J., (1988), *America*, Trans. Chris Turner, London: Verso.
Belk, R., (1993), 'Materialism and the Making of the Modern American Christmas', pp. 75–104, in D. Miller (ed.), *Unwrapping Christmas*, Oxford: Clarendon Press.
Bhabha, Homi K., (1994), *The Location of Culture*, London: Routledge.
Bhachu, P., (1985), *Twice Migrants: East African Sikh Settlers in Britain*, London: Tavistock.
Bourdieu, P., (1977), *Outline of a Theory of Practice*, trans. Richard Nice, Cambridge: Cambridge University Press.
Bourdieu, P., (1984), *Distinction: A Social Critique of the Judgement of Taste*, trans. Richard Nice, London and New York: Routledge and Kegan Paul.
Bourdieu, P., (1990), *The Logic of Practice*, trans. Richard Nice, Cambridge: Polity Press.
Campbell, C., (1995), 'The Sociology of Consumption', pp. 96–126, in D. Miller (ed.), *Acknowledging Consumption: A Review of New Studies*, London and New York: Routledge.
Caplow, T., (1982), 'Christmas Gifts and Kin Networks', *American Sociological Review* 47:383–392.
Carrier, J., (1993), 'The Rituals of Christmas Giving', pp. 55–74, in D. Miller (ed.), *Unwrapping Christmas*, Oxford: Clarendon Press.
Carrier, J., (1995), *Gifts and Commodities: Exchange and Western Capitalism since 1700*, London: Routledge.
Cheal, David J., (1988), *The Gift Economy*, London: Routledge.
Dumont, L., (1970), *Homo Hierarchicus*, London: Paladin.
Edwards, J., (1993), 'Explicit Connections: Ethnographic Enquiry in North-West England', pp. 42–66, in J. Edwards, S. Franklin, E. Hirch, F. Price,

M. Strathern, *Technologies of Procreation: Kinship in the Age of Assisted Conception*, Manchester: Manchester University Press.

Evans-Pritchard, E.E., (1937), *Witchcraft, Oracles and Magic among the Azande*, Oxford: Clarendon Press.

Featherstone, M., (1991), *Consumer Culture and Postmodernism*, London: Sage.

Finch, J., (1989), *Family Obligations and Social Change*, Cambridge: Polity Press.

Foster, R.J. (ed.), (1995), *Nation Making: Emergent Identities in Postcolonial Melanesia*, Ann Arbor: University of Michigan Press.

Giddens, A., (1991), *Modernity and Self-Identity: Self and Society in the Late Modern Age*, Cambridge: Polity Press.

Kuper, A., (1993), 'The English Christmas and the Family: Time Out and Alternative Realities,' in D. Miller (ed.), *Unwrapping Christmas*, Oxford: Clarendon Press.

Levi-Strauss, C., (1966), *The Savage Mind*, London: Weidenfeld and Nicholson.

Levi-Strauss, C., (1969), [1949] *The Elementary Structures of Kinship*, trans. J.H. Bell and J.R. von Sturmer, London: Social Science Paperbacks.

Levi-Strauss, C., (1993), 'Father Christmas Executed', pp. 38–54, in D. Miller (ed.), *Unwrapping Christmas*, Oxford: Clarendon Press.

Marriott, M., (1976), 'Hindu Transactions: Diversity without Dualism', pp. 109–142, in B. Kapferer (ed.), *Transaction and Meaning*, Philadelphia: Institute for the Study of Human Issues.

Mauss, M., (1966), *The Gift*, London: Cohen and West.

Miller, D. (ed.), (1993), *Unwrapping Christmas*, Oxford: Clarendon Press.

Miller, D., (1995), 'Consumption Studies as the Transformation of Anthropology', pp. 264–95, in D. Miller (ed.), *Acknowledging Consumption*, London: Routledge.

Schneider, D.M., (1980), *American Kinship: A Cultural Account*, 2nd Edition, Chicago: the University of Chicago Press.

Schneider, D.M., (1984), *A Critique of the Study of Kinship*, Ann Arbor: the University of Michigan Press.

Searle-Chatterjee, M., (1993), 'Christmas Cards and the Construction of Social Relations in Britain Today', pp. 157–175, in D. Miller (ed.), *Unwrapping Christmas*, Oxford: Clarendon Press.

Sharma, U.M., (1994), 'Berreman Revisited: Caste and the Comparative Method', pp. 72–91, in M. Searle-Chatterjee and U. Sharma (eds), *Contextualising Caste*, Sociological Review Monographs, Oxford: Blackwell.

Strathern, M., (1992), *After Nature: English Kinship in the Late 20th Century*, the Lewis Henry Morgan Lectures, Cambridge: Cambridge University Press.

Strathern, M., (1996), 'Enabling Identity? Biology, Choice and the New Reproductive Technologies,' pp. 37–52, in S. Hall and P. du Gay (eds), London: Sage.

Taylor, C., (1992), *Multiculturalism: Examining the Politics of Recognition*, New Jersey: Princeton University Press.

Veblen, T., (1950), [1989], *The Portable Veblen*, edited with an introduction by Max Lerner, New York: the Viking Press.

Werbner, P., (1990a), *The Migration Process: Capital, Gifts and Offerings among British Pakistanis*, Oxford: Berg Publishers.

Werbner, P., (1900b), 'Economic Rationality and Hierarchical Gift Economies: Value and Ranking among British Pakistanis', *Man* (N.S.), 25: 260–85.

Werbner, Richard P., (1989), *Ritual Passage, Sacred Journey: the Process and Organisation of Religious Movement*, Washington D.C.: Smithsonian Institution Press.

Williams, R., (1990), [1958] *Culture and Society*, London: the Hogarth Press.

Yalcin-Heckman, L., (1994), 'Are Fireworks Islamic? Towards an Understanding of Turkish Migrants and Islam in Germany,' pp. 178–195, in C. Stewart and R. Shaw (eds), *Syncretism/Anti-Syncretism: the Politics of Religious Synthesis*, London: Routledge.

Yuval-Davis, N., (forthcoming), *Gender and Nation*, London: Sage.

Consuming schooling: choice, commodity, gift and systems of exchange

Patricia Allatt

Abstract

Schooling is a relational good, its consumption founded in social reciprocities. A qualitative study of the purchase and use of schooling by
three middle class families challenges the view of identity formation as
a project of individual self-realization. Traversing the public domain of
the quasi-market of education and the private domain of the family,
schooling switches from commodity to gift, entering the associated systems of commodity exchange and moral reciprocities. The tailoring to
parental ends of the education offered by schools, and the co-labour
of consumption within the household in the form of homework,
shaped young people's identity, colonized and reproduced the family.

This chapter focuses on the consumption of schooling in the context of family relations, unravelling family processes and experiences of family members as schools are chosen and children get
on with their homework. Exploring these relational aspects of
consumption, where consumption is a joint venture founded in
social reciprocities, raises an issue at the heart of theories of consumption—the forces shaping social identity at the end of the
twentieth century.[1]

Criticising accounts which construe the formation of identity as
a project of individual self-realization, Warde (1994:892) argues
that 'current dominant approaches to consumption [by Bauman
(1988), Beck (1992) and Giddens (1991)] assume far too individualistic a model of the consumer'. Even narrowing consumption to
individualized commodities bought for purposes of display, this
dominance of the asocial individual is surprising; as Urry (1990)
notes, apart from relatively trivial purchases, such as a bar of
chocolate,[2] made by an isolated individual and immediately consumed, most consumption involves pre- and post-purchase work.

Moreover, consumption cannot be divorced from those social forces which propel individuals towards or away from particular goods and shape the manner of their consumption. 'Consumer behaviour' is 'link[ed] back' into 'status, exchange, social transition, social class, hierarchy etc.' (Warde, 1994:896).

To view education as a site of consumption thrusts its socially embedded nature to the fore. Thus different categories of educational consumer (child, parent, employer, community), have converging, though not necessarily shared, interests in the embodiment of education in the child. But, more specifically, in the schooling years, the consumption of education is inherently relational, premised upon the normatively expected and legally prescribed parent-child relationship; for however minimal, schooling cannot take place without parental involvement, even if limited to presenting the young child at school or arranging for someone else to do so. The consumption of schooling, therefore, straddles two domains, the public domain of school and the private domain of the family. Critically, in traversing these domains, schooling undergoes a transformation, changing its character from that of commodity to that of gift, thereby entering a different system of exchange. Although not a simple dichotomy, it is used here as a heuristic device to penetrate the relational character of familial consumption, uncovering social processes, divisions and tensions.

My comments stem from revisiting a qualitative study of young people and their parents in the north-east of England, conducted during 1989 and 1990, which explored the shaping of young people's economic and political identities and self efficacy within the family. Eight families, working and middle class, were interviewed, each with a 15/16 year old and an 18/19 year old most of whom were either preparing for or had recently completed public examinations. These examinations dominated the parenting careers of mothers and fathers and the education and employment careers of their children, rendering education a salient feature of family life—evidenced by family members as they described their histories, values, expectations, and daily routines.

Three middle-class families, measured by parental occupation and social mobility histories—the Jacksons, Brayshaws and Phillips—whose children attended private day schools, are the core from which the ideas in this chapter developed. The Jacksons were successful farmers with income from other sources, for whom privileged education was a family tradition. Mrs Jackson, a trained music teacher, had renounced paid employment on the birth of her first child, but for several years had taught on a part-time voluntary basis in her daughter's former prep school to ensure the continuance of her musical education. The Phillips— father a college lecturer and mother a teacher in the special schools sector—were similarly educationally privileged; and although in comfortable circumstances, they were not as materially well off as their parents had been. Consequently, educational achievement and occupational success were essential if their children were to maintain a similar lifestyle. The Brayshaws had been upwardly mobile, both parents from upper working/lower middle-class homes. Mr Brayshaw had left school at sixteen and worked his way up, taking professional examinations at evening class, and was now a qualified accountant. Mrs Brayshaw, the youngest child and first in her family to go to college, had taught mathematics but, like Mrs Jackson, had resigned her post with the start of parenthood.

I have written earlier, drawing upon Bourdieu's (1986) concept of forms of capital, on the processes by which these families laboured to transmit advantage to their children (Allatt, 1993a; 1993b). Here I adjust the lens to view schooling through the prism of consumption. I start by contextualizing schooling within the lexicon of consumption by examining definitions of 'consume' and their connection with constructs of self-identity.

Consumption: definitions and models

Consumption carries different, though not necessarily competing, models of identity formation. These lie not so much in the term itself but in the goods and services to which it is applied, since these determine the manner of consumption. The Pocket Oxford Dictionary defines consume as 'make away with, use up, devour, eat or drink up'. These convey, though less harshly, the unfavourable overtones—the general sense of destruction or waste—which persisted well into the nineteenth century (Williams 1993), and linger in modern usage. In this view, consumption is paired with production; it requires further production, replenishment, in order to continue.

Critical differences rest within these definitions, and support different models of identity formation. The consumption of food and drink, for example, differs to that of ear-rings or washing

machines. Ignoring the use value and users of the latter, ear-rings
and washing machines are outward symbolic attachments, hung
about the individual, and may eventually be used up, thrown
away or changed. In contrast, food and drink, although still
heavily symbolic, are digested, physically becoming the individual.
This interpretation exposes an alternative twinning—a consump-
tion-reproduction duo where the commodity is not replaced but
the consumer reproduced. It is represented by Bourdieu (1986) as
acculturation, whereby resources are worked upon in the
processes of social and cultural reproduction. Within this model,
self-identity is not an individualized project but one rooted in
social relationships over time. The consumption of schooling,
conceived as a process whereby identities are shaped through the
variable commodity of education, is an example of this ingesting,
digesting, reproductive view of consumption.

This reproductive view of consumption can be extended by
drawing upon Mauss' (1967) analysis of the potlatch and the gift
and the different, though inter-connected, systems of exchange
embedded in the gift and the commodity. The original meaning of
the word potlatch, the ceremonial destruction of wealth, whereby
'goods long stored are at once given away or destroyed lend[ing]
to these institutions the appearance of wasteful expenditure and
childlike prodigality' (Mauss, 1967:72) encompassed both 'to consume' and 'to nourish'. But the unspoken, yet obligatory, reciprocities inherent in the gift highlight the relational aspects, for
here social bonds are also nourished and reproduced, brought
about and maintained through moral transactions (Mauss,
1967:ix), contrasting with the commodity, where exchange relations are overtly economic.

The reproductive aspect of consumption is directly relevant to
schooling in its movement between the public and private spheres.
In the former, in the quasi-market of parental choice, schooling
takes the commodity form—whether purchased through tax,
earned income or the proposed voucher scheme (Glennerster and
Le Grand, 1995)—and is embedded in rational economic relations
of exchange between purchaser and provider. On entry into the
private domain of the household, schooling undergoes a morphological change, transformed from commodity to gift. Bought in
order to give, schooling is now embedded in a system of moral
transactions. Economic and competitive dimensions of the commodity still lurk but are transformed into over sacrifice, coloured
by love, trust, pride, and risk, and temporally graded, monitored

reciprocities. These elements were woven into the daily routines and practices of the Jacksons, Brayshaws and Phillips.

I now turn to the consumption of schooling as shaped by these two systems of exchange. Using the theme of choice, a key term within the consumption debate (Warde, 1994), I trace how choices interpenetrate school and family, and the tensions and mechanisms of their resolution. I start with the macro-choice of school and then examine the micro-choices made in the labour of consumption within the household.

Choosing a school

The consumer and the schooling market converge in the issue of school choice, entering public discourse as 'parental choice'—although unlike choice of other goods, the consumption of schooling is not voluntary but a legal requirement, responsibility for school attendance falling upon the parent (Whitney, 1995). Within this framework lie the social divisions of choice. Couched in the vocabulary of the market place,[3] underpinned by political ideologies and differential access to resources, and whilst not confined to such highly visible events[4] as secondary school transfer, it is no accident that the issue becomes heated over this staging-post in the educational career. For in the political economy of schooling, the few years between the ages of 11 and 16/18 differentially propel the young towards trajectories of opportunity and life chances.

In this quasi-market of education with its legal requirement to consume, choice is further constrained. The institutional framework of formal education circumscribes what is available; familial economic, social and cultural resources shape opportunity and orientation, indeed the survival of a household unit may be premised on non-educational needs; and the voices of parent, child and others may be variously and differentially weighted. Even Warde's (1994) preference for 'selection' rather than 'choice' is inadequate for this scenario. Indeed, in a climate of school performance league tables, schools are more likely to select their consumers—both parent and child. The data from these three middle-class families illuminate such constraints.

The social bases of choice

Only amongst the very wealthy (or, in our society, those considered to be eccentric) can education be tailored to suit what key
adults define as the needs of a child. Thus, since parents do not
perceive the education schools offer to be goods of equal value,
influence over the style and content of education is largely confined to choosing between educational environments, witnessed,
for example, in the juggling between house purchase and school
catchment area, and highly dependent upon family resources.
Moreover, choice of school is not a discrete event but embedded
in social relations over time, linking past, present and future.
Here I examine some of the processes involved under the headings of cultural heritage, happiness and control.

Cultural heritage: the moral domain

When individuals define education, or any other good, as important to their lives, to the lives of those entrusted to them or to
whom they have a sense of obligation, then resources, irrespective
of social class and however extensive or limited, are brought into
play (Allatt and Yeandle, 1992). Within the formal educational
system some families are able to weave their own pathways and
create additional openings. This was evident amongst these middle-class parents; they drew upon their cultural, social and economic resources to select institutions which provided an education
of a type they considered to be closest to their definition of their
children's needs.

The heritage of cultural capital flowing from past consumption
of schooling bestowed upon these families a range of assets. Family
consumption histories endowed parents with knowledge of both the
system and the association between educational qualifications and
future well-being—whether as material comfort, a sense of personal
fulfilment, a satisfying job, or what they defined as happiness.
Moreover, occupational experience in the system itself—one parent
in each family was or had been a teacher—and awareness of contemporary changes, underpinned parental views about appropriate
learning at particular ages and stages of the educational career,
thus enabling parents to assess teaching style and curriculum content. 'No. they seem to have pretty firm ideas about the school,
what school should be like,' replied Mike Phillips when asked if he
had influenced his parents' views on education.

Parental perceptions of what constituted good schooling included order, structure and demands for hard work. This led to dissatisfaction with the academic standards and the apparent '*laissez faire*' atmosphere of the state primary schools their children attended. These parents knew about the commodity and how they wished to consume it in the public domain of school.

Not only did these parents know how to exercise choice, they also knew the critical nature of its timing, moving their children out of the state sector either earlier than anticipated or at the stage of secondary transfer. For financial reasons, and because it was thought to be too academically formal for young children, a local prep school had not been considered. But of the state primary school, Mrs Phillips observed: 'We didn't realise how awful it was. We got him out as soon as we could.' The Brayshaws, who had not intended to use the private sector, drew upon their social capital in two ways—learning of a private school from friends whose children were already there, and asking a friend who was a teacher to assess the educational attainment of their son. Shocked by her assessment, that he was at least a year behind his expected attainment level, the Brayshaws decided to use the private sector, thus buying the commodity for competitive ends (Allatt, 1993a). Like the parents in Jackson and Marsden's (1968) study, the Brayshaws had confidence in their children's abilities irrespective of performance. Parental confidence shaped consumer choice.

Voices: the nuances of happiness and choice

Over my years of engagement in family and youth research I have been struck constantly by the parental claim, and young people's confirmation, that parents' dearest wish is to see their children happy. An apparently anodyne sentiment lodged in common sense understandings of the tenets of good parenting, the issue of school choice exposed its importance. For happiness can be differently defined, and different weight given to the voices of the actors in the drama.

Played in a setting where the child was central, in these middle-class families school choice was firmly parental. Decisions were explained in terms of the child's best interest, underpinned by parental definitions of what would make the child happy. This was not tied solely to the child's current emotional state but also took the future into account. Thus, based upon their perception of each child's personality and their own experience, parents felt not only that they knew what would enhance their child's present happiness but also that happiness in adulthood depended upon economic security, hence the need for educational success. Indeed, for the Brayshaws and the Phillips, maintenance of class position and prevention of downward social mobility could only thus be realized.

The two dimensions of happiness met in the emphasis placed on hard work in a conducive social setting. Thus, according to Mrs Brayshaw, they moved Stephen, the elder son, from the state system 'because he was unhappy at the primary school. Well, he wasn't unhappy. He was happy . . . but he likes a working atmosphere.' Whereas the younger son, John, had 'gone for a different reason . . . We felt that [he] needed a bit more pressure', an environment where work was expected. It is of note that this reasoning accommodated two competing cultural tenets of familism, individualism and fairness, treating siblings alike whilst recognizing their differences (Backett, 1982; Allatt, 1993a; Allatt and Yeandle, 1992).

In these accounts, the voice of the child had no weight, contrasting with the upper-working-class Roberts family where decisions on schooling were located in the present, taken on grounds of the child's immediate contentment. With a choice between two state schools with different academic reputations, the Roberts allowed their son to remain with his friends 'where he was happy' rather than take up a place in the school they felt to be more academically sound.

Other voices could enter the discourse of choice. Mr Jackson's own private schooling had meant that he had 'virtually left home at the age of seven'. Consequently, much to his father's annoyance, he defied family tradition; while his children's schooling remained in the private sector, he insisted that this was at day schools—thereby offering them a qualitatively different experience of childhood and adolescence. Relational aspects of schooling choice, therefore, reverberate within and down the generations; and whether family hierarchies and traditions are followed, broken or adjusted, they comprise measures against which current choice is made, shaping the way schooling is consumed and identity formed.

Control over the school

Control over what the school provides is problematic. How do parents ensure that what they are paying for meets their view of their children's needs? The evidence uncovered a twofold strategy; parental attempts at control and control as a parent-child co-operative venture.

All the parents spoke enthusiastically of the private schools they had chosen, supporting them in terms of time and fund raising, and some making a point of never criticising them to their children. As Mrs Phillips observed, revealing the commodity status of education:

> We're all positive about the school. In fact . . . if we weren't,
> we would take him away, because it would be silly to waste
> money on something we didn't feel . . . was sort of good value.

Schools, however, did not always live up to expectations. But when such occasions arose, again these parents could draw upon their stock of resources. Their cultural capital of confidence and skill, and their social capital embedded in social networks, enabled them to take matters into their own hands to supplement perceived deficiencies. Mrs Phillips, for example, had sought another first aid class amongst her contacts when Simon was barred, unjustly she felt, from the one provided at school, part of a Duke of Edinburgh Award Scheme (Allatt, 1993a). Parental influence might also be exerted by serving on school committees or associations. All the parents had adopted such roles, frequently in fund raising activity—seen as directly benefiting their children. With the Jacksons there was a hint of surveillance, the children reporting back to parents on whether recommendations, made on such committees, had been acted upon by the school.

In sum, choice and consumption of schooling in the public domain held a major place in the lives of these three families. Parents used their resources both to select an educational environment propitious to the reproduction of social advantage in their children and to hone this environment more closely to their requirements. In such shaping of the commodity, parent and child might collude.

Choice of school, however, whilst critical, was merely a peak amongst the myriad of schooling choices woven into the fabric of family life, embedded in routines, practices and rituals. I now turn to these micro-aspects of consumption, first setting them in the context of schooling's colonization of the household.

Patricia Allatt

Labouring to consume

As noted, the consumption of schooling straddles the public and private domains. In all families the years of formal education penetrate family life in at least three ways. Schooling formally timetables the major stages, transitions and turning points in educational careers and entry into the labour market. It influences the timing of household schedules, routines and plans, from the time to get up in the morning, to the use of leisure time and holidays. It also shapes the substance of family practices, for example, in the talk and help which foster commitment to schoolwork, especially visible where schooling penetrates the home in the form of homework. The latter exposes the moral bonding as schooling undergoes the metamorphosis from commodity to gift.

The gift of schooling, however, may be offered or withheld, and, indeed, refused (Bates, 1990). For the salience of education depends upon its relevance to the survival of the household, influencing how it is perceived and the extent to which its consumption is incorporated into family life. But even when the consumption of education is seen as essential it is not always willingly embraced nor a pleasurable experience, for sacrifice and work are entailed. In these middle-class families both parents and children laboured to consume; education was not an individual but a family project, a situation producing both co-operation and tension.

Whilst control over the content and consumption of education within the school was largely achieved indirectly, control over the consumption of schooling within the family was more direct, shaped and monitored through a family's values, lifestyle patterns, discipline and the forms of relationship. Thus, as well as knowing how to consume schooling in the public domain, middle-class parents understood the strategies which furthered its consumption in the private domain of the home. In this domestic consumption parental certainties led them to emphasize that goals were achieved by hard work and focusing on the task in hand; in this respect good grades in public examinations were the immediate goals. It also led to their deep involvement as agents of consumption, aware of the fragility of the endeavour, the risk that children might tire or rebel.

The micro choices of consumption

A series of minor choices over time, a hinterland of small daily decisions, cumulatively nourished the more visible timetabled markers, such as choice of school or entering public examinations. These micro-choices of consumption, made willingly or unwillingly, consciously or unconsciously, are so taken for granted that the possibility of choice is obscured.

Theoretically, such consumption choices may range from a daily decision to go to school, attention at school, the time to start homework, to meeting homework deadlines—although, as young people are aware, they have some leeway as no-one can see what is going on in their heads or the attention they are giving to a task (Allatt, 1995). As Mrs Phillips observed, although she could encourage, she couldn't 'force him'. These acts of micro-choice are embedded in family relations—in routines, practices, rituals, values, normative expectations, effort and trust.

Work, however, has to be done to maintain a flow of appropriate choices, sustaining commitment over the long years of schooling. Moreover, whilst young people devote long hours to schooling, a form of work that is insufficiently recognized (Allatt, 1993b), much work is also undertaken by parents, collaborators in the processes of investment and consumption until the young are seen to be sufficiently self-propelled. I now describe some of the processes in this enterprise.

Rendering choice invisible

One way of promoting continuity is to render the process of choice invisible, what Douglas (1975) refers to as the work of backgrounding. An aspect of invisibility is entwined in the cultural strands of family histories, well described by Mr Phillips who felt that he had probably influenced his sons' attitudes to university, but adding that the expectation of going to university had been 'just there . . . taken for granted' not only with his sons but for both himself and his wife 'in their parents' house'.

The power lies in the silence. These are those implicit background assumptions regarded as 'too true to warrant discussion' but which inform 'more coherent meanings' (Douglas, 1975:3,4) and that category of discourse which Barthes (1973:11) describes as *'what goes without saying'* (Italics in original). Their working is reflected in the younger son's response when asked about staying on at school:

My parents wanted me to stay on, but they didn't say you
must stay on. It was purely my choice they gave to me. . . . I
never thought of leaving school at sixteen.

Such backgrounding, perhaps, accounts for the absence of
parental concern about children's decisions, pointing again to
relational patterns of consumption transported across the generations.

The embedding process: systems of transferring responsibility

To retain their power cultures have to be lived. This was done
through a graduated system whereby responsibility for the self
was transfered to the young. Parents laboured to render consumption choices, if not invisible, then automatic, adopting
strategies to steer their children towards responsible choices. The
operation of this graduated system in the co-consumption of
schooling was particularly visible around the issue of homework.
Routines were established to inculcate habits, those daily acts
which serve to both constrain and release the individual (Young,
1988). These were supplemented by a background of supports
which were brought more fully into play if a young person's commitment to schoolwork showed signs of weakening.

All the families had created routines around homework.
Sometimes children were subject to promptings, sometimes they
apparently accepted the task as a part of their day. 'I've always,
like, done my homework', said Stephen Brayshaw. Parents, however, were deeply involved in its timetabling—when children
started it, where it was done, how long they spent on it, and
when it had to be handed in. The establishment of such temporal
regularities within the household routine, 'the structuring of social
life by forcing activities into fairly rigid temporal patterns', stands
the chance of being transformed into 'binding normative prescrip-
tions' (Zerubavel, 1985:xii).

Establishing and monitoring these routines makes demands
upon parental time, effort, energy and space, that is, sacrifice, the
essence of the gift. It is underpinned by love, extending beyond
the rationality of obligation (Baier, 1985), and what Offer
(Hutton, 1995) refers to as the economy of regard. These middle-
class parents poured such resources into the domestic consumption of schooling. Mrs Jackson, for example, extended her time
over the washing-up in order to be 'on call' through the hatch for

Deborah, doing her homework in the dining-room. Mrs Brayshaw, responsible for the 'school side' in the parental division of labour—Mr Brayshaw looked after the sporting interests of the children—had oversight of the daily homework routine and worked with her children to set up their revision timetables and plans at these critical times of the school year. Mr Brayshaw turned his sons' bedrooms into self-contained studies, each with desks large enough to enable them to leave their work out ready for resumption. Routines were also sustained by automatic queries of interest about the school day and insisting and encouraging a child to 'get on with his homework'. As Mrs Phillips said: 'When you're paying all that money . . . you've got to get your money's worth'—the shadow of the commodity lying behind the sacrifice of the gift and penetrating its reciprocal relations.

These routines were not static but comprised a graduated system of transfer of responsibility, a gradual release from stricter parental controls and definitions, sometimes learnt from the parenting mistakes made over an older child. Such practices nourished responsibility and a sense of independence, both highly valued in these families and key elements in the construction of social identity.

Mike Phillips comments illustrated this contained transfer of responsibility, its effect and the changes in the process with time. They also reveal the weather eye kept by vigilant parents and how, within the same style of transfer, they sustained effort when the demands of school begin to feel oppressive.

> Well not so much now they don't force me [to do homework] . . . but they just remind me that . . . they say, 'Well, if you don't do it then it's your problem. It's going to affect you in the long run' . . . Which is not actually forcing me to do it, it's making me think about it, so in the end I will do it.

And when asked if this kind of parental intervention was constant he replied:

> I think its just in the background until I don't want to do some work . . . 'I'm sick of school,' and everything . . . and then they'll just remind me, and I'll start thinking again and working.

Reflected here is a style of communication, absorbing parental time and skills but essential to co-consumption. Importance was attached to discussion: 'We don't argue, we discuss,' said Mr Brayshaw. 'We discuss things as they arise,' said Mrs Brayshaw. 'They talked things through,' said John Brayshaw.

Also reflected was a systematic development of consumer choice. This was guided by the principle of circumscribed freedom whereby advice and help were offered in a generalized form rather than in specific detail. 'I've tried to provide the experience and the facilities without really saying, 'Well, look, why don't you read?' said Mr Phillips. And Mike Phillips when asked, 'Do they tell you what to do a lot?' replied: 'They give me suggestions of what I could do, and then they let me choose.'

The boundaries of such freedoms to consume, partly shaped by inherited cultures, provided an ambience of shared assumptions, expectations and objectives. There were expectations, for example, underpinned by day-to-day routines and parental models, that you worked hard. 'It must rub off . . . He knows that we haven't got where we have by sitting back,' said Mrs Brayshaw. Whilst this relationship between work and material advancement was particularly evident in this upwardly mobile family, all three families cited work models.

Such extensive familial support, bounded by powerful implicit assumptions and set within a system which encouraged a sense of responsibility for one's own actions, transmitted a valuable form of cultural capital through the consumption of schooling. In this process parents were agents of conversion.

Consumption, reciprocities and bonds

These processes were underpinned by economic resources (stemming variously from current income, inherited wealth and aid from kin), sufficient to buy the type of education parents felt would enhance the young people's economic opportunities as well as their present and future happiness. However, two families, the Phillips, less affluent than the previous generation, and the upwardly mobile Brayshaws, were highly conscious of the economic cost of this type of education and made it clear to their children.

Economic cost, however, played two roles. A material resource, cost also symbolised the importance of education and its specially selected status. Cost highlighted not only the moral nature of the transactions in the gift system of exchange, but also the economic underpinnings of the gift itself. Mrs Phillips not only wanted her 'money's worth' but made her son aware of it.

> Yes, he might as well be aware of the fact that he's had a very expensive commodity. Mm . . . don't sort of rub it in all the time, but . . . he's quite aware . . . Yes, I think you have to be aware of it.

The young people also were conscious of the symbolic value of economic cost. Education was a valuable 'commodity' to which Simon Phillips referred as 'mostly a bonus'. Implicit was the understanding that this education was something over and above that which others received 'at ordinary comps', who were likely to be disadvantaged in the examination stakes. In this rendering it was a gift that parents were providing over and above that which parental obligation would dictate.

Economic investment in education was woven into family norms and practices in ways which furthered the consumption of schooling, creating cultural capital via educational success. Thus parental economic investment and sacrifice was paralleled by normative expectations of obligation and reciprocity between the generations. There was a bargain to be kept, clearly expressed by Mr Brayshaw.

> Sorry, but if you don't keep your side of the bargain, y'know. It's costing us . . . It's costing me a lot of money for you to go to school. If you don't utilize it, then you don't expect me to support you the other way.

Young people's side of the bargain was to repay in kind, displaying their appreciation through hard work, effort and the achievement of as good examination results as possible.[5]

The concept of the gift has a temporal dimension, the notion of delayed reciprocation and repayment of debts. These family narratives, however, showed that such repayment was not simply a matter of distant future success but fell within a temporally graded system of monitoring. Shimmering in the distance stood the ultimate measure—entry into a good job and the prospect of a happy life; more proximate were university or college entry, public examination grades and termly school reports; but, most critically, and underpinning these medium and longterm outcomes, reciprocity was woven into the routine of family life in the form of effort. Whilst children have few resources, they can show that they are trying; for effort is a resource to which children share access with adults, hence it is coinage in parent-child relations (Allatt, 1995, 1996). Consequently, if obligations were met, for a matter of trust was involved, children became more deeply involved in the consumption of schooling, the co-creation of their own cultural capital and identities, and the strengthening of moral bonds.

Familial bonding through educational consumption was further deepened by a paradox. Independence, highly valued in these families, competes with two other highly regarded familial tenets—solidarity and fairness (Backett, 1982; Allatt and Yeandle, 1992). Yet it was both controlled and sustained by its integration with these two familistic themes. For example, familial solidarity was displayed in the sharing of leisure time activities or the support members gave each other in their various interests, attending concerts or matches. Further, commitment to schooling carries the danger of differential success amongst siblings and the engendering of rivalry or despondency; the Brayshaws and the Phillips were worried about the effect of a highly successful elder brother on the attitude and performance of the younger. Attempts to contain such threats were made by enfolding them within a reward system which, while recognizing and lauding the individual, treated siblings alike and celebrated the family as a unit.

This system emphasized the pleasure of achievement for its own sake, young people said they 'would work hard anyway'; a place at Cambridge would be enough for 'thirteen years hard work'. But parents also recognized the lesser milestones of achievement—'with a book or a kiss'. Mr Brayshaw observed of an 'A' grade for an 'O' level taken a year early: 'It's a cause for saying . . . "That's one under your belt. We'll go out, even if it's only a bar of chocolate but we'll get something. We will do something that will recognize you." ' Additionally, however, reward was frequently embedded within a family celebration, such as going out for a meal. The ritual both acknowledged a policy of fairness, of 'doing the same for both of them', while publicly affirming the collective nature of the family-household. It comprised a system which incorporated control and encouragement, attempting to sustain family solidarity whilst celebrating individual achievement. It also revealed how the co-consumption of schooling spilled into other areas of social life. Education was a resource which reproduced the family as well as colonizing it.[6]

Conclusion

The language of consumption has penetrated education, from public rhetoric to lay accounts and, here, the narratives of parents and young people in the private sector of education (see also Roker, 1992). Yet, whilst this vocabulary is coloured by notions of individualism and individual advantage, the consumption of schooling cannot be viewed in an individualized way. By its nature, it is hooked into the social relations of generation, traversing the institutions of school and home, and changing chameleon-like from commodity to gift as it switches into different systems of exchange. Moreover, consumption and the manner of consumption is shaped by a family's culture, social and economic circumstances. Indeed, it could be argued that rather than turning to theories of consumption, the most powerful analytical tool is still the mapping of schooling onto the social divisions of class.

An earlier analysis of these data used the concepts of social and cultural reproduction to identify processes at work in the transmission of advantage (Allatt, 1993a). Two questions, therefore, remain. One is whether the concept of consumption enhances understanding of the data and the real world. In this regard, the focus on choice led beyond choices made at major stages and turning points, bringing to the fore the micro-choices running through the educational career, and revealing processes through which an educational culture was backgrounded and maintained.

The second question asks if the analysis of the consumption of schooling illuminates the concept of consumption itself. Here, the relational aspects of schooling, and its span of both public and private domains, provided a unique empirical ground. The inspection of the term consume revealed a kaleidoscope of interpretation, extending the notions of 'using up' and image creation to include nourishment, reproduction, and goods which undergo morphological change—from commodity to gift, respectively embedded in economic and moral systems of exchange.

Parents and young people laboured to consume, both sides working to 'get as much out of [schooling] as they could'. Processes of consumption integrated past, present and future; familial systems, underpinned by the principle of circumscribed freedom, were rooted in the past by a legacy of educational cultures and reached into the future through a vision of developing identities. The moral bonds of reciprocal relations of consumption inherent in the gift—through parental sacrifice, support, surveillance, obligations, effort, rewards and the repayment through children's effort—and the co-consumption of schooling itself, seem likely to be powerful and enduring anchors of identity. As Quicke (1993:119) noted of the sixth formers he studied: 'Parents were still principal agents in maintaining the students' sense of self and identity in the world'. This is not to deny the role of symbolism in the presentation of the self, nor the place for adjustment, development, or, indeed, rejection over the life course. It is, however, a model which sharply contrasts with the notion of an apparently unhampered self dipping into the consumer bazaar to construct yet another image.

Notes

1 The chapter is based on data from the *ESRC: 16–19 Initiative: Family Processes and Transfers in the Transition to Adulthood* (Grant No. XC 05250019).
2 Even the individual purchase of a bar of chocolate may resonate with social constraints. In some children's spending money such purchases fall within the category of 'fritter money' as opposed to money spent on more substantial purchases or saved.
3 A reader describes Tony Blair, leader of the Labour Party, as 'fuelling the mindset of those who deploy their consumerist skills and strategies in a relentless and compulsive pursuit of the "good school" '. (John Cocking, Formerly Chair of Governors, Islington Green School, *The Guardian*, December 1994: 21).
4 The social divisions of choice also reside in the lesser, though critical, choices presented by modularization and the wider range of subject choice. Confidence and knowledge are needed to negotiate these internal markets to advantage.
5 These parents did not remark, and indeed it would be improper in our society, that good educational performance brings reflected glory and accruals of status to a family. However, whilst parents were proud of their children, bent their efforts to help them and did not invest in their education merely with regard to family status, in Veblen's sense in his discussion of conspicuous consumption, the children were 'vicarious consumers', the parental 'investment' increasing parents' 'good fame' (Veblen 1970:66). Schooling was a positional good, and a competitive dimension in terms of status and shame, success and failure was latent. Thus, whilst not ignoring their repressive aspects, both pride and the accrual of family status arising from the children's success held the potential for a strengthening of bonds.
6 I am grateful to David Chaney for this insight.

References

Allatt, P., (1993a) 'Becoming Privileged: The Role of Family Processes'. In I. Bates and G. Riseborough (eds), *Youth and Inequality*, Buckingham: Open University Press.

Allatt, P., (1993b) 'Time, Work and Generation: Children's Homework'. Paper presented at the 10th Annual Conference of the Association for the Social Studies of Time, *Time and Work*, Dartington, July.

Allatt, P., (1995) 'Family Work Configurations: Youth, Family and Work in Times of Economic and Social Change'. Keynote paper presented at the *First International Petrozavodsk Youth Research Conference: Youth in a Changing World*, June.

Allatt, P., (1996) 'Conceptualising Parenting from the Standpoint of Children'. In J. Brannen and M. O'Brien (eds), *Children in Families: Research and Policy*, Brighton: Falmer Press.

Allatt and Yeandle, (1992) *Youth Unemployment and the Family: Voices of Discordant Times*, London: Routledge.

Baier, A. C., (1985) 'What do Women Want in a Moral Philosophy?' *Nous* XIX, 1, 53–63.

Barthes, R., (1973) *Mythologies*, Frogmore: Palladin.

Backett, K., (1982) *Mothers and Fathers*, New York: St Martin's Press.

Bates, I., (1990) 'No Bleeding, Whining Minnies: The Role of YTS in Class and Gender Reproduction'. *British Journal of Education and Work*, 3, 91–110.

Bauman, Z., (1988) *Freedom*, Milton Keynes: Open University press.

Beck, U., (1992) *Risk Society: Towards a New Modernity*, London: Sage.

Bourdieu, P., (1986) 'The Forms of Capital'. In J.G. Richardson (ed.), *Handbook of Theory and Research for the Sociology of Education*, New York: Greenwood Press.

Douglas, M., (1975) *Implicit Meanings. Essays in Anthropology*, London: Routledge.

Giddens, (1991) *Modernity and Self Identity*, Cambridge: Polity.

Glennerster, H. and Le Grand, J. (1995) 'Tickets Please, Children.' *The Guardian Education*, 4 April: 5.

Hutton, W., (1995) Priceless Gifts Within Everybody's Reach'. *The Guardian* 27 December: 15. Citing, Offer A., (1995) *'Between the Gift and the Market: The Economy of Regard'*, Oxford: Nuffield College.

Jackson, B. and Marsden, D., (1968) *Education and the Working Class*, London: Penguin.

Mauss, M., (1969) *The Gift: Forms of Exchange in Archaic Societies*, London: Cohen and West. First published (1950) Paris: Presses Universitaires de France.

Quicke, J., (1993) 'A Yuppie Generation; Political and Cultural Options for 'A' Level Students'. In I. Bates and G. Riseborough (eds), *Youth and Inequality*, Buckingham: Open University Press.

Roker, D., (1993) 'Gaining the Edge: Girls at a Private School'. In I. Bates and G. Riseborough (eds), *Youth and Inequality*, Buckingham: Open University Press.

Urry, J., (1990) 'The "Consumption" of Tourism', *Sociology* 24, 1, 23–35.

Veblen, T., (1970) *The Theory of the Leisure Class*, London: Unwin Books. (First published 1899).

Warde, A., (1994) 'Consumption, Identity and Uncertainty', *Sociology* 28, 4: 877–98.

Whitney, B., (1995) 'Truancy: Prosecute and Be Damned.' *The Guardian Education*, 4 April, p. 8.

Williams, R., (1983) *Keywords: A Vocabulary of Culture and Society*, London: Fontana Books.

Young, M., (1988) *The Metronomic Society: Natural Rhythms and Human Timetables*, London: Thames and Hudson.

Zerubavel, E., (1985) *Hidden Rhythms. Schedules and Calendars in Social Life*, Berkley: University of Chicago Press.

Expelling future threats: some observations on the magical world of vitamins

Pasi Falk

Abstract

The chapter focuses on the consumption motives and marketing strategies of a specific category of contemporary magical substances, that is, the expanding range of vitamin (and mineral) products. The consumption of these products—located ambiguously in the demarcation of 'medicine' and 'nutrition' (symptomatically also characterized as 'protective foods')—has increased very dramatically in the Western world during the last two decades. The trend is most articulated among the educated middle classes whose diets are hardly characterized by nutritional deficiencies. Thus the grounds for the consumption boom must lie elsewhere, indicating other kind of motivational factors. On the other hand, even though the marketing strategies of these products cannot be conceived of as the manipulative force causing the increase in consumption, the advertising arguments promoting the use of vitamin products may be analysed as (implicit) reflections and interpretations of the actual motivational factors.

The analysis of these advertising arguments—related to the historical roots of nineteenth century patent medicine advertising—acts as a starting point for the interpretation of the motivational factors of consumption (of these products) then contextualized in the changing meaning structure of 'food'—broken down into four dimensions: fuel, poison, medicine and (oral) 'pleasurable' (corresponding to the German term Genussmittel)—as it has evolved from early twentieth century to the present configuration. As it appears, the tendency manifests a shift in the meaning of 'food' giving an ever more emphasized role to the duality of medicine/poison. This tendency is expressed not only in the 'nutritional scientific' discourse—especially in its mass mediated versions—but also within two other related (and more recent) discursive lines: 'environmental' and 'fitness & beauty' discourses, as I have named them.

The interesting point is, as I am arguing in this chapter, that the motivational disposition towards the use of vitamin products fits well with the behavioural patterns outlined by these three discursive lines. Whether these products are used as substitutes or supplements, their specific magical character appears to lie in their future orientation and specifically in their supposed efficiency in keeping the evils to come afar—in the last instance, postponing not only ageing but death itself. In this respect the use of vitamin products resembles the more traditional case of talismans and amulets protecting against the evil eye (*mal occhio*) etc.

Who wants to live forever . . .
Freddie Mercury (*Queen*)

Introduction

My aim in the following is to focus on the motives for consumption and marketing strategies of a specific category of contemporary magical substances, that is, the expanding range of vitamin-mineral products. The consumption of these products has increased dramatically in the Western world in the last two decades. The trend is most obvious among the educated middle classes whose diets can hardly be characterized by nutritional deficiencies. Thus the grounds for the boom in consumption must lie elsewhere, indicating other kinds of motivational factors.

The category of vitamin-mineral pills and elixirs is located in the ambiguous borderline between 'medicine' and 'nutrition'. They are composed of the basic elements of the so-called 'protective foods', a term which was coined in the 1920s—amidst the great era of nutritional discoveries, detecting the various vitamins etc. (see Levenstein 1988:148)—referring to foodstuffs, such as vegetables and fruits, acting as major vehicles of these health-securing essences.[1] On the other hand, these products have also been characterized as 'preventive medicine' in reference to specific nutritional deficiencies and whatever further illnesses they may cause.

These terms have been used both by medical doctors and nutritionists in a more strict sense in reference to specified and named nutritional deficiencies. However, both in the lay vocabulary of consumers and in the advertising argumentation of the marketers the words 'protection' and 'prevention' tend to allude rather ambiguously to all manner of negative things which may threaten one's health and well-being.

In linking the perspectives of (potential) consumers and marketing, I am not saying that the latter would act as a manipulative force which cause the increase in consumption. What I am arguing is that the statements made in advertising for the use of vitamin products may be looked upon as—more or less implicit—reflections and interpretations of the actual motivational factors. In other words, the adverts do not actually create needs or desires by identifying and naming 'good objects' which deliver satisfaction and compensate for anything *lacking*; the naming in advertising concerns more fundamentally the *lack* itself or—in an inverted mode, typical of contemporary advertising in general—the positive state of being characterized by the absence of the *lack*.[2]

However, this procedure of naming is realized primarily by representational means; the physical products are transformed by the imagery of 'well being' and 'feeling good', that is, into messages which while operating primarily on a positive register necessarily remain undefined and ambiguous (see Falk, 1994). After all, how else could the good or perfect state of being which lacks any lack be turned into a representation? The point is that this is precisely the mode of representation (and naming) which makes the resonance of these messages among recipients—the potential and likely consumers of these products—possible in the first place. Thus we also have to thematize the site of this resonance, that is, the motivational (deep) structure lying beneath the disposition to consume these products.

To put the matter differently: if and when the consumption of these products does not follow the principle of 'rational' medical care of some detected (and diagnosed) ailment and, furthermore, if and when the protective and preventive functions of these substances remain unspecified and ambiguous—in the last instance referring to the absence of ills and the continued presence of well-being and feeling good—one simply cannot avoid relocating the meaning of the words 'protection' and 'prevention' in a dimension which surely is less rational (but not to be equated with the irrational) and probably to a similar degree more 'symbolic' (Sperber, 1982)—and magical.[3]

Now, what could be the specific character of the magical thinking which figures both in the consumption and marketing of these products? There is nothing mysterious in the pursuit of happiness, of social, mental and bodily well-being or simply 'feeling good'. Neither is it very strange to regard good health as an aspect of these desirable states or as a precondition for their realization. From this perspective the use of vitamin products—even in the protective and preventive mode—is simply goal-oriented action which appears to be as 'rational'—or at least as sensible—as other forms of taking care of oneself, especially of one's own body.

Obviously, most of the medical authorities of today, leaning on the scientific status of school medicine, would consider these as 'false' means in the pursuit of the unquestionably 'right' end—reminiscent of Sir Edward Tylor's definition of magic as 'false science'. However, from the consumers' point of view, this is just a truth of one—though official—discourse opposed by others, including not only those of the naturalists and alternative medicine but also the whole pharmaceutical industry which dominates the production of these goods nowadays, and which actually enjoys a corresponding scientific and 'official' status as part of the modern medical complex.

In the present context I will not proceed to the analysis and evaluation of the competing 'truths' in the different discourses. Instead I will elaborate the theme further by arguing that in order to get an idea of the magical character of the (use of) vitamin products we have to problematize—and historicize—the very aim of consuming these products, that is, the quest for health. To question this unquestionable value will be the topic of the following excursus.

The quest for health and . . .

In problematizing the positive category of health, I will not focus on the configurations in which the binary opposition of health and illness is inverted or blurred in terms of positive/negative charges. As an example of the former (inversion) one might refer to the medieval ascetics for whom illness and the decay of the body meant a step towards the positive state of pure spirituality. A paradigmatic case of the latter (value ambivalence) is surely the disease of melancholy—especially in the way it was (re)formulated between the sixteenth to the eighteenth century when it had a certain positive identity as a sign of the subtle and sensitive constitution of those suffering from the malady.[4] But, as I said, this need not concern us here.

Instead I will outline the changing ways in which (the question of) health is positioned in the context of life, and how health is related to the other 'good things of life'. I will illustrate the changing position of health in a condensed history starting from the classical dietetics of Greek Antiquity (based primarily on the Hippocratic Corpus) followed by a huge leap to the 'regimens' formulated primarily in the seventeenth and eighteenth centuries and finally jumping to the twentieth century.

In its widest sense classical dietetics was a corpus of principles for the art of living. These principles derived from the Hippocratic system structured according to the cosmological scheme of a micro-macrocosmic continuity (eg, Lonie, 1977). Harmony was the key principle of dietetics ranging from the balance in the 'mixture' (temperament) of the four elements (in the bodily/microcosmic scale, humours) of the cosmological continuum to the balanced mode of life—in the 'use of pleasures' (Foucault, 1987, 1988), in relations to others and in whatever practices one's life involved. All these 'goods' of life—from health to beauty and moral virtue—formed a unity in accordance with the idea of harmony and balance. Each element should maintain its right (relational) measure, including the concern with one's *health*, not to speak of prolonging one's life—out of proportion, as it were.

In other words, the formula 'health and long life' which sounds like a truism, almost like a tautology (health = longevity) even to us, did not have a place in the classical dietetics—simply because the formula fights against the holistic principle of harmony between *all* the good things of life. It is not until the sixteenth century that health and long life is linked together in the medical and dietetic discourses—coined into a formula which has enjoyed an unquestionable status to the present day.

Now, before I make the leap to the sixteenth (to eighteenth) centuries and to the ways in which this formula figures in the discourses, I shall try to answer the probable objections evoked by my argument (above). It is certainly true that the dream or idea of eternal life—life without death—is about as old as the idea (consciousness and fear) of death, that is, as old as human culture. Likewise the idea of an extraordinary long life is at least older (in the Western tradition) than the Hippocratic dietetics. So for example Herodotus (the contemporary of Hippocrates) tells in the third book of *Histories* his version of the mythical Ethiopians, living in the country of the Sun which nourishes them 'to the quasi-divine standing of the *makrobioi* [long-lived] (Vernant, 1989:164–9).

The point is, however, that both the eternal and the long-lived are elsewhere. These dreams and ideas are *projections* into the mythical realm, into another world somewhere else, in another age—from the Lost Paradise to God's Kingdom to come (in the Christian tradition); projections which are more or less directly constructed as negations of this worldly life (*no* hunger, *no* suffering, *no* disease, *no* death). The Medieval carnevalistic *Land of Cockaygne* is only one of the inverted projections (*mundus inversus*) of the experiences of 'real life'.

The configuration is fundamentally different in the medical and dietetic discourses which began to take shape from the sixteenth century onwards. The formula of 'health and long life' relates now to this worldly life—not as projection but as *project*. To be more precise, life was regarded more and more clearly as an *individual* project. In this respect the 'regimens' formulated especially in the seventeenth and eighteenth centuries were a continuation of the classical dietetics of the 'free men' of Greek Antiquity—the forerunners of individuality and self-relatedness.

However, there are certain essential differences. Even though the Hippocratic system is still the basis of the (more mechanistic) humoural medicine of those times, the cosmological (micro/ macro) scheme lost its central place, giving way to a scheme which contextualized the individual body and self in society— relating it to the societal and especially productive practices.

This scheme should, of course, be explicated in relation to the rise of the 'Protestant ethic' (Weber) and Puritanism. Nevertheless, for obvious reasons I have to skip all this and focus merely on the redefinition of health in these regimens for 'health and long life'. As it appears, the formula contains a double instrumentalization: first, 'health' as a means for obtaining longevity, and second, 'long life' (+ health) as a means for implementing one's vocation to the fullest efficiency. The life of the 'professional man'—the term used by George Cheyne in his *Essay of Health and Long Life* (1724)—is conceived of as a productive project to be implemented, implying the care for one's bodily/mental 'capital'. It is surely symptomatic that in contrast to the classical dietetics, in these regimens the principles of temperance and moderation were applied to a whole range of practices from diet to sociability, but not to productive activity (labour)—neither to longevity.[5]

In a sense the formula of 'health and long life' in regimens like the one presented by Cheyne expressed the emerging idea of (societal) *progress* writ to the scale of the individual life span and the individual's bodily constitution. Man's life as a project was given a primary role in relation to the otherworldly projections. This progressivistic point of view was explicitly stated by Antoine-Nicolas de Condorcet—a key representative of the idea of progress—on the eve of the French Revolution. As McDannell and Lang note, for Condorcet 'the infinite improvement of the human mind and *the prolongation of physical life on earth* made even heaven seem irrelevant' (McDannell & Lang, 1990:205–6; italics added). In Condorcet's progressivistic vision the paradise would be brought (back) onto earth and those coming after us would end up in 'an Elysium created by reason and graced by the purest pleasures known to the love of mankind' (Condorcet, 1955 [1793]:202).

This could be the right moment for the final jump in this condensed history of 'health'. I will move to our times, first focusing on the turn of the nineteenth and twentieth centuries—to the rise of the so-called consumer society (especially in the United States)—and then proceed to the contemporary scene.

The turn of the century is the historical juncture (in Western civilization) of the old production-oriented cultural code and a consumption-oriented one. Leaving aside the whole complexity of this economical, social and cultural change I will focus on the new ways in which health is thematized in individual 'life projects'.

First of all, the individual life (as) project becomes increasingly detached from the production-oriented progressivism characteristic of the 'health and long life' formulas of the seventeenth- and eighteenth-century regimens. The mode of individuality emerging and gaining in societal generality (from the upper classes to the middle classes) in this shift is not a mere continuation of the self-controlled 'bourgeois subject' but articulates a break with it, characterized by a certain kind of self-relatedness.

This shift in the mode of individuality has been conceptualized in various ways: as a move from 'self-control' to 'self-expression' (Lears, 1981, 1983, 1984; Taylor, 1989), from 'utilitarian' to 'expressive individualism' (Bellah *et al.*, 1985), from 'character' to 'personality' (Susman, 1984) and from 'inner-directed' to 'other-directed personality' (Riesman, 1955). The first three of these formulations emphasize the central role of self-concern (*who/what am I really? what shall I become?*), while the last stresses the social determination of the same concern with oneself (*how do I appear to the other(s)? what should I be like?*).

Nevertheless, all these formulations point to a common denominator of the modern individual self: the individual life (as) project becomes increasingly autonomous and self-contained in terms

of the meaning given to it—and the means and ends of its implementation. These individual choices may be largely 'other-
directed', yet the choices must still be made by the individual.
There is no *Gemeinschaft* to make the choices for you and The
Great Project of Progress—the modern cosmology—is losing
its role as a structuring frame for the individual life project.
However, the individual life project is still there—as self-
realization and self-actualization—and so is the principle of
progress, but now as a striving for *self-completion*.[6] And this is
surely something other than the 'professional man's' aim to fulfil
his earthly vocation.

According to this configuration, 'health' is redefined in a way
which is in some respect reminiscent of classical dietetics. Health
regains its place as one of the 'good things of life' (pleasures, success etc.). Yet, contrary to the classical setting, there are no regulating principles of harmony and balance to keep the health
concern within its 'right' proportions. Thus health may be conceived of both as a means (for enjoying the other good things of
life) and an end in itself, structuring the life project into a health-
oriented 'way of life', that is, realizing the quest for self-
completion primarily at the bodily level ('self-building as body-
building', the latter in an extended sense of the term).

So 'health' figures as an element of self-completion in the individual life (as) project—the latter being merely a temporalized
formulation of the former. In this context 'health' becomes linked
to the specific mode of future-orientation characteristic to the
individual life project. It is related to an 'open future' in the modern condition(s) of uncertainty and contingency. Now 'health' is
not merely a state of being to be obtained (cure) and/or maintained (care) in the *present* but also—and one might add in an
increasingly emphasized way—a condition alluding to the *future*
and all the potential threats it may contain. In this context
'health' acquires the meaning of *prevention*—of the ills lurking in
the days to come. One leads a healthy life in order to protect oneself against future ills or illnesses and consumes 'preventive medicine' for the same reasons.

All this sounds very sensible indeed—even though the latter
could be considered to be fallacious means for the purpose.
Nevertheless, we should pose the tricky question: preventing
what—what kind of threats? An obviously sensible answer would
be: protecting us from and thus preventing specific illnesses and
diseases—like a vaccination against certain harmful diseases. But

surely this is not what it is all about. The ills remain largely undefined. So, we have to formulate the answer anew, in more general terms: preventing illness whatever that may be. And thus the object to be prevented escalates to almost anything that may be imagined as a threat to one's body and self—anything that endangers the striving for self-completion.

However, the description above seems to lead us to a motivational pattern which is unlikely to be very typical of 'normal'— more or less health-oriented—individuals, including those consuming vitamin-mineral products. The description points rather to a 'pathological', generalized phobia reminiscent of an (earlier) description of a 'freely floating' (neurotic) anxiety characterized by 'a tendency to an expectation of evil' (Freud, 1976 [1917]:446).[7]

So we have to reformulate the question in order to make the positive dimension in the future-orientation of the life project visible. The question could be posed as follows: how should we characterize the generalized future threat which endangers the task of self-completion? Actually the answer is to be found in the question. This feared 'thing' is precisely the counter image of the idea(l) of completeness, that is, the falling apart and decay of one's (bodily) self, a process whose end point is death.

In mental terms this fear may be conceived of as a basic (and 'normal') anxiety of the modern individual self and its existential condition which tends to be experienced as a state of ontological insecurity (see Falk, 1994, Chap. 5). This approximates to a constellation Jackson Lears seem to have in mind when analysing the specific nature of the health-concern emerging in the United States at the turn of the century. According to Jackson Lears,

> [t]he quest for health was becoming an entirely secular and self-
> referential project, rooted in peculiarly modern emotional
> needs—above all the need to renew a sense of selfhood that
> had grown fragmented, diffuse, and somehow 'unreal' (Lears,
> 1983:4).

What this means is that an excessive concern for one's health may be interpreted as a fear—not only for ills threatening one's physical health (illness) but for all evils threatening one's well being in general. In other words, 'health' acts as a representative for the state of *well being* more generally. Thus, to take an example from the contemporary scene, the anxiety evoked by the apocalyptic visions of global environmental catastrophe could be 'acted out' in the form of compulsive care for one's own health. (On the other hand, there is always the possibility of a projection in the opposite direction: projecting one's own anxieties onto the problems of a global scale.)

But let us move back closer to the bodily dimension. At first sight the fear for (bodily) decay is nothing else than the age-old fear of death. However, a second look reveals that this is not the case. What this specific fear signifies is rather a *denial* of death. The fear concerns the process of bodily decay in itself, a process which probably involves a number of illnesses but which actually refers to *ageing*.

Thus we end up with a new formula which seems to be a kind of synthesis of the old 'health and long life', and a more recent one, namely 'health, beauty and fitness'. The latter formula fits well with the 'other-oriented personality type' (introduced by David Riesman [1955]) being especially sensitive to others' looks and responses and thus giving 'health', at least to a certain extent, an instrumental role as a means of obtaining and keeping up appearances. On the other hand, the synthesis of these two formulas is something other and more than this. Undoubtedly longevity still figures in the contemporary health-related formulas, for example in the numerous (mostly American) self-help books. Nevertheless the scope has changed. This could be illustrated by a relatively recent (1982) best seller by Durk Pearson and Sandy Shaw entitled *Life Extension: Adding Years to Your Life and Life to Your Years*. In other words, 'life extension' is not so much a matter of prolonging one's life but more a question of conserving one's youth-fullness (youth as fullness)—remaining 'forever young' (to use the words of Bob Dylan in a somewhat altered sense).[8]

In this context the two key terms linked to the vitamin-mineral products—protection and prevention—acquire a new meaning which is more aptly expressed by a third term—*preservation*.[9]

Protecting against the signs of ageing, preventing the biological clock from fulfilling its function—or even turning the hands of the clock backwards; face-lifting makes you (look) ten years younger. Rejuvenating body lotions which are *balms* in all three senses of the term; a pleasant aromatic resin, a healing ointment and a means of embalment with the aim of making one's body as eternal as possible. The first sense excluded the concept of balm applies also to the vitamin-mineral products which promise to keep the future threat of ageing at a distance or alludes to a preserved state of well being and youthfulness as if the time itself could be stopped.

A cultural configuration in which the universally human fear of death is replaced with the fear of growing old seems to fit very well to the depiction of the 'culture of narcissism' presented by Christopher Lasch (1980, see esp. Chap. 9)—which is surely more than a coincidence. The autonomized project of self-completion taken to its extreme as preservation—the embalment of one's live body and life—corresponds very accurately to the narcissistic syndrome in which the idea of giving up or away something is experienced as death (of the self).

From the narcissistic perspective there is no continuity beyond and outside the self. The continuity—the life as project—lies wholly inside the boundaries of the self, implying that the end of the self is equated with the end of the world (Lenzen, 1989). Consequently there is a tendency to disregard the continuity in which one is related to those to come—the next generation, to a certain extent also in relation to one's own children: the almost impossible thought of *giving away* which is equated to giving up *(one's self)*, the inability to see the life of those who will follow as a continuation of one's own life. There is no cosmology which would define an individual life as a part of a greater whole (holy) and even the 'Great Narrative' (Lyotard, 1984) of progress has (largely) lost its role as a frame for trans-individual continuity. Furthermore, modern society lacks the ritual means for transferring its members from one stage to the next in the life cycle (Lenzen, 1989) thus, again, emphasizing the autonomization and closure of the individual life (as) project.

The mental image of individual life in the form of a graph does not have the form of a cycle or parable intertwined with the ones to come. Rather it is conceived of as a line, first ascending (growth) and then continuing horizontally towards an end point out of sight (embalment). The narcissistic 'fight for life' is not a confrontation with actual threats here and now but rather a fight against time related to the future *per se* as a threat.

Contemporary patent medicines

The general pattern outlined above figures in a more or less articulated manner in the advertising of all those body-related products—to be used externally (on skin) or internally (ingested)—which operate within a future-oriented scope, expelling future threats of ageing and conserving youth-fullness. Thus defined, the category of these products is much wider, ranging from actual amulets & talismans (eg magnetic bracelets) to immaterial products such as therapies and (bodily) self-care programmes. Here, however, my interest is in the mode of magical thinking linked to the specific—though paradigmatic—case of the vitamin-mineral products. First I shall consider the ways in which they are represented (in adverts) and then open up a more differentiated perspective on the different user types of these contemporary 'patent medicines'.

In order to understand the ways in which the vitamin-mineral products are represented in contemporary advertising we have to deal briefly with the overall tendency in the century-long history of modern advertising which could be characterized as a move to the positive register of representation. This tendency manifests itself in a condensed way in the patent medicine advertising around the turn of the century. Earlier in the nineteenth century patent medicines (cure-alls) were advertised primarily by means of the negative register, presenting open-ended lists of ailments to be cured and using mythical images (dragons, skeletons etc.) of the evil 'things', especially the invisible enemies called microbes, which the panacea promised to exorcise.

However, as the evil thing expanded to a general category of ill-being the medicine was consequently turned into a representative of generalized well-being—a state of being which escalated beyond the boundaries of a more narrowly defined concept of 'health'.

The general reason for the move towards positive representation in advertising is to be found in the formation of 'the world of goods' (of the consumer society) in which the goods are offered as (potential) 'good objects' (Klein, 1932) to be used as the building-bricks of the consumers' self-completion (Falk, 1994). However, in the case of patent medicines one should focus now on the specific mode in which this tendency is realized.

One obvious reason for the move to use the positive register in representations of patent medicines was that the producers wanted to expand their markets to include not only people who were (or felt) ill but also those who were (or did) not. By the end of the nineteenth century all patent medicines had redefined themselves not only as a cure for the sick and frail, but also as a preventive elixir for the healthy. A patent medicine called *Pure Malt*

Nectar, for instance, was advertised under this slogan in the United States; 'invigorating tonic, alike for invalids and those in health' (Petersen, 1969:321). At the same time, advertisements started to identify and visualize the 'good' that followed for those who decided to use the product, defined either as a succession of specific 'good things' or in more ambiguous terms, as in this slogan for a latent patent medicine: 'HADACOL—for a better tomorrow!' (see Brigham and Kenyon, 1976).

Adverts like this no longer focused exclusively on the identification of a deficit but moved on to naming the desired (good) state of being that can be attained by the goods (ie the products) specified. The ailments to be cured were still listed but the emphasis shifted to the positive side. Another, even more specific reason for this was the formulation of the rules and legislation for 'truthful' advertising which banned the use of 'false promises' characteristic specifically of patent medicine advertising. Nevertheless, even the later representative of these products—HADACOL, which was introduced in the early 1940s—still used an open-ended list of ailments in its advertising along with the slogans alluding to 'happy days' ahead.[10] On the other hand HADACOL may be regarded as an early example of more contemporary patent medicines. It was composed not only of the more traditional magical ingredients but also included the modern invisible helpers, especially vitamin B.

As early as the beginning of the twentieth century, however, the redefinition and expansion of the identity of patent medicines tended to pull down the barriers between different categories of oral consumption; the line between preventive medicines and foodstuffs was blurred. Preventive medicines promised to keep the evil (illness, ageing and ultimately death) away and turn 'normal' life into a better one by providing extra energy, happiness, beauty, etc.[11] The same arguments were used also in the marketing of corn flakes, rice crispies, etc., in the name of 'good health'.[12] This trend was then reinforced by innovations in organic chemistry and nutrition science, which shifted the focus of attention somewhat away from invisible enemies, the bad 'microbes', to the good invisible helpers, ie vitamins (most of them discovered in the 1910s and 1920s) and other protective nutrients (Levenstein 1988:147–8).

A look at the adverts of the contemporary vitamin-mineral products gives the impression that no essential change has taken place since the HADACOL days—except for the fact that the naming of the negative (in terms of ills) has vanished almost completely. When choosing some examples of the adverts for these products—limited to only those sold in the ('official') chemist's shops—I even came across one which hardly differs from the HADACOL-slogan; a product named KAROLE (A and E vitamins + selenium) offers its users 'a better day after tomorrow'. Another called symptomatically LONGO VITAL (A, B, C, D and E-vitamins + herbs) promises both 'efficiency' and a 'new grip on your life'; BEROCCA (B-vitamin mixture) puts 'a smile on your face' and so forth. The most professional sounding heading accompanied a product named BIO-SELEN (A, B and E-vitamins + beta carotene, zinc and selenium): 'more resisting power!—protects your cells against symptoms of premature ageing'. A smart formulation which gets the message through without getting into trouble with 'false promises'. After all, it does not promise to stop the ageing—and in fact in the bottom of the advert one finds a text in small print reading: 'medicine-like product—efficacy not proved according to the norms applied to medicines'.

So at least the adverts of the contemporary patent medicines seem to back up the general frame of interpretation formulated above. Then again, this is not directly translatable into a monolithic motivational pattern shared by a homogenous mass of consumers. First of all, the category of vitamin-mineral products also contains 'medicines' for specified ills and symptoms; compounds with calcium against *osteoporosis* (especially for women in their menopause), B6-vitamins likewise for women (menstruation & depression), and the vitamin-mixtures for the treatment of hangover (for men?). In these cases the use is closer to medication; in the first case it is preventive, in the second it may be both preventive and actually curing, while the third is designed for cure. On the other hand, those products in this category which are not targeted to specific use may still be used for different, more or less specific, reasons.

Nevertheless, these different reasons are located in the realm of the individual consumer's free choices simply due to the fact that the vitamin-mineral products belong to the OTC-category, that is they are sold freely 'over the counter' as distinct from medicines, the availability of which is controlled, that is, the drugs sold on prescription.[13]

In the following I will make some preliminary interpretations of the different types of use based on the material in a study

(Klaukka, 1989) dealing with the trends in Finnish medicine consumption including some comparisons with the rates of consumption in other countries. The rate both of the overall medicine use and the use of vitamin-mineral products is rather moderate compared with other Western countries. Compared with Finland the overall medicine consumption is considerably higher in almost all West European countries and even higher in both Japan and USA—the latter of which happens also to be the leading country in the consumption of vitamin-mineral products. On the other hand, in spite of the differences there seems to be a general trend towards growth in the consumption of these products in the Western world.

In the study by Klaukka (1989) there is an analysis of the Finnish data dealing with the different motives of the use of the vitamin-mineral products. According to these findings the use of these products is concentrated primarily in the educated, urban, middle-class, young and middle-aged groups. Among these social groups there seem to be two contrasting grounds for the use of these vitamin products—as a *compensation* for 'unhealthy' manners (smoking, drinking) and as a *complement* or *continuation* of what is considered to be a healthy lifestyle; eating vegetables, physical exercise—a pattern which is more common among men than among women within the same social groups, at least in Finland. These two different uses could also be characterized as follows:

(1) the first (compensatory) is close to the principle of curing— even though the ills (unhealthy habits) are better conceived of as potential health problems projected into the (near) future, thus emphasizing the preventive character of these 'medicines'. Furthermore, these ills are not seen as threatening outside agents but as self-induced (potential) problems demanding compensation. The vitamin products are used as antidotes against the effects of the chosen pleasurable 'poisons'. This is a motivational construct which is still in accordance with the principle of medical care. On the other hand this is a rather marginal case in the consumption of these products as a whole.

(2) in the second configuration the identity of these products moves along the dimension of (preventive) medicine to (protective) nutrient, from the former towards the latter. Now the use of these products are rather conceived of as a logical complement and continuation of the health-oriented way of life—as just

another additional element in the metonymic chain of 'health'. In this case the use of these products is part of the healthy 'regimen' which includes not only the healthy foodways but also all the other dimension of bodily self-care (exercise, sufficient rest etc.).

Furthermore, the study includes a reference to the consumption pattern of the vitamin-mineral products in the United States which differs from both of those described above. The 'American pattern' appears to be more or less independent of the health concerns both in the negative/compensating and the positive/complementing forms.

So what does this consumption pattern indicate and, furthermore, what could the motivational factors be in this case? Should the use of these products be understood as a (dead) ritual or 'ritualism' devoid of any meaning to the consumer? Is it just a habit? If so, why would these specific products become the objects of habitual use? Even though social conduct contains a whole range of rituals and also ritualisms, this would not be a satisfactory explanation of the phenomenon. At first sight this mode of use, detached as it is from health concerns, appears to be just another mode of oral consumption, like eating candies or chewing gum, or even more generally, just another realm of consumption where the 'manipulative' advertising apparatus persuades people to buy and use (up) without any particular reasons or meaning.

The latter argument is surely too simplistic and thus does not deserve further consideration[14] while the former argument has a certain relevance; after all, these products have an ambiguous identity (especially along the dimension of medicine/food)[15] which pushes them closer to the other (non-medical) categories of oral consumption. And furthermore, as noted above, the use of these products also as 'medicine' has from the earliest days (Levenstein, 1988), had the identity of 'preventive medicine', considered by most medical authorities—today more than before—as unnecessary, excessive and even unhealthy when taken in excess.

In other words, there is no actual illness to be cured, only a good health, good condition, good looks and good 'feeling' to be perfected,[16] maintained and—protected from future threats. Thus preventive medicine and protective food/nutrients are really indistinguishable—not only conceptually but also in the practice of consumption. And finally, as products dominating the OTC category[17] the vitamin-mineral pills and elixirs are freely available on the market as objects for consumer choices—like any other products for oral consumption, and for that matter, like consumer goods in general. And this applies to the marketing and advertising of these products too. Even though there is some market segmentation, the majority of these adverts are targeted indiscriminately to the 'big audience'—as products 'for you', actually referring to 'all of you'.

Now, it could be argued that even though magical thinking figures in each of these three motivational patterns, the third—the 'American pattern'—represents the specific mode of the future-oriented magic in its purest form. In distinction to the two former types—the compensatory and the complementary—the third could be characterized as *supplementary*. The supplementary use of these products seems to be independent of health concerns because it is not related to health behaviour in the two senses presented above. Consequently it seems plausible that it does not concern 'health' in any narrow sense but rather in the diffuse sense of a continuous well-being pointing towards the idea of preservation. However, in this modified sense 'health' still figures also in the supplementary type but now in a plain and passive consumerist mode. The benevolent powers of the product are incorporated in the simple act of ingestion without any need for other action. So one does not have to do anything else for the cause of 'health'—no abstinence, no exercise etc.—except taking the pill. An idea which was aptly formulated in a recent Finnish advert for a product named BIO-QUINONIN (with coenzyme Q 10): 'just sit back and get fit!'.

One is really tempted to speculate on the possibility that this supplementary type explains to a significant degree the expanding consumption of these products in the Western countries in general.

Be that as it may, these products make for an ideal marketing item at least for the two latter future-oriented motivational patterns. No one can say they don't work because there is no argument that the effects are visible here and now. The promises of future health, longevity, youthfulness etc. cannot be falsified unless one lives one's life all over again in a 'control group'. This has to do with more than just the placebo character of a product. The utility of this product is equally verified by the presence and absence of any effects; after all things could have been worse if . . . And last but not least, these pills do not cause too much inconvenience, so why not take them, just in case?

Notes

1 A later derivative of the term 'protective foods', modified to protective 'nutri-
ent(s)', referred specifically to these necessary nutritive essences: vitamins, min-
erals and protein. In the Finnish nutritional discourse the ambiguous character
of these substances is manifested in the use of 'nutriment' and 'nourishment' as
interchangeable terms (suoja*ravinne*, suoja*ravinto*). A recent Finnish advert
(*Pharma Nord*) for these products uses a term (possibly a neologism) which is
even more symptomatic: 'additional' or 'supplementary nourishment'. The
symptomatic character of the term is made explicit further below.

2 I have dealt with this theme in more detail in an analysis of the advert representations of nineteenth-century patent medicines and their transformation at
the turn of the century (Falk, 1994, Chap. 6).

3 This much can be said without accepting the problematic postulate of the
mutually exclusive relationship of the relational vs. magical thinking. A more
thorough elaboration of this topic would imply an analysis and deconstruction
of the binary opposition and the ways it has been formulated, especially in the
anthropological tradition—from Tyler, Frazer and Lévy-Bruhl to more recent
discussions (see Tambiah, 1993). However, this is a task which, for under-
standable reasons, cannot be pursued systematically in the present context.

4 Melancholy was both a disease and a sign of those belonging to the social élite
and due to this the symptoms of the illness were even imitated (in the eighteenth century) by those who wished to be counted as one of the chosen.

5 Likewise symptomatic is the fact that Cheyne did not locate the happy state of
the human condition in the Lost Paradise but in the Loss itself, caused by the
Fall of Man. In Cheyne's words,

> not merely a *Punishment*, but also a remedy against the Disorders his
> Body would be liable to in his new State of the Creation, and against the
> poisonous Effects of the *Forbidden Tree* he had eaten the Fruit of. I am
> the more confirmed in this Belief, that I observe, the *absolute* Necessity of
> *Labour* and *Exercise*, to preserve the Body any time in due plight, to
> maintain *Health*, and lengthen out *Life*. (1724:90).

6 The striving for self-completion becomes articulated in different guises; doing
one's career, perfecting one's 'collection' of consumer goods, finding one's true
inner self etc. The point is, however, that this striving is first and foremost a
self-referential project.

7 Then again, one could still refer to Freud's thesis according to which the
extreme (pathological) cases merely articulate and make visible the dispositions
of those considered 'normal'. So, for example, if we look at the endless list of
symptoms George Beard, the inventor of 'neurasthenia', ascribes to this civilization disease—which he regarded as a threat to almost all Americans—we
will realize how central phobias are:

> . . . fear of lightning, or fear of responsibility, of open places or closed
> places, fear of society, fear of being alone, fear of fears, fear of contami-
> nation, fear of everything . . . (Beard 1881, 7).

8 Bob Dylan rather represents the specific case of the sixties generation which
refuses 'adulthood' equated to conservatism, or at least experiences the move
as problematic. This may be exemplified with the Hollywood 'mid-life crisis'

movies which started with people in their thirties, moved on to those in their forties and in the latest versions dealing with people in their fifties. The funny thing is that this is the same 1960s generation experiencing a mid-life crisis every ten years—and never seems to get beyond the point. So we will probably see also the next parts of this series, the crisis of septuaginarium . . . ? However, for the sixties generation staying 'forever young' is more an issue of a societal, social and lifestyle orientation—surely something other than a striving to conserve one's youth and eternalize one's bodily self to the point of choosing to be deep frozen instead of being buried—in the expectation of resurrection. The ultimate example of the denial of death.

9 It is interesting to note that the term preservation in the fifteenth century English not only referred to protection and defence but had also a more specific meaning as preventive medicine, which in those days signified the overall magical character of medicalization.

10 The product was created by Dudley LeBlanc who started his business with patent medicines in the 1920s. Later he founded the 'HAppy DAy COmpany' from which the name of the product derives—with the added L for LeBlanc (Brigham and Kenyon, 1976).

11 This effectively implied a redefinition of 'normalcy' as a deficit, which was no longer understood in terms of specific ailments but which had already been reduced to a general sense of 'not feeling well'. Or as Jackson Lears notes:

> As early as 1873 an advertisement for Tarrant's Seltzer in *Harper's Weekly* noted that 'thousands of people who are not actually sick complain that they are—never well . . . (Lears 1983:25).

12 In the marketing of certain types of cereals a more 'pharmaceutical' identity was favoured. An example is provided by the adverts for Postum Cereal Company's flakes, in which the product was represented as a medicine for a self-invented (named) illness called 'coffee neuralgia' (Carson 1959:161).

13 The boundaries between these two medicine categories vary from one (western) country to another—for example the antibiotics are found in the OTC category in some European countries, but not in the Nordic countries who apply a more strict control over the sale of drugs.

14 Whatever role 'manipulation' has it presupposes something—meanings linked to motivational dispositions—to be worked on. Thus we end up where we started.

15 Today the ambiguity figures also in relation to the pole of 'pleasurables'; the effervescent vitamin tablets dissolved in water into fizzy sweet fruit-flavoured drinks, not to mention the latest (American born) fad of energizing 'smart drugs' sold by name such as 'Powermaker.WoW!!' and 'Brain III Formula', or the 'smart bars' established in avantgarde discos and restaurants offering their customers hyper-healthy (vitamin etc.) drinks such as 'Power Punch' and 'Psuper Psonic Spyber Tonic'.

16 'Perfection' in this context does not actually refer to a state of (physical) deficiency as an illness to be cured but as a 'normal' state of being which could always be 'better'—a kind of progressivist principle writ to the scale of the individual's life (project).

17 The category of OTC medicines is, of course, much wider (varying from country to country according to the legislation), containing a whole range of medicines for specific ills (for skin problems etc.). One significant subgroup are the painkillers (and antipyretics—both combined in the classical case of *Aspirin*)

which have had a steady place in the non-prescription medicine consumption for quite a while in the Western world (the world conquest of *Aspirin* began about a century ago). Even though the painkillers are used for specific and actual ills they still have a tendency to induce modes of use which have a less specific character. This is due to the fact that painkillers are (meant to be) used as remedies for *symptoms*, experienced as pain, rather than specified (diagnosed) illnesses. So even though say headache seems to be rather easily definable as 'feeling ill', there is still an open route for expanding the use of painkillers to more ambiguous experiences of 'not feeling well'. Even though the consumption of pain-killers in Finland has been rising steadily in recent decades, however, the fastest-growing subcategory of OTC medicines, from the mid 1970s onwards, has been the vitamin-mineral products.

Bibliography

Beard, M., (1881) *American Nervousness*, New York: G.P. Putnam's & Sons.
Bellah, R. *et al.*, (1985) *Habits of the Heart*, New York: Harper & Row.
Brigham, J.C. and Karlie K. Kenyon. 'HADACOL—The Last Great Medicine Show,' *Journal of Popular Culture* 10, no. 3 (1976): 520–33.
Carson, G., (1959) *Cornflake Crusade*, London: Victor Gollancz.
Cheyne, G., (1724) *An Essay of Health and Long Life*, London: G. Strahan.
Condorcet, A.N. de, (1955) *Sketch for a Historical Picture of the Progress of the Human Mind*, New York: The Noonday Press. (Orig: Esquisse d'un tableau historique des progrès de l'esprit humain. Paris 1793).
Falk, P., (1994) *The Consuming Body*, Theory, Culture & Society Books, London: Sage.
Foucault, M., (1987) *The Use of Pleasure*, Harmondsworth: Penguin.
Foucault, M., (1988) *The Care of the Self*, Bungay: Allen Lane/Penguin.
Freud, Sigmund, (1976) *Introductory Lectures on Psychoanalysis*. Vol. 1. The Pelican Freud Library, ed. Albert Dickson. Harmondsworth: Penguin Books. [1916–17].
Klaukka, Timo, (1989) *Lääkkeiden käyttö ja käyttäjät Suomessa [The Use and Users of Medicine in Finland]*. Helsinki: Kansaneläkelaitos.
Klein, M., (1932) The Psycho-Analysis of Children. London: Hogarth Press.
Lasch, C., (1980) *The Culture of Narcissism*, London: Abacus.
Lears, Jackson, (1981) *No Place of Grace*, New York: Pantheon Books.
Lears, Jackson, (1983) 'From Salvation to Self-realization.' In *The Culture of Consumption*, ed. R.W. Fox and Jackson Lears. 1–38. New York: Pantheon Books pp. 1–38.
Lears, Jackson, (1984) 'Some Versions of Fantasy. Toward a Cultural History of American Advertising, 1880–1930'. Vol. 9. *Prospects. The Annual of American Cultural Studies*, ed. Jack Salzman. New York: Cambridge University Press pp. 349–405.
Lenzen, Dieter, (1989) 'Disappearing Adulthood: Childhood as Redemption.' In *Looking Back on the End of the World*, eds. Dietmar Kamper and Christoph Wulf. 64–78. New York: Semiotext(e).
Levenstein, H., (1988) *Revolution at the Table*, New York: Oxford University Press.

Lonie, I.M. 'A Structural Pattern in Greek Dietetics and the Early History of Greek Medicine,' *Medical History* 21, no. 3 (1977): 235–60.

Lyotard, J., (1984) *The Postmodern Condition*. Minneapolis: Minnesota University Press.

McDannell, C. and Lang, B., (1990) *Heaven, A History*, New York: Random House/Vintage Books.

Petersen, William H., 'Devils, Drugs, and Doctors. Patent Medicine Advertising Cards,' *Palimpsest* 50, no. 6 (1969): 317–31.

Rieseman, D., (1955) *The Lonely Crowd*, New Haven: Yale University Press.

Sperber, D., (1982) 'Is Symbolic Thought Prerational?' In *Between Belief and Transgression. Structuralist Essays in Religion, History, and Myth*, eds. Michel Izard and Pierre Smith. 245–64. Chicago: The University of Chicago Press.

Susman, Warren I., (1984) *Culture as History*, New York: Pantheon Books.

Tambiah, Stanley J., (1993) *Magic, Science, Religion, and the Scope of Rationality*, Cambridge: Cambridge University Press.

Taylor, C., (1989) *Sources of the Self*. Cambridge, Mass.: Harvard University Press.

Vernant, J-P., (1989) 'Food in the Countries of the Sun.' In *The Cuisine of Sacrifice among the Greeks*, eds. Marcel Detienne and Jean-Pierre Vernant. 164–9. Chicago: The University of Chicago Press.

'Bastard' chicken or *ghormeh-sabzi?* Iranian women guarding the health of the migrant family

Lynn Harbottle

Abstract

Based on ethnographic data, derived from Iranian migrants, in central England, this chapter examines women's domestic food-work, from a health perspective, and considers how ethnic identity may be variably performed through specific food consumption practices. 'Bastard chicken' and '*ghormeh-sabzi*' serve as metaphors, representing British (perceived to be under-developed) and Iranian (highly elaborated) cuisines, and as vehicles allowing play around the notions of positive and harmful incorporation. I contend that, through the selective application of sophisticated Iranian cooking techniques, these women are able to positively transform the (inherently dangerous) food they serve to their families, to ensure their good health and maintain their identities.

Introduction

Consumption processes are socioculturally, geographically and historically contingent. Falk (this volume) has demonstrated the changing understandings of health over time, and has shown how symbolic health practices, including the consumption of certain nutrients, has become important in the enactment of social identities, in modern societies. This paper considers those practices from the perspective of a specific migrant group—Shi'ite Iranians in central England. Through the exploration of women's food-work, ie their everyday domestic provisioning and household meal preparation, it also examines the social (re)construction of this group of consumers and emphasizes the inter-relational, rather than individualistic, aspects of consumption processes in the performance of identity.

Health or Well'th?

Although the World Health Organization, in its 'Health for All by the Year 2000' charter, (W.H.O., 1982) recognizes the wider social context of health, nevertheless in many quarters, and particularly within the biomedical discourse, health tends to be perceived in terms of an absence of organic disease. A pervasive, western, mind/body dualism is reflected in the semantic distinctions between 'health' and 'well-being', the latter being considered to comprise (less valued) emotional and material influences. However, in traditional Iranian cosmologies, no such dualism exists, rather, there are powerful links between environmental factors, the emotions and the body. In order to overcome the 'health' 'well-being' divide, it may be more helpful to combine the terms ie 'well'th'[1] (this also appropriately connotes material influences).

Food provides one of the most direct, easily available and consistent means by which people may influence their health status (Kandel and Pelto, 1980:345). As in most cultures, it is the women within migrant Iranian communities who are regarded as largely responsible for the day to day provision of food, for guarding the health of their families and for treating sickness through the preparation of special foods, herbal remedies and other medicinal treatments (Lock, 1980; Tan and Wheeler, 1983; Kerr and Charles, 1986). For Iranians, food is much more than simply a means to physical health; meal provision and commensality are vital in maintaining emotional well-being, spiritual harmony and in reinforcing cultural identity (see Figure 1).

During data-collection, derived from informal interviews and participant observations with about thirty women, in dispersed

---

Food, Health and Well-being

Aesthetic Pleasure ⎫
Emotional Security ⎪
Socio-cultural Solidarity ⎬ Well-th
Physiological Homeostasis ⎪
Political Power ⎭

Figure 1

areas within central England, I sought to interrogate emic understandings of health, enacted in daily experience, and to understand
the multiplicity of ways in which food serves as a means of pre-
serving the well'th (health and integrity) of Iranian migrant families. The accounts obtained demonstrated consideration of the
nutritional/physiological properties of foods, interwoven with concerns relating to cultural consumption and identity; Fischler's
description of the principle of incorporation (1988) offered a useful and holistic theoretical perspective by which this data could be
analysed. Incorporation is the action in which we 'send food
across the frontier between the world and the self' (Fischler, 1988).
It is a basis of identity; to incorporate food is to incorporate all or
some of its properties. Hence, we become what we eat: a) as nutrients are used in the synthesis of new tissue and to maintain vital
metabolic processes; b) as the symbolic characteristics of food are
absorbed and shape our individual and collective identities.

Therefore, we are able to manipulate the diet and to re-make
ourselves, both metabolically and symbolically, ie to increase or
decrease body size and boost our immune systems or to retain,
modify or transform our individual and/or collective identities.
Fischler poses the question: 'If we do not know what we eat, how
can we know who we are?' (1988) In the particular situation of
Iranian exiles and refugees, I propose that one of the chief means
by which they are able to determine and define who they are is
through specific food preparation and consumption practices.

Returning to the title of the paper, *Ghormeh-sabzi* is a stew
(*khoresh*) made of a mixture of beans and meat, vegetables and
dried limes. Not only is it highly nutritious and considered
'healthy' (for its high fibre and relatively low fat content) within
the current biomedical discourse, but symbolically, the individual
ingredients and overall recipe signify Iranian cuisine and
identit(ies). It seems to be one of the most widely-known and
popular recipes and was commonly mentioned in interviews.

> Safieh: 'Some foods are basic, everyone likes, for example
> *ghormeh-sabzi* . . . because I think it's our traditional food and
> everywhere you can find it but maybe there is some little
> difference. For example, my mother and me like red beans in
> *ghormeh-sabzi* but my husband likes the (black)eye bean.'

Although *ghormeh-sabzi* is consumed throughout Iran, different
styles of cooking, and/or slight variations in the ingredients, have

served to mark different regional identities; for example, apart from the use of different types of beans, there may be variation in the type and amount of fat used, in the quantities and proportional contributions of the herbs and limes and contestation over whether tomatoes should or should not be included. In Britain, the dish becomes an appropriate medium by which to represent the multivalency of Iranian identity, according to regional, ethnic, religious and family backgrounds, reflected in subtle alterations to the basic recipe. It is also symbolic of positive incorporation, ie of safety and of self, as such it has the power to (re)incorporate the eater into Iranian cuisine, culture and cosmology.

Mistakenly requested in a supermarket by one informant who was shopping for a self-*basted* bird, 'bastard' chicken serves as a charged metaphor, representing the dangers of modern technology and of harmful incorporation. Nutritionally, it is high protein and valued dietetically for its low fat contribution; but it has been contaminated by the addition of a number of additives, including hormones and polyphosphates, as well as by the plastics in which it comes encased. To Iranian migrants, it also symbolises the threat of western culture. Together, *ghormeh-sabzi* and 'bastard' chicken offer the means to think about and understand the food-work and consumption concerns of Iranian migrant women and to play on notions of self/other; safety/danger and food/poison.

Traditional concepts of health

In Iranian cosmology all aspects of lifestyle influence health status, while ideologies of individual and social health invoke concepts of balance, harmony, integration and wholeness. Historically, popular health beliefs have been derived from Galenic-Islamic medical principles, elaborated by Ibn Sina, from Arabic, Greek, Latin and Indian philosophies. Within this system, individual temperament is believed to be derived from a distinctive balance of the four humours and their associated properties (blood—hot and moist; red bile/bilious—hot and dry; phlegm/serous—cold and moist; black bile/attrabilious—cold and dry). Temperament is considered variable according to age, sex, race and climate (Pliskin, 1987:135–6). The body is also believed to be physically sensitive to elements within the environment and at certain stages in the life-cycle, such as early childhood, individuals are particularly susceptible to alterations in climatic conditions.

207

Diet (through the notions of hot and cold—*sarde-garme*—foods) interacts with climatic influences and individual temperament to affect health. 'Hot' or 'cold' qualities (referring not to thermal temperature but to perceived intrinsic properties) are ascribed to body conditions, foods, and medicines. The proper bodily function of an individual is maintained through consumption of a diet balanced in relation to the intake of foods with these qualities. Illness is perceived to be caused by an imbalance in the hot/cold equilibrium, and results in specific reactions such as digestive problems, skin eruptions, sore throats and headaches (Pliskin, 1987:140). This can be rectified through the consumption of foods with opposing qualities and/or specific medicinal treatments.

Theoretically, then, health is maintained by an active and constant process of balancing one's body base, which demands daily attention to food consumption. Equilibrium encompasses a range of states, as individuals have different bases, according to inherited characteristics, birth circumstances, sex, season and lifestage. The action of diet, drugs, tonics, herbs and the environment all influence the equilibrium. The base state of children is regarded as 'hotter' and less stable than that of adults and they tend to be more susceptible to 'hot' illnesses (Pliskin, 1987:137). Men usually have 'hotter' bases than women, and they demonstrate a greater degree of tolerance to changing conditions.

A large body of research exists for identifying different frameworks based on humoural principles (impacting on food and health ideologies) throughout the world (eg Greenwood, 1981; Messer, 1981; Tan and Wheeler, 1983). Those operating in the Middle East, Europe and the 'New World' are believed to be derived from the Galenic system; parallel systems apparently exist in the Far East, Southeast and South Asia (Messer, 1981). Although the general structural principles may be shared worldwide, there are significant variations in the detail and practice of these systems both within and between cultures (Greenwood, 1981; Tan and Wheeler, 1983). For example, in formal Auryvedic and Chinese systems, the 'hot-cold' distinction is the major idiom for discussing moral, social, and ritual states, in addition to the specific qualities of foods and medicines, yet at a folk level, only discrete elements of these beliefs may be adhered to and these may be interwoven with other concepts (both traditional and modern) relating to food and health. Similarly, in Morocco, elements of the Galenic humoral system have been integrated with Islamic medicine in present day pluralist practices; and a wide degree of intracultural variation in classifying foods has been demonstrated, according to personal knowledge and experience (Greenwood, 1981). Meanwhile, in Japanese popular health beliefs, only remnants of the 'hot-cold' framework remain, consisting of pairs of foods which are thought to cause food poisoning if consumed together (referred to as *kuiawase*) eg mushrooms and spinach (Lock, 1980:97).

Migration and Syncetism

Research by nutritionists and medical sociologists, among migrant groups in Britain, has tended to proceed from an applied perspective in which it is hoped that knowledge of traditional beliefs will enhance the provision of health education and/or meal provision within state-run institutions. In the current study, establishing the importance of hot-cold beliefs offered a useful and non-threatening starting point, in interviews, from which to explore wider influences upon consumption patterns and food-work. According to the existing literature, maintenance of traditional practices may vary according to level of education, as well as prior exposure to and current knowledge of traditional and alternate belief systems, such as biomedicine. For example, Chinese mothers in London reportedly maintained a high level of regard for their traditional practices, even if they felt constrained and prevented from fulfilling their requirements by environmental circumstances (Tan and Wheeler, 1983). Second generation Punjabi women in Glasgow were more variable in their adherence to hot-cold beliefs (Bradby, 1995) but appeared to retain a reasonable level of knowledge concerning them. The majority of women interviewed in this study, however, declared themselves to be sceptical (a few were completely dismissive) and many had only a superficial awareness of *sarde-garme* principles. Some considered themselves to adhere to the system but in practice this simply meant limiting intake of very hot or cold foods.

Amongst those with some awareness of *sarde-garme* beliefs, meat and very sweet foods, such as dates, sugar and chocolate were generally regarded as 'hot', milk and rice as 'neutral' and vegetables and most fruits as 'cold', although there were anomalies, such as yellow melon. There were also regional differences in classification; fish, for example, was considered to be hot in some areas and cold in others.

Mehri: 'In my city (Mazandaran) people believe fish is hot but in his city (Kerman) they believe it's cold. They eat fish with hot things. They don't eat yoghurt with fish because they believe it's cold . . . but we do! (to cool it down)'.

As in the Mexican system (Messer, 1981), many women only paid attention to the 'hot-cold' qualities of the diet if they considered themselves or any family member to be especially vulnerable, due to sickness, age or physiological state (eg pregnancy); at such times diet assumed even greater importance. For example, it was suggested that babies tend to be prone to coldness which can be counteracted with a small amount of *nabat*. In old age, the body base also becomes 'colder' and individuals may become susceptible to cold illnesses.

Zahra: '(L)ike (my father is) cold and he doesn't eat much cold food, because he believes every time he eats more cold food, it hits him—affects his digestion and his digestion goes bad . . . (H)e gets too much water in his mouth . . . that's the way he finds out he's got coldness'.

In Iran, as in many other places, certain foods have been ascribed specific medicinal properties (Lock, 1980; Pliskin,

---

TRADITIONAL HEALTH PRACTICES

Daily Health Maintenance

Balance {
    individual temperament
    environment
    lifestage
    diet (*sarde-garme*)

Foods

    Hot ——— neutral ——— cold
    eg meat   rice   yoghurt

Diet in Sickness
1. Light diet eg *kateh, ash*
2. Manipulation of hot-cold foods eg. *nabat*, fruit juice
3. Medicinal items—mint, liquorice, quince seeds.

Figure 2

1987:141). The use of these remedies in sickness continues to comprise a major part of popular Iranian medicine (see Figure 2). Frequently, the foodstuffs assigned such medicinal qualities are marginal substances, falling 'betwixt and between' the categories of food and non-food; herbs and spices, for example, are common medicinal ingredients (Lock, 1990:96). A range of dried flowers, seeds, leaves and berries may also be used and are drunk (steeped in water) for a range of conditions such as digestive ailments, coughs, sore throats, fevers, nerves and fear (Pliskin, 1987:141).

> Mehri: 'Sometimes if they catch a cold (or) stomach (ache), then (I use) *nabat* with tea . . . We use some dried herbs from (a) special shop . . . When we have coughs, we use (quince seeds) . . . I don't believe it very much. I think when you catch (a) cold you have to go to the doctor. You can use (herbal medicines) because (they won't) damage anything but sometimes people just use them and don't go to (the) doctor. Especially with children . . . (they) may have a problem in future because they don't kill all the microbes . . . I saw a child in the hospital, they didn't take him to the doctor when he had a sore throat, so after a few months he had a rheumatic fever, so I'm very aware if my children ha(ve) a cold . . .'

In contrast to synthetic medicines, herbal concoctions are often thought to be controlled and not to cause side-effects (Lock, 1980; Pliskin, 1987). Although western medicine is believed to be more powerful than traditional treatments, most interviewees in this study commonly used a number of herbal remedies, in particular mint water and *nabat*, for minor ailments; these might also be used before resorting to pharmaceuticals and/or in addition to them, to offset their heating effects. In addition to specific remedies, modification of dietary intake was widely reported by informants during sickness. Soups, fruit juice and plain foods were generally thought to be better tolerated and fries and spicy foods were avoided (whether these modifications were derived from Galenic-Islamic, or more recent biomedical, influences is difficult to ascertain).

> Monir: 'If, for example, you get flu or a cold you don't eat spicy foods, you eat very plain foods, like just *kateh*—steamed rice, with yoghurt, or you eat soups . . . watery soups—not too much spice in it'.

A number of conditions required the therapeutic use of more commonly consumed foods, for example, honey, sugar and chocolate (although still marginal in terms of their overall quantitative contribution to the diet and the ambiguity of their structural position). For example, one informant described being prone to low blood pressure, particularly at the end of her menstrual cycle. Her account reveals the way she intuitively senses which foods to eat, on the basis of bodily sensations, and reveals her resistance to accept the biomedical diagnosis, in the light of her successful self-treatment.

> Soraye: 'My blood pressure is a bit low . . . I'm better off with the hot (foods) because when I eat too much cold food I feel dizzy. I start getting headaches . . . Here it's more noticeable— I don't know why—because of weather . . . here you feel (you need) to eat more chocolate but (not) in Iran . . . I went to the doctor. They said they think it's migraine . . . but I don't think so, because yesterday I had 3 glasses of milk with honey. Everytime I felt I was getting a headache I had one glass of milk and honey and it stopped.'

In contrast to this informant, who had no formal biomedical training, another woman, trained as a midwife in Iran, applied her knowledge in a description of the use of *sarde-garme* principles by couples wanting a child of a specific sex (hot foods are believed to encourage the development of a boy and cold ones to increase the chances of carrying a girl).

> Safieh: . . . 'My cousin used *sarde-garme* for (the) sex of (her) baby. She wanted a girl and she can't get a girl . . . and she said to me she used this (and it worked). I think I believe some food could have (an) effect on (the) sex of (the) baby because it changes (the) pH of (the) body and (has an) effect on (the) move(ment) of sperm in (the) body of women'.

Her explanation for the success of the method illustrates the way traditional and modern concepts are syncretized and how the traditional may be reinterpreted and translated in terms of dominant ideologies, such as biomedicine. She personally does not have confidence in the Galenic tradition, partly because she lacks the experiential physical evidence of its efficacy and in part owing to her training. Yet, recognizing the prevalence and persistence of this classificatory system, she offers a rationale for its success, couched in terms of the hegemonic medical discourse.

> Safieh: 'I don't believe hot-cold but I think its connected to sympathetic and parasympathetic nerves . . . for example yoghurt is *sard* and I think it works on . . . the gland . . . in our mouth and it makes water in our mouth . . . because they say the *sardi* makes water in the mouth . . . My mother-in-law believes you shouldn't eat fish and yoghurt together . . . but I've never obeyed . . . (the) present generation doesn't believe . . . When I was a child somebody said don't eat yoghurt or *kaskh* (fermented yoghurt) with *ash reshte* but I did and nothing happened. I think . . . in addition the energy of the food. Because the sweet and the chocolate is *garm*. The yoghurt is cold (less energy)'.

She also considers herself, as a member of the younger generation, to be more enlightened than older people. This was a theme drawn out by most informants, not just with regard to dietary traditions but also in relation to other aspects of lifestyle. In this study, the age range of the women interviewed was from the mid-twenties to early fifties and length of residence in the UK was between two to ten years (some had also spent several years in other western countries). All had been exposed to nutritional information, in Iran and in Britain. Many women regarded *sarde-garme* to be outdated and to be based on superstition; it was thought to be more suited to the older generations, younger women find the scientific 'facts' more persuasive.

Even amongst those most convinced of the value of *sarde-garme* beliefs, they were not the dominant concern in ensuring a physiologically sound diet for the family. Rather, these principles were dynamically and variably integrated, or used in conjunction, with popular understandings of biomedical nutrient classifications. Some foods, particularly fruit, were widely perceived to be good for health—'I think if a child has fruit enough . . . she will be healthy.' (Goli, 1991). This was partly due to an awareness that they were considered 'healthy' by dietetic standards and were preferred as a means of restoring balance to other alternatives. In some instances there was real ambivalence demonstrated towards foods which were valued for their heating qualities but regarded as dangerous in terms of nutritional contribution, in particular towards chocolate—also a marginal substance within the British diet (James, 1990).

> Soraye: 'I don't want to give her chocolate . . . Dates are hot and better than chocolates, because eating too much chocolate can make you fat . . .'

In contrast to the scepticism often acknowledged towards traditional wisdom, no informants expressed any disbelief of the nutrition information they had acquired. Like British Asian women in Scotland (Bradby, 1995) these interviewees used their nutrition knowledge to rationalize and confirm the logic of systemic beliefs but unlike the Scottish group, they did not appear reciprocally to apply traditional principles to interrogate scientific 'reductionist' knowledge.

Despite the privileging of the biomedical discourse over traditional knowledge, women commonly indicated that as their nutritional awareness had grown, so they were increasingly convinced of the natural goodness and superiority of the diet in Iran. This was most strongly articulated by an informant who had spent half of her life abroad.

> Monir: 'In Iran they don't talk about foods the way they do here. It just comes naturally because all the diet, the Iranian diet is very good, when you think about it. (When) you get more information about healthy food . . . then you realize that what you had—the diet that you had in Iran—was healthy . . . The people don't have any knowledge about what healthy food is, it comes naturally because it's been given to them, generation from generation.'

The preparation of healthy food was considered to be an intuitive ability, born and bred into Iranian women. For those well versed in the professional discourse, such as one interviewee, who had recently completed a Masters course in Nutrition, this provided reassurance as to the soundness of the Iranian diet and of the reliability of their instinctive knowledge.

> Hamideh: '(Before) I didn't know much about it but I just realized that, I think, it's so nutritious and its variety and you know, combination of . . . beans and meat and herbs, I feel, I realize it's really worth it . . . It's not just a lot of meat—you know, you just worried about cancer—too much fat but . . . the protein of plants is much more healthy) . . . I mean after the course I understand . . . (and) I trust it.'

If health information had generally shaped women's opinions, the nutrition message which had most powerfully influenced their day-to-day food preparation was a concern over dietary fat intake. Although all informants, without exception, mentioned fat as a consideration, this was manifested in different ways. For those who had lived in the UK for relatively short periods (two or three years) the predominant focus was on avoiding heart disease.

> Mehri: 'I use a little bit of fat . . . I don't fry the chicken or meat . . . Some Iranian women, they used fat a lot, but not now . . . Because the oil is expensive, you know, in Iran now, so they have to be careful . . . Before—my grandfather's time . . . they ate fat a lot, because they work(ed) a lot . . . so they used the fat, they spent a lot of calories . . . but now people use cars all the time . . . people use vacuum cleaners or washing machines . . . They don't work a lot, so they don't need a lot of calories, so they must be careful . . . We have a programme on the TV to tell people to be careful. And when you see your friend has (a) heart attack and the reason is he or she (is) eating too much fat or a lot of sweets, you just wake up to yourself and be careful . . . I use fish a lot, I don't know (if) its true or not (but) I heard it's good to keep out the heart attack'.

Her lay theorising interweaves an understanding of the biomedical discourse (ie the impact of changing lifestyles on energy expenditure and balance), with observations of the influence of socioeconomic changes, and she illustrates how personally relevant experience may prove to be a catalyst which transforms theoretical knowledge into behavioural change (Davison *et al.*, 1991).

Amongst those who had lived in Britain for longer periods, concern with fat intake was more clearly articulated in relation to weight control. A number of women reported having put on weight here; this was often attributed to the need to eat more in a cold climate, and in some cases, to lack of exercise; three informants joined 'Weight-Watchers' during the course of this fieldwork!

> Monir: 'We are quite conscious about (our) weight. We tend to choose less fat in our diet . . . and we don't have any sauces, apart from salad cream and a little bit of olive oil and some fresh lemon juice but we tend to completely avoid sauces—mayonnaise and all that stuff.'

215

Others reflected approvingly on the fact that they had initially lost weight when they came to Britain, due to the change in routine. From their accounts, it appears that the pressure to conform to western societal norms, regarding body image, may be experienced more intensely as the length of exposure to them increases. A significant difference between Iranian and British conceptions of ideal body size was remarked upon by some women.

> Soraye: '(H)onestly, in (Iran) you just notice they are fat . . . but when you compare it, (it's) not like here, I think they are much more comfortable in Iran.'

> Zahra: '(In Iran) people were not that fussy because, I think, they all wear these long veils, so they're not really bothered about weight, you know, having (a) big bum or big bust or anything like that, it's not showing . . . I don't think people like it, you know, (being too) slim, you know, like size 8. They won't like that at all . . . I think people prefer size 12, back home (and) they don't mind size 14–16 . . .'

It was also noted that weight loss was often met by resistance from family members (especially parents) in Iran. This was explained in terms of a generational change in ideals, with large proportions, as an indication of a plentiful diet, being more highly valued among older people.

> Farah: 'I think sometimes older . . . women like people to be a bit fat, rather than skinny . . . I think because we think about being fashionable, maybe and they don't. That's why, when I married, my mother-in-law liked me being chubby . . .'

> Soraye: 'They think it doesn't suit you—being skinny, you're better being a bit (chubby) . . .'

> Farah: 'I think when you lose weight, it affects your face and that's why they don't like (it). Really, I don't like (it either) . . . You have lines and everything but your body is good, it looks nice, but not your face and that's why they don't like (it).'

Although these women discuss weight loss primarily in terms of aesthetic appearance, I have suggested elsewhere that additionally, for parents of Iranians living in Britain, the transformed body symbolises a change of identity which, in a culture where the harmony and stability of the family is so important, may give rise to a significant degree of sociocultural dissonance (see also Harbottle, 1995: 35). An alteration in facial characteristics is cause for particular concern, as the face is so prominent and is a focal area for inscribing identity, eg through hairstyle and make-up (Synnott, 1993). This may be intensified, in a society where the rest of the body is shrouded from public view, as in the Islamic Republic of Iran.

Incorporation, Identity and Well'th

The links between identity and health were more clearly articulated in some interviews. For example, after discussing the ways one woman attempted to lower her family's dietary fat intake, I was intrigued to discover why she used shoulder of lamb, in preference to the leg—a leaner and more highly valued cut on the British market. Her husband interjected, explaining the religious underpinnings to what has now evolved into a cultural preference; in Islam the shoulder is considered cleaner and tastier—'it has less blood left in . . . whereas in (the) leg there is more blood' and it is regarded as only semi-*halal* (Mahmood). His response indicates how even the organoleptic properties of food (considered to be physiologically determined) are psychologically, socially and culturally moulded (Lalonde, 1992). Mahmood then went on to describe the loss of traditional Iranian consumption patterns and replacement with western dietary practices.

> Mahmood: 'Most of the Iranian foods are made of grains. Gradually during the Shah's time it became a mode . . . to have more meat in food because they sa(id) those grainy foods are old-fashioned . . . they don't have any protein . . . (but) chickpeas . . . are the best source of glutamic acid . . . which is the kind of nutrient that neurons usually consume . . . We not only have this in our . . . main food . . . but we also fry these and we mix them with raisins and we give (them) to children to take to school . . . They say, "take these things away, they're no good and go and have more meat. Look, westerners are eating more meat . . . let's have more meat"!'

Ironically, he uses the biomedical discourse to criticise the western diet and to lament the impact of the former Shah's modernization programmes.

Grains humble food Iranian	↑fibre ↓fat	nutritionally and morally sound
Meat ↑status Western	↑fat	↑risk heart disease and 'diseases of affluence' morally unsound

Figure 3 Food nutrition and morality

In Mahmood's account, there is a powerful resonance with the notion of *gharbzadegi* (west-toxification), a term applied in Iran to express the cultural intoxification of Iranian youth with western secular values and material goods (Farmaian and Munker, 1993; Sreberny-Mohammadi and Mohammadi, 1994). Here the toxic effects of the western diet, manifested by high levels of heart disease, are paralleled with the damaging effects of western culture upon Iranian society (see Figure 3). Just as 'damage-limitation' measures have been taken by the government to protect the Iranian people from the cultural invasion, so a campaign has been mounted to combat the high prevalence of heart disease.

Although in one sense Iranian migrants may be considered to have physically embraced the west and to have been incorporated within it, nevertheless they demonstrate a high degree of ambivalence towards western standards and considerable resentment over the sustained political and economic interference, particularly by the British and Americans, in Iran's modern history (Farmaian and Munker, 1993; Zonis, 1991). Interestingly, conversations about food and diet frequently seemed to precipitate the expression of anxieties regarding identity issues, and politico-economic and socio-cultural concerns were inextricably interwoven with attention to the physiological properties of the diet. At times these issues were deeply embedded within the narratives but at other times they were more clearly articulated. For example, Mahmood interjected again, later in the same interview; this time he directly considered the impact of other cultures and cuisines upon Iranian national (and upon his own) identity.

Mahmood: 'We have lost our identity . . . we seem a sort of bewildered people. Some people think like that, they have lost their identity, they don't know where they are. We have been

attacked by so many tribes and countries . . . We have been
influenced by so many cultures that it's got sort of mingled,
amalgamated culture . . . Adaptation always (causes) a lot of
stress and pressure on the person . . . We are very adaptable,
very hospitable, very respectful to foreigners . . . but it (isn't)
necessarily good . . .'

Other interviewees expressed concern regarding the potentially
harmful aspects of the diet in exile. Although the wide variety of
foods available in Britain was commented upon, nevertheless,
many women considered the diet in Iran to be superior because
of its 'naturalness',[2] and experienced considerable anxiety over
the pesticides, additives and other contaminants in the modern,
British, highly processed diet.

Mehri: 'I had a problem . . . I feel the hair on my body is more
than before . . . I think myself it's—they put hormones in the
meat, especially in the chicken . . . maybe that's why. Or fruit
and vegetables, because they take them (a) few times a year, so
it won't be normal. I mean in our country we use one time
from the trees or the land—one time or twice, not more than
that . . . My children's teeth are not very good here . . . they
(are) marked . . . and the water actually is not very good here.'

Although at one level, this angst may represent a broader and
very modern mass manifestation of the fear of harmful incorporation (Fischler, 1988), at another level there is a particular political
specificity of meaning in an Iranian context. The chemicals and
pesticides referred to by this informant may not only be considered to be personally harmful, but in representing the 'other' of
the dominant society, also symbolize pollution and transformation by an unhealthy social environment.

The fear of ingestion of hormones may signify other and perhaps more urgent dangers. Although these substances are not
clearly defined in modern lay understanding, they have strong
sexual connotations, for example hormone replacement therapy
and the contraceptive pill (Fischler, 1988). Currently, in Britain,
there is controversy over falling male sperm counts over the last
decade. One explanatory hypothesis is that oestrogenic substances, migrating from food-packaging materials to ingested
food, may be responsible; hence men's bodies are under threat of
contamination and demasculinization by female substances.

In the preceeding account, Mehri was distressed by apparently noticeable alterations to her own body, brought about by consumption of hormone-containing British foodstuffs. In her case, the concern relates to the development of male secondary sexual characteristics.[3] In the light of other discussions with women regarding sexual matters (see also Harbottle, 1995:23), I would suggest that underlying her explicit anxiety may be a more insidious and powerful fear of contamination by western sexual morality and specifically the threat of uncontrolled female (ie less differentiated from male) sexuality.

Even those who did not remark upon the dangers of the British diet found that it did not satiate their appetites but left them still hungry. Regular consumption of familiar meals was vital, not only to nourish the body but also to satisfy the psyche and to strengthen the social body.

> Goli: 'When I have Iranian food . . . I am not any longer hungry . . . it satisfies me but with English food I am not satisfied . . . I'm looking for something else . . . especially with rice, I have to eat rice.'

Incorporation offers the opportunity for the transfer and reinforcement of beneficial traits and desirable transformation, both of the individual body and of collectively valued characteristics (Fischler, 1988). For those who would soon be going back to Iran, a major priority for women was to ensure that their families did not lose their Shi'ite faith. One woman was particularly diligent in ensuring the consumption of home-prepared, fresh, halal food: if her children wanted pizza or burgers, she made them herself. By reworking the pizza recipe, she effectively transforms it into an acceptable and distinctly Iranian Shi'ite product and, by so doing, ensures her children's retention of Muslim values.

> Mehri: 'I want to keep our diet, our food, because we won't live here forever, soon we will have to go back there and I don't want a lot of changes. I don't use . . . ready meals, because my children don't like (them) and I don't (either). It's not our taste . . . I make burgers myself because in the shop its not halal meat, so we don't use it. English children don't like the pizza we make . . . with meat, because we can't use sausage . . . (and) tomato and green beans and cheese. I don't like (mozarella) because it doesn't taste (of) anything, just like

glue—but I use cheddar cheese. I think the taste is better, but it's not like (in the) shops.'

In Islamic beliefs, food laws comprise part of a system which assures the believer of spiritual health in this world, as well as the possibility of an afterlife (Tapper and Tapper, 1986). Foods are either permitted and lawful (*halal*) or forbidden (*haram*). In the case of those families who adhered closely to Islamic dietary injunctions, the interlinkages between religion, aesthetics and health were clearly stated.

Mehri: 'When (they) cut the head off the sheep or chicken, the way Muslim people do it, all the blood comes out from the body, to make it clean—it's better. The meat is more delicious, it's very healthy, because if they keep the blood inside the body it's no good.'

The incorporation of *halal* foods, together with their purity and cleanliness, is seen to be health-promoting. In contrast, consumption of *haram* or impure foods (including meat from animals not killed in the prescribed way and blessed in the name of Allah, pigs, and blood from meat) may be dangerous.

Safieh: . . . 'we don't obey exactly the same things but in my heart, I like (to) eat *halal* . . . I don't like (pork).'

Even though most interviewees did not strictly follow the food code, it retained a residual significance. Few ate only *halal* meat, but almost all respondents reported avoiding pork and ham completely, although they would occasionally buy frankfurters or other pork-containing products. Those who had eaten pork had seemingly developed a culturally-conditioned aversion to it and disliked the taste; most saw no need to integrate it into their well-established culinary repetoire.

For expatriates in Britain, trips to Iran are highly important events (Harbottle, 1995) for the reaffirmation of cultural identity and reinforcement of family ties. Throughout such visits, food provides a powerful vehicle to communicate the care of the host relatives (and may serve as a means of expressing dysphoric affect). During the stay, family members prepare for the impending separation and return of the visitors to Britain. As part of this process, food supplies are gathered and prepared (with the investment of a considerable amount of labour) which will serve to maintain kinship and cultural ties until the next visit. The specific items chosen to maintain links may be those instrumentally considered unobtainable, expensive or of inferior quality in Britain; significantly, they are often those marginal substances particularly valued for their medicinal and restorative properties. Many are of key symbolic value in that they are essential for the preparation of Iranian dishes, eg saffron, dried limes, *sumac*, *zeresht* and herb mixtures; others are served individually as markers of ethnicity, eg the nuts and sweets to be offered to guests and served at parties.

> Soraye: 'pistachios (and) nougat . . . I always bring 2–4 kgs . . . dried (limes) definitely. My mother prepares them . . . *zeresht* (small red sour berries) definitely, almonds and pistachios (and) walnuts—you can buy them here but they taste funny—they are not as fresh. When you buy them fresh they are a bit sweet . . . *sumac* for *chelo kebab* and . . . I use lots of dried mint— and (my mother) . . . dries it.'

Summary and Conclusions: Recycling the Culinary Triangle

Research in the medical arena has previously tended to privilege western reductionist definitions of health and has failed to observe the holistic, dynamic and shifting context in which diet and health perceptions are enacted. Yet, within popular Iranian health beliefs, mind/body and body/spirit dualisms are absent. Rather, an interrelationship between mind, body and spirit is accepted, such that any imbalance in the emotions, caused by individual, familial or socio-cultural stressors, may lead to physical sickness and any spiritual disturbance, for example caused by sin, may lead to emotional and/or physical manifestations (Pliskin, 1987).

Amongst the Iranian migrants interviewed in this study, daily concern with food and diet is apparently important, not only to prevent sickness but also to secure a state of optimal health through the preservation of individual well-being, familial harmony, social relations and ethnic identity. In Britain, these women face the daunting task of attempting to maintain the well'th of their families in the face of specific threats of negative incorporation. They continually manipulate food consumption, so strengthening and equipping the family to withstand absorption into a foreign culture.

Although Levi-Strauss' culinary triangle (1966) has been extensively criticised for its static and highly formalized structural analysis, I suggest that it can be effectively recycled, if reinterpreted and applied in terms of actual cultural practices, which are historically contingent and subject to modification and contestation (see Figure 4).

a)	IRANIAN DIET	raw food (nature)———	*sophisticated cuisine*	———cooked food (culture)	
			additives	*no cuisine*	
b)	BRITISH DIET	raw food (nature)———	spoiled food ———(denatured)———	cooked food ———(toxic culture)	
			additives	*sophisticated cuisine*	
c)	IRANIAN MIGRANT DIET	raw food (nature)———	spoiled food ———(denatured)———	cooked food ———(restored culture)	

Figure 4 Possible food transformations

Possible food transformations

a) As previously stated, foodstuffs in Iran are generally regarded by these women as pure and unspoiled; the application of regional recipes and cooking methods then works a simple nature–culture transformation, producing healthy, nurturing food (represented by *ghòrmeh-sabzi*).

b) In the case of British food, the raw ingredients are perceived by these women to undergo an intermediary transformation, prior to cooking (the 'bastard' chicken); this fits with Levi-Strauss' description of a rotting or denaturation process. Upon application of English cooking methods, considered to be unelaborated and lacking in skill, by interviewees, the final cooked food is then of dubious food value and represents western toxic culture.

c) My argument is that Iranian women migrants, when preparing food for the family, are able to work another transformation. Although they are obliged to use denatured or spoiled ingredients,

I suggest that through their personal application of a highly sophisticated and elaborated cuisine, together with the use of specific medicinal and/or restorative agents, such as saffron, pistachios, *sumac* and dried limes, they have the power to reclaim the spoiled food and make it not only edible, but tasty, satisfying and sustaining.

Food occupies a central position in the social lives of these female Iranian migrants and daily food consumption practices provide one of the most important and accessible means by which they may reinforce, modify or transform their identities. Women hold a key role in food consumption processes; through engaging in their everyday household provisioning activities, they maintain the well'th of their families, not simply by selecting and acquiring specific ingredients but then by transforming them through particular culinary practices. This performance may be variably enacted by women, according to their different understandings of and needs to maintain the ethnic identities of themselves and their families and the range of alternate means available by which they may do so. Additionally, there may be times of special need, eg during sickness or when under threat for any reason; then extra input of foods considered to have beneficial effects, for their medicinal or symbolic value, may be required. Special meals and events such as *No Ruz* and *Moharram* may then also be interpreted as providing a tonic to boost the symbolic immune system of the family and/or social group.

Acknowledgements

I wish to express my gratitude to all the individuals who participated in this study and especially to 'Farah' for her tale regarding the 'bastard' chicken. I would also like to thank Ronnie Frankenberg, Fatimeh Rabiee and Azam Tourab for their very helpful insights and criticisms of the draft paper.

Notes

1 Frankenberg uses the notion of ill'th in a similar way (1986).
2 However, in Iran people are also concerned at the increase in modern commercial processing methods, such as battery farming (Rabiee, pers. comm.)
3 Total body hair removal is commonly practised by Muslim Iranians who consider body hair to be unhygienic as well as unfeminine. An apparent increase in

hair growth, then, provokes anxiety in a culturally specific way (Rabiee, pers. comm.).

References

Bradby, H., (1995) 'Of Heating and Heart Attacks: Understandings of Health and Food among Young British Asian Women,' Paper given to *B.S.A. Medical Sociology Group* 22–24 Sept 1995, York.

Davison, C., Smith, G.D. and Frankel, S., (1991) 'Lay Epidemiology and the Prevention Paradox: The implications of coronary Candidacy for Health Education', *Sociology of Health and Illness*, Vol. 13, (1): 1–19.

Farmaian, Farman S., with Munker, D., (1993) *Daughter of Persia*, Second Edition, London: Corgi.

Fischler, C., (1988) 'Food, Self and Identity', *Social Science Information*, Vol. 27(2): 275–292.

Frankenberg, R., (1986) 'Sickness as cultural performance', *International Journal of Health Services*, Vol. 16: 603–26.

Greenwood, B., (1981) 'Cold or Spirits? Choice and Ambiguity in Morocco's Pluralist System', *Social Science and Medicine*, Vol. 15(B): 219–235.

Harbottle, L., (1995) ' "Palship", Parties and Pilgrimage: Kinship, Community Formation and Self-Transformation of Iranian Migrants to Britain', Working Paper No. 9: Representations of Places and Identities, Keele, Keele University Press.

James, A., (1990) 'The Good, the Bad and the Delicious: The Role of Confectionery in British Society', *Sociological Review*, Vol. 38(4): 666–68.

Kandel, R.F. and Pelto, G.H., (1980) 'The Health Food Movement,' Chapter 11 in *Nutritional Anthropology: Contemporary Approaches to Diet and Culture*, New York: Redgrave Publishing Company.

Kerr, M. and Charles, N., (1986) 'Servers and Providers: the Distribution of Food within a Family', *Sociological Review* Vol. 34(1): 155–55.

Lalonde, M.P., (1992) 'Deciphering a Meal Again, or the Anthropology of Taste', *Social Science Information*, Vol. 31(1): 69–86.

Levi-Strauss, C., (1966) 'The Culinary Triangle', *New Society*, Dec. 22: 937–940.

Lock, M.M., (1980) 'East Asian Medicine in Urban Japan', *Comparative Studies of Health Systems and Medical Care*. Number 4, Berkeley: University of California Press.

Messer, E., (1981) 'Hot-Cold Classification: Theoretical and Practical Implications of a Mexican Study', *Social Science and Medicine* Vol. 15(B): 133–45.

Pliskin, K., (1987) *Silent Boundaries. Cultural Constraints on Sickness and Diagnosis of Iranians in Israel*, New Haven: Yale University Press.

Sreberny-Mohammadi, A. and Mohammadi, A., (1993) *The Body Social: Symbolism, Self and Society*, London: Routledge.

Synott, A., (1994) *Small Media, Big Revolution. Communication, Culture and the Iranian Revolution*, London: University of Minnesota Press.

Tan, S.P. and Wheeler, E., (1983) 'Concepts Relating to Health and Food held by Chinese Women in London'. *Ecology of Food and Nutrition*, Vol. 13: 37–49.

Tapper, R. and Tapper, N., (1986) ' "Eat This, it'll Do You a Power of Good": Food and Commensality among Durrani Pashtuns.' *American Ethnologist*, Vol. 13(1): 62–79.

World Health Organization (1982) *Plan of Action Implementing the Global Strategy for All*, Geneva: W.H.O.

Zonis, M., (1991) *Majestic Failure: The Fall of the Shah*, Chicago: University of Chicago Press.

Consuming the past

Gaynor Bagnall

Abstract

This chapter reports preliminary findings from case studies of two heritage-based sites in north west England: Wigan Pier and The Museum
of Science and Industry in Manchester. The research has involved
examining both the production and consumption processes at work at
these sites. The author focuses here on the area of consumption and
presents data, collected in interviews with visitors to the two sites
which suggest that visitors use emotional, imaginary and bodily maps
to make sense of the past. The authenticity of the experience is sustained by an 'emotional realism' which enables and enhances the
process of consumption. The author also argues that the manner in
which these sites are consumed supplies one way of understanding the
definitions and significance of the concept of heritage articulated by
the visitors.

Introduction

Museums and heritage-based attractions have become important
and significant sites of leisure consumption in the 1990s. For
instance, the most popular new UK tourist attraction to open in
1994 was 'Anything to Declare', HM Customs & Excise National
Museum in Liverpool, with 312,000 visitors in its first year
(BTA/ETB Research Services, 1995). In 1994 visits to museums
accounted for 16 per cent and visits to historic properties a further 20 per cent of all visits to tourist attractions. In the year
March 1994 to February 1995, The National Trust received
£41,753,000 in membership subscriptions, and generated revenue
of £34,275,000 from admission fees, shop trading, restaurants and
tearooms (BTA/ETB Research Services, 1995). This information

begins to illustrate the popularity of heritage-based attractions for people having a 'day out' in the UK.

As John Urry recently pointed out, however, there has been little research looking at how people react to, and make use of, heritage sites. Urry argues that we can presume that different visitors will 'read' museums and heritage sites in various ways (1996). Macdonald too, asserts that museum studies should be wary of constructing a 'passive and unitary public' and be sensitive to the 'interpretative agency of visitors' (1996:5). Yet, much work on heritage-based sites has assumed that they transfer a straightforward nostalgia from object to consumer. To date, writing in this area has provided little empirical evidence to allow the reader to understand how visitors consume such sites. My research involves case studies of two heritage-based sites in the north west of England: Wigan Pier and The Museum of Science and Industry in Manchester. Part of my remit was to talk with visitors at these sites to gain a better understanding of how they 'consume' heritage-based locations.

I was interested in looking at the meanings people invest in the idea of heritage, and heritage sites, and how we can relate these to their lifestyle and consumption activities. In particular, I was concerned to discover how visitors negotiated the sites. How did they make their way around them? How did they respond to their visit? The aim of the research was to move away from 'one-sidedly quantitative methods' (Fyfe and Ross, 1996:131), with their use of highly structured questionnaires, towards a more detailed and flexible approach. I interviewed people while they were visiting the site in an attempt to avoid decontextualisation (Hughes, 1986). Conducting interviews at heritage sites is not easy as people often visit such places in groups, therefore all the interviews were tape-recorded to enable a detailed analysis of them to be undertaken. Adopting such a technique also allowed me to capture and specify each person's contribution. In all thirty-five interviews were conducted at each site, and the people interviewed were selected randomly from the visitors.

In this chapter I do not propose to discuss every aspect of the interviews. Instead I will focus on the ways in which visitors map their consumption at the two sites. The idea of mapping is derived from the work of Kevin Lynch (1960), who uses the concept in his spatial analysis of the city. Lynch suggests that urban alienation is linked to the mental unmappability of city space. In his writings on 'cognitive mapping' Jameson (1991) extrapolates this to the difficulties any political form of postmodernism faces in mapping global totality. I will suggest that in making sense of the past at the sites I studied, visitors emotionally, imaginatively and physically map their consumption. These forms of mapping enable and enhance the visitor experience. Visits to such sites are not necessarily the cognitive experience that has previously been associated with such visiting. The key is an emotional realism (Ang, 1996), the ability of the sites to engage visitors on an emotional and imaginary level, to engender feelings which are meaningful. However while the visitors respond to the sites on an emotional level, they also seem to need the information presented by the sites to be genuine, authentic, based in 'fact'. Thus, there is a duality to the authenticity required of the sites. Alongside the pleasure visitors gain from the 'real' emotions stimulated by the sites is the requirement that the stories told there are accurate, legitimate. Furthermore, the way in which visitors consume these sites allows us to comprehend the salience of the idea of heritage and gives us an understanding of the definitions of heritage that the visitors supplied.

The sites

Many people have now written about the 'new museology' (Vergo, 1989). The changes in museums that have allowed them to become more accessible, more reflexive, and more visitor-centred (Ross, 1994). There has also been a good deal of writing about heritage and heritage sites (Hewison, 1987; Urry, 1990; Wright, 1985, 1989). Heritage is a difficult and value-laden concept. Therefore, it is tempting to adopt Hewison's argument that heritage has turned history into a commodity which has diminished our critical capacity for understanding the past (1987). Such definitions of heritage, however, take little account of the bedrock of popular support it receives. Nor do they acknowledge the role of the other forces at work in the representation of history, such as historical novels, biographies, electronic media, television, and film. Nor do they take account of the different forms of heritage offered to the public gaze, the different historical narratives that are now available for consumption. As Samuel argues, an expanding historical culture now extends into previously unnoticed areas and utilizes a range of new documentation, from football scarves to CD-Rom (1994).

The two sites that I have looked at exist as museums and heritage sites; either term could be used to describe or define them. Their content and method of representation highlight the changing nature of museums and emphasize some difficulties associated with the concept of heritage. Both display a move away from the cultural élitism previously associated with many museums, towards a more populist approach in which the barriers between high and popular culture are eroded; there is a process of de-differentiation[1] (Lash, 1990).

The sites are in the north west of England and are regionally important tourist attractions, economically and culturally. Both attractions can be found at canal side locations, inside historic industrial architecture, and are comparable in terms of size, admission charges,[2] and visitor numbers. The Museum of Science and Industry is operated as a registered charity, while Metropolitan Wigan Leisure Department manages Wigan Pier. A theme of industry is identifiable at both attractions and the past and locality are used as unifying themes. However, the sites do differ, in the employment of actors at Wigan and the display of science in Manchester. Both are promoted as museums, while Wigan Pier also describes itself as part theatre. They invite visitors to 'Step back in time to Victorian England and rediscover life in a bygone age' (Metropolitan Wigan Leisure Department, undated), and to 'discover what life was like in cotton mills in their heyday' (The Museum of Science & Industry in Manchester, undated).

At Wigan the foremost attraction is 'The Way We Were' exhibition which attempts to show the lives of everyday working people in the period 1890 to 1914. It does this by using a range of exhibits, models, and reconstructions of shops, pubs, houses, a music hall, a market, a railway carriage, a schoolroom and a coal mine. Perhaps the aspect of the exhibition that the Pier has become most famous for is its employment of actors, who perform in promenade plays around the different settings of the 'Way We Were', and in playlets within specific locations like the Victorian schoolroom. Wigan Pier is promoted as a family day out, a 'mixture of entertainment and education together with a feeling of re-living the past. Everything you could possibly wish for in a great family day out' (Metropolitan Wigan Leisure Department, undated). The site also has a cafe, water bus rides, concert, conference and corporate facilities, a play area, shops, an education centre and a pub.

At Manchester the museum covers a seven-acre site, with galleries which include Air & Space, Xperiment, Changing Exhibitions, Underground Manchester, Making of Manchester, Power Hall, and Gas and Electricity. The museum's promotional leaflets invite the visitor to 'Feel the past, Touch the Future', to 'discover what life was like in cotton mills in their heyday and meet an alien—all in a single day out'. It is a place 'with working exhibits bringing the past vividly to life' (The Museum of Science & Industry in Manchester, undated). The museum has working exhibits, a hands-on interactive science centre, steam train rides, and reconstructions ranging from sewers to a sitting room. It aims to 'demonstrate the wealth of the region's heritage' (Greater Manchester Museum of Science & Industry Trust, 1989). The site also offers other facilities and attractions such as a shop, cafes, conference centre, educational and library services, train rides, and lecture theatres. Thus while we can describe both attractions as heritage sites, in that they offer us history as a product to be consumed, they also offer more to the visitor, a whole range of activities and experiences to consume.

The Visitors

A key concept discussed in the consumption debate is 'choice' (Warde, 1994), so who does choose to visit such places? Why do they visit? What choices do they make while there? How does this affect their consumption?

At both sites two thirds of the visitors I interviewed were from the local area; that is they lived within 30 miles of the site. The other third consisted of visitors from abroad and from other parts of the UK, either on day trips, or staying in the area and visiting the sites while on holiday. Most people visited in groups, although at Manchester there was some evidence of men visiting alone. At both sites many groups contained children. These included parents and children, and women bringing their child relatives such as nieces or nephews. At Manchester there was some evidence of men visiting the museum with their children; this was not so at Wigan. We can connect this to the theme of the museum, particularly the scientific aspect; it appears that the site was seen as an appropriate place for a father to take children to. Most visitors to both sites thought that they had an equal appeal to men and women; however, a significant minority at

Manchester thought the site had a specific appeal to men. At both sites the other all-adult visitor groups were made up of friends, partners, relations, and people brought together through organized trips.

There was a good deal of diversity in the ages of the visitors to the sites. However, there was little evidence of visitors in the 18-to-25 age group at either site. There were a number of visitors over the age of 65 to be found at Wigan Pier. In terms of occupations the diversity of visitors to Wigan Pier is great; hairdressers, tattoo artists, ships captains, teachers, social workers. The range was perhaps less great at Manchester, with many people having some occupational connection to industry, science, or the field of education. There was very little ethnic diversity at either location: White visitors predominantly peopled both sites.

Of the thirty-five interviews conducted in Manchester, more than 48 per cent of the groups interviewed contained at least one person with a degree, or included someone who was currently in higher education. It was interesting that while there was the unsurprising phenomenon of university educated parents bringing their children, there were also young adults currently in higher education taking their non-university educated parents to the museum. Indeed 65 per cent of the visitor groups included somebody with either a degree or a professional qualification such as a teaching certificate, and 29 per cent had undertaken some form of vocational or technical qualification such as City and Guilds. Thus 94 per cent of those groups interviewed contained at least one person who had received some form of further education.

The type of occupation and its connection with the science and industry theme of the museum provided one explanation for the sort of people who visited. However, many other visitors were employed in the health, welfare and educational fields, giving some credence to the notion of 'cultural capital' (Bourdieu, 1984). This can be conceptualized as, 'forms of cultural knowledge, competences, or dispositions' (Bourdieu, 1993:7). Such knowledge can be utilized by social agents to make sense of cultural relations and artefacts. Those who possess such knowledge can decode the encoded meanings that give value and interest to cultural products. This cultural competency can be transmitted by the pedagogical action of family members, or educated members of the social group (Bourdieu, 1984). Thus cultural competencies can be passed on, to transmit advantage.

At Wigan Pier 20 per cent of the interview groups contained at least one degree educated person, 20 per cent had a professional qualification, and 20 per cent had a technical or vocational qualification such as City and Guilds. While there were fewer visitors educated to degree level, 60 per cent of the interview groups still contained at least one person who had undergone further education. The higher age cohort visiting Wigan also contributed to the level of educational attainment identified. However, these findings seem to imply that we could have different social groups visiting each site or perhaps more specifically, different facets of social groups. It does seem that a site like Wigan Pier holds little attraction for parts of the middle classes, those private sector professionals with cultural practices of 'commodified high living' (Savage *et al.*, 1992:110). This may be connected to the content of the heritage on offer at Wigan, which is predominantly working-class. While represented at the Manchester site, this group were still only minimally evident. The other social groupings of the middle classes and their attendant lifestyles, articulated by Savage *et al.*, were represented at both sites: the 'ascetic', which is associated with public sector professionals who are high in cultural but not economic capital and the 'undistinctive' which can be found in managers and government bureaucrats and is associated with a stolid 'boring' lifestyle (Savage *et al.*, 1992).

If these are the people who visit, why do they choose to visit these particular sites? At both sites some visits were made because of a clear choice, and we can connect this with the transmission of cultural capital. Thus, at Wigan Pier:

> 'Well I was coming with erm, to take my mum who's never been, I've been once before and I wanted to take my mum, I thought she might be interested and the children, er that's my nephew and niece.' (Female 38, Comprehensive School Teacher[3]), or: 'Er its a place we've heard about quite a lot, I've never had chance to come before, me wife's brought the children in the past and we tend to enjoy going out to museums and the such, we don't go too far out at the weekends so here we are.' (Male 38, Hairdresser).

At Manchester too, the exercise of choice can be seen:

> 'I think we're interested in Museums', (Male 52, Primary School Teacher), or: 'I thought it would be ideal for the children and it's been excellent', (Female 36, studying for a BEd).

233

However, this was not always so, for some visitors the decision was more arbitrary:

> 'Erm, the weather, we were originally going to go to the Lakes, erm, but with it being such a bad day for weather we decided to come here instead.' (Male 41, Ships Captain), or: 'Er well actually we were heading for Granada Studios but it was so packed, we decided to come on somewhere else and this was close.' (Female 42, Classroom Assistant).

Thus, we can see that there is a diversity to the people who visit and the reasons supplied for their visit. However the sites do seem to have a particular appeal to what in general terms can be called the middle classes. From the evidence of my interviews, it seems that the sites do not attract everybody. In my sample there was little evidence of the unemployed visiting the sites,[4] nor was there any black or ethnic minority representation among the people interviewed, a feature of heritage sites that other writers have identified (Urry, 1990). Hence while most people interviewed thought that both sites would appeal to anybody, this 'everybody' is perhaps better conceptualized as 'people like ourselves', (Female 42, Classroom Assistant).

Heritage: a physical experience

We have looked at who visits and why, but how do people consume while at the site, how do they navigate their way around the site? I want to suggest that the visit is organized by physical experience, there is a bodily mapping of consumption at both sites. Moreover, it is this physical mapping that stimulates both the imagination and emotions which visitors employ to make sense of their experiences at both sites. Thus, visitors to both sites utilize physical, emotional and imaginary maps in order to organize and understand the visitor experience.

Wigan Pier claims to provide the sights, sounds and smells of the time. The Museum of Science and Industry invites the visitor to feel the past, touch the future. Thus, a visit to Wigan Pier or the Museum of Science and Industry is not just a cognitive experience, rather it is a bodily, a physical experience.[5] While I would agree with John Urry (1990) that the visual has a key role, I would challenge the idea that it is all-important; rather the visitor experience at both sites is much more pluri-sensorial. My interviews with visitors to Wigan suggest that the physical encounter with the Pier involves an invocation of the past that they achieve through the medium of sight but/which is also secured through other bodily experiences—such as the smells and noise in the mine, the soundtrack in the Way We Were, the dialogue of the actors, the sounds of steam trains, the taste of sweets from a 'bygone era'.

'You, you don't all the time notice the sort of soundtrack that's going on around you but every so often you hear something and think, you know it's, er, you know it does tend to bring it to life rather than just walking round in silence,' (Male 35, Structural Engineer).

At Manchester the experience was also about physicality, the getting to grips with Xperiment, the hands-on science centre, climbing in and out of old planes, hearing, smelling and tasting the steam train, listening to the deafening noise of the machinery in the Power Hall or in the Textile Gallery. Many people claimed their favourite part of the museum was a section that involved a heightened physical experience, from hands-on science to the smells in Underground Manchester or the noise of the Power Hall. Thus, the navigation and the consumption of both sites is achieved physically as well as cognitively and frequently the physical has primacy:

'I like the hands-on, that's especially good for school children but really I like to play with them myself' (Male 51, Primary Head Teacher); 'Its nice to see the steam and gas engines working, the noise and the smell' (Male 53, Aircraft Engineer); 'I liked the smell of it' (Sewers) (Female 36, Purchase & Ledger Clerk).

From the responses above, we begin to get a sense of how the visitors to both sites were able to map their visit by physical experience. The significance of this physical mapping is that it enables the visitor emotionally and imaginatively to map their consumption and so give meaning to the versions of the past offered. This stimulation of emotions and imagination was particularly noticeable at Wigan Pier, where the use of actors certainly heightens the encounter. However it could also be detected at

Manchester. Thus, there is an interconnection between the physicality of the experience and the emotions and imagination engendered.

Emotional mapping

I will now discuss how the interrelation between the physical and emotional maps is displayed. It is important to note, however, that this interconnected mapping does not necessarily lead to an acceptance, a confirmatory reading, of what the site offers. It can promote a quite different response—a rejective mapping, a rejection of the information or message exhibited. Thus two forms of emotional mapping can be identified, the confirmatory and the rejective.

The Confirmatory Emotional Map

This was the most common way of experiencing both sites. The emotional response stimulated by the physicality of the experience led visitors to feel that they really were consuming the past or getting a good idea of what life was like in the past. The content of the sites allowed visitors to experience an emotional realism. Visitors could identify with the emotions generated by the offerings at Manchester and Wigan; there was an authenticity to the feelings activated by the sites.

The use of actors to recreate the past at Wigan Pier is very important in stimulating the emotions and imagination of the visitors. The promenade playlets, which the visitor follows around the site, and the other performances in which the visitor participates, seem to enhance the visit and allow the visitors to experience a feeling of reliving the past:

'Erm, I think it was erm quite realistic, it gave you an idea more than just looking at displays. . . . I think that the smells and the sounds are very important in creating that feeling without which they would just sort of be images' (Male 33, Fieldwork Social Worker); 'Er he went in afterwards, so the acting was very real and it frightened him' (Female 38, Teacher Comprehensive).

Thus the displays at the Pier can provoke an emotional response that enabled the visitor to feel as if they had experienced a realistic version of the past. They might have encountered real coal in a plastic mine, but there was no doubting the emotional impact it could engender or the feelings that it could mobilize. This process could also be detected at Manchester:

'I think the textiles certainly have an interest to all, especially when they have these machines running and you think that people worked in that for nigh on 12 hours a day' (Male 58, Electrical Engineer); 'Erm well I always like the reconstructions, like in the sewer, I think they're great 'cos it really brings it home what it was like then,' (Female 52, Midwifery Manager).

Thus one of the primary ways that these sites invoke the nostalgic impulse is by an invitation to 'feel' something. It has been argued that these 'heritage feelies' (Fowler, 1989:62) where the visitor is invited to feel, as well as to see, contribute to self-delusion, since visitors can never know what it was 'really' like. However, other writers argue that it is important to promote a response, that heritage needs to be 'hot' and engage with the emotions. This 'hot' approach is seen as preferable to the adoption of a 'cool' approach which entails a freeze-framing of history (Uzzell, 1989). Feelings are seen as one way of opening the door to the past (Craig, 1989). It is not possible to avoid twentieth century values in any heritage construction. As Lowenthal says, it is 'contingent on our own views, our own perspective, and above all our own present' (Lowenthal, 1987:217). Hence, it is argued that plausibility is more important than 'fact', as meaning is not a collection of facts but the sum total of the experience (Craig, 1989). Thus, it is argued that heritage sites should strive for plausibility rather than accuracy.

One method of achieving this, is the concept of 'ceremonial time'. This is not a linear construction of time, but when past and present are one, moments in life when remembrance of an event seems especially real, times when we feel in touch with our own sense of place (Craig, 1989). Thus, emotions can play a key role in bringing the past to life. They can enable visitors to explore the past themselves and make history more meaningful to their lives and personal experience.

Gaynor Bagnall

The Rejective Emotional Map

As I noted earlier, however, there is no one visitor experience. It is possible for this invocation of emotions to stimulate a rejection of the picture that is presented. One way this is achieved is through the notion of personal memory, which can challenge the constructed nature of sites like Wigan and Manchester. Ann Game (1991) engages with the work of de Certeau, to argue that, while such texts can delimit a field and structure relations, personal memory can be used to rewrite these texts. These re-writings act as anti-texts allowing us to read against the text, to 'open up space to something different' (de Certeau, 1984:106–7). These are ordinary, everyday practices so that whilst the museum fixes and delimits, memory operates by dispersion so that the memorable is also dispersed. These remnants can't be seen or put into representation, as they are fragmentary pasts that cannot be read by others. Thus, it is possible that in certain landscapes, places, sites, a space can be opened up for the transformation of stories (de Certeau, 1984; Game, 1991).

At both sites there is a tension between museums delimiting the field, and an appeal to personal memory. Heritage, with its discourses of nationality, pastness and memory, does have a tendency to homogenize, to reduce heterogeneous history to heritage. However, at such sites there is a space for personal memory, a 'place for retelling' (Game, 1991:163). If we look at Wigan, there is a way of being there that rejects the constructed structure of the site. The pier was able to stimulate personal memories that allowed people to reject the homogenization of history. Thus in response to my question concerning the ability of Wigan to make History come alive:

'I think it's tempered with what people like, you know, your grandparents and that tell you, little things that you might say ooh I remember them saying that, those things, so it depends really . . .' (Female 34, Housewife prev Insurance Clerk); 'er at the pithead, there was a coal reel and a lift for coal, well I did that. It was only for two years but I did that, aye' (this was the job of cleaning and sorting coal at the Pithead). . . . 'Well you know it was a hard life and I was brought up erm among the miners, you know I had three brothers and a father and I remember the 1926 strike and it was something terrible, oh, and that's the true picture for me anyway, 'cos I lived through it all' (Female 83, Retired).

At Manchester I was also able to identify the use of personal memory to provide a rejective emotional mapping:

'We were saying that the most interesting bit is the sewer bit, that was extremely interesting because there was actually lots of things there that we can remember when we were children. We were coming out and saying "My God, we must be museum exhibits already!" ' (laughter), 'it's frightening, and 'cos a bit of that I can remember from when I was a child it's not as old as they're depicting, they're saying when it started but not when it finished.' (Female 51, Betting Shop Cashier)

We have seen that people do make use of emotional mappings to make sense of their visit. These can take the form of confirmatory or rejective maps. Connected to these emotive chartings is the use of the imaginary, the ability of imagination to enhance our consumption at such sites. I will turn briefly to this next.

Imaginary mapping

It has been argued that unlocking the imagination can lead to a heightened sense of place (Craig, 1989). Looking is one means through which imagination is stimulated, emotion is another. It is important to find a place for imagination when discussing heritage-based tourism. However, it is an imagination mediated by social context. In a provocative book Colin Campbell (1987) argues that consumption is as much a matter of emotion and feeling as rational behaviour. Individuals are capable of manipulating belief, by suspension of disbelief. Thus, the individual can adjust the level and nature of the emotional experience (Campbell, 1987). This requires skilful use of the imagination, as it is difficult to imagine sensations. However it is easier to imagine events or situations which produce an emotion in the imaginer. Nostalgia is an appropriate emotion for it is largely self-referential. Thus, the sites at Wigan and Manchester can successfully utilize nostalgia and the emotions it generates as a means to stimulate the imagination. Moreover, individuals now have a greater capacity for imagining because they are continuously bombarded with images and, frequently, images from the past. This is not a free-wheeling imagination, but one that is located within specific social processes and is dependent upon social factors. The images provoked can be mediated by issues such as gender, class, and ethnicity, or cultural location.

Thus, at both sites visitors used imaginary maps alongside emotional maps. It is the way in which the two maps interconnect that allow the visitor to experience the sites. There is a circularity among the three maps, physical, emotional, and imaginary as they feed in and out of each other during consumption; a circularity that we can see in the interview data provided. For example the physicality of the experience promotes an emotional response which allows the imagination to be stimulated:

> 'In a way yes, but er, the children they were both frightened in the mine and I thought that was quite realistic, the feeling of being closed in, and in fact you're not even on a lower level, it's quite well done' (Female 37, School Nurse); 'because then you can sort of picture it, you know, in your own mind as if you were there and it was happening', (Female 31, Building Society Cashier).

However leaving the story there would be remiss, for underpinning these maps is a desire, a need, for the information offered for consumption to be authentic, based upon 'facts'.

Authenticity: who needs it!

As we have seen, both sites seem to give the visitor a sense that they are consuming reality. These tangible reconstructions of the past can stimulate emotions, memories and the imagination. We can connect this to an article by John Urry (1996), in which he suggests that we need to develop a theory of 'reminiscence'. Reminiscence is a spatial practice in which performativity plays a key role, it is not a passive consumption process. Instead it involves concentrated viewing and performance, by visitors, actors or workers at a site, to produce and stimulate memories. Thus, no one account of history is available at heritage sites. Although people are aware that the performance is staged, it is still able to reawaken dreams and desires. Thus to reminisce 'is collectively to effect a performance' (Urry, 1996:55). I would suggest that it is the reality of the emotions felt by the visitors that contributes to their ability to 'perform' at the sites.

Moreover in my research authenticity was considered extremely important and was to some extent used as a legitimation of the visit. Thus, while visitors may feel 'freed from the constraints of high culture on the one hand, or the untrammelled pursuit of the pleasure principle on the other' (Urry, 1988:38), the majority still seemed to need a legitimation, a justification for their play, and their emotional and imaginary engagement. Education and the validity of the knowledge offered provided this authority. Thus, at Wigan Pier:

'Mmmm, oh yes definitely, otherwise there's no point in doing it' (Female 42, Housewife married to Chemistry Lecturer); 'Yes, well I think, I mean a lot of us get our knowledge from these sort of things so if they weren't authentic we'd be learning something that wasn't true, wouldn't we' (Female 55, Housewife); 'Erm because as well as being somewhere to go for a day out it's also educational for kids and it's important you see the life in the past without any sort of rosy glow put over it' (Male 41, Ships Captain).

This could also be identified at Manchester:

'Yes I think that's important' (Female 56, Receptionist); 'Aye I think so, well absolutely, I'm surprised at the question, yes of course it should be authentic,' (Male 52, Primary Teacher).

In the next two examples, the visitors acknowledge the possible inauthenticity of the experience:

'Personally yes, erm it's very very difficult to do I don't think it can be achieved' (Male 38, Hairdresser); 'You know the shops and that have got like plastic fish and they're obviously plastic, I mean I know you can say well you can't put a real one down, but erm I dunno for youngsters it's probably very authentic, you're just probably a bit more cynical and that' (Male 35, Police Officer).

Thus it seems that there are two levels of engagement at work in the consumption of these sites. At one level there is an emotional realism (Ang, 1996) in which it is the tangibility of the emotions engendered that is the important aspect of the consumption process. However, this emotional realism is underpinned by a desire for the experience to be based in fact, to be genuine.

Perhaps this is a lingering remnant of the days when museums were seen as the repositories of all knowledge, of cultural elitism. Another explanation is that for the social groups who were visiting the sites, leisure consumption required justification or legitimation; and the desire to learn, to be more educated, provided that mandate.

What is heritage?

I would now like to look briefly at a recent book on Scottish Heritage by McCrone *et al.* (1995) which begins to tap into the emotional and imaginary mappings I have identified. McCrone *et al.* (1995) interviewed life-members of The Scottish National Trust and looked at how they conceptualized heritage. While heritage was identified as a salient concept, it was understood in different ways. In the main there were two ways of understanding heritage. One emphasized the physical artefacts, while the other McCrone *et al.* equate with the French word 'patrimoine', which suggests possession of certain values and culture, the idea of inheritance. Among those interviewed there was a commitment to this heritage and the objects used to represent it. These objects can confer identity and act as vehicles capable of bringing the past into the present. Hence, there is an appeal and engagement with an 'imagined community' (Anderson, 1983) which can result in the dissolution of inequalities and differences. However, as Stuart Hall has argued, in contemporary society people have to be members of several imagined communities. Identity is always an unfinished game. It is always under construction (Hall, 1993). Yet, importantly for our discussion here, it 'always moves into the future through a symbolic detour through the past' (Hall, 1993:362). McCrone *et al.* take this further to argue that heritage also 'has an identity-conferring status, not simply (or even) in collective and national terms but in individual and personal' (McCrone *et al.*, 1995:181).

In my research, heritage as a concept was not always as tangible as McCrone *et al.* discovered, although this is not surprising, as the audience for the sites I studied is more diverse than the National Trust Life members that formed the basis of their research study. However, while some visitors did struggle with the term, many more were able to articulate similar understandings of the word heritage to those unearthed by McCrone *et al.*:

'Things which are important of the past. And that does include the industry of the past as well as oil paintings of the past and stately homes of the past' (Male 33, Software Engineer); 'Something that's old, that's been there for years and years and you know it's your heritage, your ancestry, it tells a story of where you all came from, how we got here, you know' (Female 33, Coach Owner); 'Well that's your . . . your heritage is what you really are' (Female 83, Retired, Prev Manual work including Pit Work); 'Oh this is getting hard, I'm in need of a degree,' (laughs), 'I would say its something to do with the past, er being kept basically into the present for the future, for the future generations' (Female 40, Domestic).

I would suggest that heritage as material artefacts and heritage as representative of culture, values, and inheritance can be identified in the above. Moreover, it is possible to connect these definitions of heritage with the emotional and imaginary maps employed by the visitors. Heritage is not an abstract idea, it is associated with, and articulated through, emotions, memories, and imagination. However it was also a term that carried negative connotations for some visitors:

'Gosh I can't say as an archeologist, but well people shudder I think in archeology, ah heritage oh gosh its going to all be turned into a kind of funfair, I think if it's done properly if its done like say York (Jorvik Centre) is done, okay' (Female 41, University Researcher, Archeology); 'Erm, well I suppose that's what it means the glossy bits, I don't think erm, it's not a word I would use myself really it's just the nice things, maybe its wrong, but I always imagine it as what rich people did and how they lived' (Female 43, Housewife/ Computer Operator); 'Erm well its about Britain's heritage, history it's our, well it's not mine, no, you see my parents are foreign so my heritage, so my heritage I suppose is different, my parents are Ukrainian, so I've got this idea of my heritage being somewhere else but I suppose this is British people's heritage, remembering the past and what it was about and how we developed from there' (Female 38, Comprehensive School Teacher); 'I think it is er for people who are British er but not necessarily for, I mean like the school where I teach you know with 50 per cent Asian children, even though we brought them here, the way of life in the past doesn't really apply to them, it was a bit difficult for them to understand.' (Female 39, Primary School Teacher).

The last few quotations are interesting as they are the only ones to raise the issue of whose past is represented, and they begin to problematize the notion of heritage, and its frequent construction as white and peculiarly English or British. The irrelevance of, in this instance, Wigan Pier to the lives of Asian school children as articulated in the last quotation may offer the beginnings of an explanation as to the lack of black or ethnic minority representation in my interview sample. Some black and ethnic minority groups may not have the necessary resources with which to negotiate these sites. They may not have the biographies and memories that allow them to connect and identify with what is on offer[6] and that could enable them to map these sites emotionally and imaginatively. Moreover, these quotations also highlight the point Hall raises about a feature of contemporary societies being that people are often members of several imagined communities. The vast majority of respondents do not articulate this view, although that is not to deny that in other circumstances they might. However it does highlight the ability of both sites to use heritage as a unifying, organizing principle that can construct communities and divert attention away from differences.

Conclusion

In this chapter I have suggested that the process of consumption at The Museum of Science and Industry and at Wigan Pier is constructed around physical, emotional and imaginary mappings. In talking about the notion of heritage, visitors articulated a set of ideas that we can connect to the mappings employed in the negotiation of the sites. Heritage is about physical, material objects, but it is also about culture, values and inheritance. It is by engaging with imagination and emotions that visitors can give some significance to the concept of heritage.

Yet operating alongside these maps and the idea of heritage articulated, is the visitor's requirement that the sites be authentic. However, there is a duality to this authenticity. Visitors do derive genuine pleasure from the ability of the sites to provoke an emotional response, to stimulate their imagination so that they 'feel' as if they have had a taste of re-living the past. They can relate to the feelings mobilized by their journey around the sites; and it is this emotional realism which sustains the process of consumption and provides much of the pleasure. However the sites have to do more than this, more than just provoke an emotional response. They also need to convince the visitor that the experience is based in 'fact', and has some historical or educational value. Most visitors expect and require the stories told to be 'true'. Moreover, it would appear that the experience of consumption would be devalued and undermined by the removal of the foundations of truth from the visit. As museums and heritage-based sites change to a more populist approach, it could be argued that it is the desire to hold onto some form of 'cultural capital' that is the motivating factor in the desire for the authenticity. For it is only their attachment to a factual-based history which separates some of these sites from other forms of entertainment. Thus, for many visitors, authenticity acts as a legitimator during consumption; it justifies the choice they have made. They have the opportunity to 'feel' something and they perceive that the visit had educational value as well.

Acknowledgements

I am very grateful for the suggestions and advice of Brian Longhurst, and the helpful comments of the participants in the sixth seminar of the ESRC Seminar Series: Conceptualizing Consumption Issues, held at Keele University. The research has been supported by the Institute for Social Research/Department of Sociology at The University of Salford in the form of a studentship awarded to Gaynor Bagnall.

Notes

1 However not isolating this process of de-differentiation from the political and economic workings of late capitalism is important (Jameson, 1991). The changes that have occurred need to be understood in the context of the requirement for sites like The Museum of Science and Industry in Manchester and Wigan Pier to survive in the market economy. To do so they have to deal with the impact of changes in public and private sources of funding, and the effects, pressures, constraints and tensions of consumer markets.
2 Currently and up to 13/2/97 the adult entrance charge at The Museum of Science and Industry in Manchester is £4.00, with a concessionary entry of £2.00. However during Star Trek: The Exhibition, 29/3/96 to 14/7/96, the museum's admission charges increased to £5.00 for adults and £3.00 for concessions. At Wigan Pier the current adult admission charge is £4.40, with a concessionary rate of £3.30.

3 The quotations from visitor interviews used in this chapter are a representative sample of the data contained in my interviews. Due to lack of space only a small sample could be shown, however, for a fuller exposition of the interviews please see my forthcoming PhD.

4 One can suggest reasons why this group is missing from my sample. The cost of admission to the sites could be a contributory factor though concessionary rates are available. Another consideration could be the lack of interviewees in the eighteen to twenty-five-age group, an age range which has a comparatively high level of unemployment (CSO, 1996). However, without further research it is difficult to isolate whether it is age, unemployment, or a combination of the two, which is contributing to this group's limited appearance in my sample.

5 It has to be borne in mind that the promotional information itself can and will have affected the responses to my questions. However, assessing the impact of this material is difficult as most visitors had not read the literature provided, had read it sparingly, or intended to read it at some time in the future.

6 However, this is not to deny that many black and ethnic groups would have the resources required to map these sites emotionally and imaginatively, nor is it to deny that there are heritage sites and museums where some black and ethnic minority groups would be better able to map the sites than the predominantly white middle class visitors that I interviewed. It is also important to note that the locations studied recognize that they need to attract these groups to their sites in greater numbers and have instigated measures to try to achieve this, particularly through their educational programmes.

Bibliography

Ang, I., (1996), *Living Room Wars*, London: Routledge.

Anderson, B., (1983), *Imagined Communities*, London: Verso.

Bourdieu, P., (1984), *Distinction: A Social Critique of the Judgement of Taste*, London: Routledge & Kegan Paul.

Bourdieu, P., (1993), *The Field of Cultural Production*, Cambridge: Polity Press.

BTA/ETB Research Services, (1995), *Sightseeing In The UK 1994*, London: BTA/ETB Research Services.

Campbell, C., (1987), *The Romantic Ethic and the Spirit of Modern Consumerism*, Oxford: Basil Blackwell.

Craig, B., (1989), 'Interpreting the Historic Scene: The Power of Imagination in Creating a Sense of Historic Place,' in D. Uzzell (ed.) *Heritage Interpretation Vol. 1*, London: Belhaven Press.

Central Statistical Office, (1996), *Social Trends 26*, London: HMSO.

De Certeau, M., (1984), *The Practice of Everyday Life*, Berkeley: University of California Press.

Fowler, P., (1989), 'Heritage: A Post-Modernist Perspective,' in D. Uzzell (ed.), *Heritage Interpretation Vol. 1*, London: Belhaven Press.

Fyfe, G. and Ross, M., (1996), 'Decoding the visitor's gaze: rethinking museum visiting,' in S. Macdonald and G. Fyfe (eds), *Theorizing Museums*, Oxford: Blackwell/The Sociological Review.

Game, A., (1991), *Undoing the Social*, Milton Keynes: Open University Press.

Greater Manchester Museum of Science and Industry Trust, (1989), *Museum of Science and Industry*, Manchester: Museum of Science and Industry.

Hall, S., (1993), 'Culture, Community, Nation', *Cultural Studies*, Vol. 7: 349–363.

Hewison, R., (1987), *The Heritage Industry*, London: Methuen.

Hughes, J., (1986), *Sociological Analysis: Methods of Discovery*, London: Nelson.

Jameson, F., (1991), *Postmodernism*, London: Verso.

Lash, S., (1990), *Sociology of Postmodernism*, London: Routledge.

Lowenthal, D., (1985), *The Past is a Foreign Country*, Cambridge: Cambridge University Press.

Lynch, K., (1960), *The Image Of The City*, Cambridge: MIT Press.

McCrone, D., Morris, A., Kiely, R., (1995), *Scotland—the Brand*, Edinburgh: Edinburgh University Press.

Macdonald, S., (1996), 'Theorizing museums: an introduction', in S. Macdonald and G. Fyfe (eds), *Theorizing Museums*, Oxford: Blackwell/The Sociological Review.

Metropolitan Wigan Leisure Department, (n.d.), *Wigan Pier*, Wigan: Metropolitan Wigan Leisure Department.

Museum of Science & Industry in Manchester, (n.d.), *The Museum of Science & Industry in Manchester*, Manchester: The Museum of Science & Industry.

Ross, M., (1994), *Interpreting the New Museology: A Case Study of Museum Workers*, Working Papers No. 8. Keele University: Department of Sociology and Social Anthropology.

Samuel, R., (1994), *Theatres of Memory*, London: Verso.

Savage, M., Barlow, J., Dickens, P. and Fielding, T., (1992) *Property, Bureaucracy and Culture: Middle Class Formation in Contemporary Britain*, London: Routledge.

Urry, J., (1988), 'Cultural change and contemporary holiday-making', *Theory, Culture & Society*, Vol. 5: 35–55.

Urry, J., (1990), *The Tourist Gaze*, London: Sage.

Urry, J., (1996), 'How societies remember the past,' in S. Macdonald and G. Fyfe (eds), *Theorizing Museums*, Oxford: Blackwell/The Sociological Review.

Uzzell, D., (1989), 'The Hot Interpretation of War and Conflict,' in D. Uzzell (ed.), *Heritage Interpretation Vol. 1*, London: Belhaven Press.

Vergo, P., (1989), *The New Museology*, London: Reaktion Books.

Wigan Tourism Association, (n.d.), *Wigan: discover the Unexpected*, Wigan: Wigan Tourism Association.

Warde, A., (1994), 'Consumption, Identity-Formation And Uncertainty', in *Sociology*, Vol. 28, 4: 877–898.

Wright, P., (1985), *On Living in an Old Country*, London: Verso.

Wright, P., (1989), 'Sneering at the theme parks', *Block*, 15: 38–55.

The consumption view of self: extension, exchange and identity

Rolland Munro

Abstract

This paper explores self as a site of consumption. Arguing that most views of self are caught in a production metaphor, the paper goes on to suggest that the limitations to Mary Douglas's theory of consumption lies in its lack of theorizing in terms of consumption of self. The paper then examines the notions of extension and exchange as they have been elaborated by Marilyn Strathern. Pointing out that there can be no 'return' from extension to a core self, merely exchange to another configuration, the paper illustrates how appropriation of artefacts makes possible performance on a scale.

When the 'inner' life of a person which is opposed to the externality of the social life is exalted, when the individual is called upon to return to himself, in order to become emancipated from pressure, briefly, when the 'social I' is characterized as the 'superficial I', as opposed to the 'profound I' . . . a flagrant error of analysis is committed.

Georges Gurvitch *Journal of Philosophy* Vol. 38, 1941: 488.

Introduction

What are we to make of this movement; a going out *from* self *to* the social, and then returning? Is this an age-old myth, one of reversibility? That self, whatever its performances, its extensions and exchanges, always recovers itself *as* self?

And what might this require in terms of contemporary explanation? That the concept of self is underwritten by a metaphor of throw-away architecture? Self, in a production view, imagined as a prosthesis of disposables, pithily captured in the term 'lifestyle shopping'. A logic of addition and subtraction, with a handbag here and a new job there. Or is it more, in what can be called the consumption view, a metaphor for (endless) travelling? The 'individual subject's journey of interpretation' (Strathern, 1992:9) becoming no more than a grazing of cultural spaces, one that consigns the postmodern self to the sociality of a tourist?[1]

Consider the following statement, one that occurs towards the end of a recent article on consumption:

> Following a line of argument that began with the recognition that goods are *building blocks* of life-worlds, we have suggested, as have others, that they can be understood as constituents of selfhood, of social identity. (Friedman, 1990:327, emphasis added)

Friedman's examples given earlier in his article, such as a display of imported cans of coke (not locally made bottles) in the windshield of one's car in Brazzaville, seems to me to catch the current mood of much work on consumption. Goods are not 'used' for their own sake, in reduction to some notion of 'physical' or 'mental' ingestion. Rather, as artefacts, they are seen as part of complex processes of prosthesis; additions or subtractions which go with producing and reproducing 'distinction': class, status, membership and other social realities of an adding culture.

Friedman's statement insinuates that we have a new, and more robust theory of identity; one in which all categories of what passes for art, education, ethics and even history are traceable to what Friedman calls 'global strategies' of persons in their attempts to build a life world. Of course, Friedman seeks to go beyond Bourdieu's (1984) thesis of distinction as 'show', a docile replication of garnered cultural capital. For those in Brazzaville, distinction moves on 'genuine "cargo"', one that 'always comes from outside' as 'a source of wellbeing and fertility and a sign of power' (1990:315). The other-directedness here is intensified best in the figure of the *sapeur*, an 'authentic clothes freak' who scrimps and saves in order to spend everything in the quest for Parisian or Italian design labels. According to Friedman, the *sapeur* is unlike the *flaneur* in that there is no insinuation of a 'real person' lurking below. You are what you wear in Brazzaville, not because clothes make the person but because clothes are the immediate expression of the life-force possessed by a person, and 'life-force is everywhere and is always external'

(1990:316). Not so much, then, a myth of reversibility but rather a metaphor of endless travelling. Through a consumption of goods, identity becomes less a prosthetic extension of a self lurking below and more a continuous transmography of self.

The seduction of this consumption view is the offer of an improved notion of identity. The notion of exchange value is picked up anew and, once revitalized into a consumption view, becomes a circulation metaphor. The circulation metaphor helps strip exchange value from its supposed affinity to use value. Contrary to the accumulation assumptions implicit in economic theories, where an exchange value of goods can be interpreted as a *deferral* of use value, relations between use value and exchange value then come to seem arbitrary and broken. It is not something intrinsic to self, in the form say of preferences, that determines use value. Instead, exchange value represents a potential motility to self; one that we index through the more contemporary term 'identity'.

In the consumption view, identity work involves a relative positioning *vis a vis* goods. It is goods, as will be discussed more fully in a later section, that helps create and construct identity. But who or what is doing this 'positioning'? Who or what is creating, constructing or carrying these 'global strategies'? We do not know. A consumption view of identity does not stretch as far as providing a consumption thesis for self. This then is my difficulty. That in order to accomplish an accurate rendering of identity work, we have had to give up on a satisfactory theory of self.

In line with Cohen's (1994) recent attack on anthropology, talk of identity in the consumption view looks to act as a way of obviating 'self'. Even in Friedman's analysis, references are seldom to persons, but more to 'the Congolese', 'the Ainu'. We are told 'Hawaiians do not feel a need to . . .', 'Hawaiians are acutely aware of . . .', 'Hawaiians do not wish . . .'. Of course, Friedman's analysis is a sophisticated and reflexive account that has moved on past some of the more blank renditions of cultures. In contrasting, for example, how the Congolese 'appropriate otherness' with how the Ainu 'produce selfhood for others', Friedman does evoke a sense of resistance to any mechanical 'globalization' process. But, while local in variation, these remain 'global strategies'. By ignoring the interpretative work that persons may be putting into effacing their difference *as* Congolese, or *as* Ainu, or *as* Hawaiian, Friedman does little to celebrate what Cohen calls the 'triumph' of cultural performance: the *appearance* of common behaviour. I am left with the uncomfortable feeling that, in respect of self, this new notion of identity does little more than swap 'global strategies' for anthropology's earlier reliance on 'stereotypes'.

So what then *is* a consumption view of self? The question, as I see it, exists in two parts. First, what is the nature of self that is implicit in the 'consumption view'? This matter is, of course, partly a descriptive question, one that has us running to the texts, either to argue over interpretations of terms or dispute sources as requisite authorities. But perhaps some leverage might be gained from asking, instead, how this nature of self is different from that implicit in a 'production view'? Who, or what, is 'building' (sic) the life-world in Friedman's analysis? Is Friedman merely attempting to 'supplement' a consumption view of culture with a production notion of the individual? It will be fairly clear from what follows that I duck opportunities for scholarly enquiry here in favour of some more or less bald assertions. Nevertheless, I am suggesting that, to the extent there can be said to be any residual view of self at all left within a consumption view, that 'remainder' is either null, or mainly rehearses a production view.

Second, there is the question of how *should* those taking a consumption view understand the nature of self? I add a normative force by underlining the 'ought', since this part of the question follows directly from the ambitions of the consumption thesis to overthrow over-narrow production concerns. If there is any ground at all to my suspicions that extant theories of consumption harbour production views, then the question arises as to whether, so far, the consumption project has not fallen short in its critique. Until there is a clear view of self, one that is recognizably freed of any production underpinnings, the consumption project stands incomplete. It looks impure; its expulsion of neo-classical economics unfinished.

But wait. Could there be any such thing as a 'consumption view' of self? Here I am less certain. I grant, certainly, some haste in my readiness to move debate on from the question of description, but I am in no hurry to settle normative issues. For the moment I do not see how any *theory* of self could altogether escape a production mode. Indeed, in sympathy with Friedman who gives emphasis to consumption *and* production, I am as unconvinced about a consumption thesis that deletes production as I am sceptical of a production view that belittles consumption. What I do wish to ascertain, however, is that the insights of the consumption thesis over the social are followed through and that those who profess a consumption view, such as Mary Douglas, deliver persons who are, in her own terms, more than 'puppet consumers'.

After a preliminary discussion on traditional theories of self, therefore, I briefly rehearse some aspects of the consumption view, drawing particularly on Douglas and Isherwood (1980). Although I offer some criticisms of what I am calling the consumption view, it should be clear that I do not seek to dismiss or replace this view. Indeed, quite the contrary. My reasons for reiterating the consumption view are because I consider that the insights it offers for a view of self are missing from much current work on consumption. The major part of the paper is then devoted to analysis of Marilyn Strathern's analysis of self as 'extension'. In juxtaposing an analysis of self as 'extension' with that of identity as 'exchange', I hope first to undermine the dogma that seeks to separate, and hierarchize, use value with exchange value and, in so doing, settle some aspects of the vexed relations between self and identity.

Producing selves

Traditional theories of self are inherently production views. Or so it seems. Persons produce and reproduce themselves in terms of either identity, personhood, or persona. The labour of self is assumed to be one of prosthesis, building up extensions from a foundational core.

Of course, such theories of self vary in ways that mystify this common theme. First, theories vary according to differing conceptions of the core. The core may be made up, for example, of 'values', 'beliefs', 'attitudes', 'wants', 'needs', 'preferences', 'motives', 'impulses' or 'desires'. All these, sometimes uniquely, sometimes in combination, are understood to be the elements that help to determine, fix, or shape 'action', 'conduct', or 'behaviour'.

Second, competing ontologies offer different materials to be worked on for all this production. Across different theories, the 'building blocks' for producing selves hypostatize a range of artefacts, from an accumulation and exchange of 'goods' to an accumulation and exchange of 'symbols'. Depending, then, on differing conceptions of the core, and differing conceptions of building materials, what is deemed to be 'consumed' can vary enormously. This is so even where consumption is construed in terms of 'satisfactions'; for example, the influential American economist, Irving Fisher, defined income in terms of 'psychic satisfactions'. Or in cognitive models of self, it is not so much satisfactions, as it is 'information' that is being processed, presumably endlessly. Or in the case of much extant social theory, it is 'meanings' that are being consumed, say, as confirmatory evidence for beliefs; and, in so doing, this consumption goes towards the creation and reproduction of class, ethnicity and gender.

There are, then, important differences in ideas of self, differences which have to be noted and accounted for if we are to return to settle accounts between a production view and a consumption view. Nevertheless, the overall picture is clear: a production view of self is one of persons sometimes expanding *their* empires[2] sometimes retreating in disarray to a core, or minimal self. One can think of an air-bag, expanding with the drawing in of air and then contracting on its expulsion. The metaphor of self is one of inflation and deflation: first out, then in.

This aspect of expansion and contraction is also helpful in reflecting on the dilemma in which the consumption view finds itself. Most notably in the economic based literature of decision-making, individuals are moved 'in' *as if* for analysis and then selves are moved 'out'. Out of the way, that is, of analysis. Freed from the tumescent weight of distended, embodied persons, an 'objective' perspective on the distribution of goods, wealth and labour can continue unimpeded. Once selves are imputed to be the Other of rational choice, they can be treated as inherently 'subjective' and excluded as things to be *subtracted* from analysis.

Of course, selves cannot be disposed of completely. Their deletion takes place more as a sleight of hand. Not all of self can be removed. Something must be doing the decision-making, the choosing, the revealing of preferences, must it not? So why not call this part *agency* and then delete the rest *as* self, as 'individuality'? For here is the sleight of hand. Only those 'parts' recalcitrant to analysis are to be excluded from analysis. Only those parts requiring deletion are to *be named* as 'self'. That common part of the person required for analysis is then universalizable as the core. With one hand we are assumed to all have agency, in the form of 'wants', 'needs', or 'preferences' and so on. With the other hand these are decreed to vary, their content changing in line with our individuality.

The universals alter with fashion, but the effect is the same. It is to divide self. Separating out from persons that which is to be regarded as 'individual', or 'subjective' (in the form of beliefs, interpretations and desires), from that which is taken as 'universal', or 'objective' (such as rationality, or class, ethnicity and gender). In division, everything of the person is excluded, except that which is required for theory-building.

In this way, theory can be made stable. But stability alone is not enough. Simple deletion alone would not make theory immune from falsification. The (subjective) self, that which is left out as 'residual' to analysis, has to be re-turned to as 'supplement'. The (subjective) self, the repressed, can be added back on any occasion in which 'deviations' from analytic predictions require 'explanation'. For example, economics draws on this division of persons in order to theorise conditions that will impede optimal decision making. Persons are seen as irrational, say in resorting to barter and thus restricting the flow of money; or over indulging in private exchanges of information that give rise to market frictions such as 'insider trading'. Thus, in order to explain theory's deviation from everyday experience, the 'subjective' self—that remaindered part of persons—is brought back 'in'; persons re-enter, but in an asymmetrical way that leaves them existing only to account for empirical 'deviations'.[3]

This is not all. Together these moves also produce a moral order. That which is 'right' in the person (agency, rational choice) is held to sustain that which is 'right' in society (markets and, more recently, hierarchies). That which is 'wrong' in the person (individuality, irrationality) accounts for that which is 'wrong' in society (gaps in the market, lack of optimality). At work is a division of labour. As Bloor (1976) and Latour (1993) explicate in different ways, theory not only explains the good, deletions from theory can explain the bad.[4] And this division of labour has its correlate in self, since the discarded part of self is useful to explain 'deviations' from theory's predictions.

Nor need the picture be static. There can be a sense of progress. As theories come and go, so notions of self as 'containing' this, or containing that, come and go. Whereas previously persons may have been conceived of in terms of motives, or drives, or beliefs, now people are 'filled' with attitudes. The genealogy is clear: what remains unscathed across production views of self is a particular conception of knowledge. Knowledge as 'external', as 'objective', as 'universal' remains. Indeed, it is this assumption, the inviolate status of knowledge, that the consumption view has been successful in challenging. Nevertheless, as we will see, a consumption theorizing of 'identity work' is still liable to be supplemented with production views of self.

The consumption view

In setting out an anthropology of consumption, Douglas (1966; 1975) seeks to avoid an effacement of the social by the economic. She accomplishes this, surprisingly, through emphasizing goods. Instead of seeing the world of goods as too mundane and looking for more hermetic forage, such as high art or myth, she treats goods as culture. By arguing, for example, that some goods are taboo because they are 'good to think', Douglas rescues 'culture' from its displacement by economics as a 'given'. The critical difference to economists is over how to look at goods. Thus, where economists would study a world of *goods,* Douglas is interested in a '*world* of goods'. This inversion requires some clarification.

Against its marginal status in the production frame of economics, where culture has no place within analysis, beyond its possible status as another good, Douglas reasserts the centrality of the social in any exchange of people, goods and words. In contrast to Levi-Strauss's division of social life into three communication systems of goods, women and words, Douglas claims to synthesize these:

> The meanings conveyed along the goods channel are part and parcel of the l meanings in the kinship and mythology channels. (Douglas & Isherwood, 1980:88)

In this way the consumption thesis theorises the social as a *sharing* of culture.

Douglas & Isherwood (1980:76) insist that 'any choice between goods is the result of, and contributes to, culture'. According to *The World of Goods,* studying consumption is about seeing the relations between the consumption of goods and the intractable problems of knowledge:

> Goods, in this perspective, are ritual adjuncts; consumption is a ritual process whose primary function is to make sense of the inchoate flux of events. (Douglas & Isherwood, 1980:65)

But Douglas and Isherwood are also returning culture to the matter of goods in a way which is intended to avoid equating consumption merely with processes of socialization. Against much structuralist theory in sociology, with many of its traditional views entailing 'cultural dopes', persons are conceived as being *active* agents in the sharing of goods.[5]

Douglas makes a 'sharing' of culture active by drawing attention to the *expressive* nature of materiality. This expressive nature of materiality is crucial for understanding the consumption view. Consumption 'uses goods to make firm and *visible* a particular set of judgments in the fluid processes of classifying persons and events' (Douglas & Isherwood, 1980:67, emphasis added). In an extension of the ethnomethodological approach, goods make us visible (and hence account-able) to each other as an 'us'.

For me, this is the critical turn in the consumption thesis: the value of goods lies in their use by 'members' to make their judgements on each other visible to each other. Thus the notion of visibility is central to understanding possibilities for sharing. But there is a further point here:

> No one likes to recognize that the capacity to share all three [bed, board and cult] is socially endowed, a result of current decisions, and not an ineluctable fact of nature. (Douglas & Isherwood, 1980:88)

The social is not to be thought of as something which, by being *naturalized,* lies outside analysis. Rather, as will become clear in a moment, its naturalisation *as* culture makes it all the more important that it be brought back inside analysis.

So how is 'culture' active? As I read it, the key phrase in the following quotation is *admission*:

> Studies of the ancient Israelites . . . contemporary Thai villagers . . . and contemporary Lele tribesmen in the Congo show how the world is organized in a recursive system of metaphors dealing with *admission* to bed, board and cult. . . (Douglas & Isherwood, 1980:88, emphasis added)

Persons are active over making things present and making other things absent. Their explicit consumption of people, goods and words, alongside any apparent non-consumption, instantiates their *belonging*.

Identity, in the consumption view, is therefore an effect constructed and created through adherence to systems of exchanges that guarantee inclusion and exclusion. Clearly there are processes of structuration and stabilization implicit in this analysis of the constituting of membership. The question which I now wish to press is whether these possibilities allow for a sharing of culture, without recourse to a cultural determinism similar to Durkheim's. If we are only talking identity, has this analysis excluded a space for self?

Exclusion and self

According to Mary Douglas, writers like Trollope, by tying the exchange of women intricately to the exchange of information (how *could* Mr Wharton let his daughter marry a man Wharton didn't know?), suggest a powerful relationship between the social and the economic: between matters of 'exclusion' and the effect of non-consumption .

In following this thread, it is important to note how *exclusion* is intimately tied to the consumption thesis:

> Sharing goods and being made welcome to the hospitable table
> and to the marriage bed are the first, closest fields of inclusion,
> where exclusion operates spontaneously long before political
> boundaries are at stake. (Douglas & Isherwood, 1980:88)

This suggests a first important thesis implicit in the consumption view: 'sharing goods' always involves exclusion. For example, when Ben and Sharon share their sweeties behind the bicycle shed then I may feel excluded. Or if I don't own a car, then I may be seen as excluding myself from some trips or parties. This principle may also be extended from the exclusion of persons to forms of knowledge. For example, if the 'shared goods' of a research programme are understood to be theories, then a researcher's everyday consumption involves exclusion of other theories. Other people's theories don't really constitute knowledge, do they?

But more is entailed than simple refusal. It is important to see *how* exclusion is intimately tied to the consumption thesis. The 'naturalness' of exclusion has to be asserted:

> . . . whenever exclusion is operated to define a category of
> outsiders, the segregated category tends to be accredited with a
> different nature . . . (Douglas & Isherwood, 1980:88)

This suggests a second important thesis: whatever is left *outside* consumption has to seem 'natural'. And again this dictum has its correlate in research programmes. It becomes natural to exclude some matters from discussion. Like culture, at least to the economist. Or, as I am going on to suggest, like self to the culture theorist. Only some problems count as problems; not all gaps in knowledge count as 'anomalies'. And so on. A researcher's consumption of theories involves assertions of the different *nature* of other research programmes; it installs their concepts *as* the Other.

Together, the 'exclusion' and the 'naturalness' of the Other give rise to an *unspeakability* of the Other. The question of who, or what, gets 'forgotten' can be understood to be intimately related to the current 'state' of knowledge. To explicate relations between these, the unspeakability of the Other, a 'forgetting', and the state of knowledge, Douglas focuses on pollution. Drawing on a number of sources, she examines the relations between what is taken to be 'dirt', that which is somehow 'below consumption', or too mundane to be other than implicit, and the backgrounding of cosmological knowledge, which is also implicit since it is 'too true to warrant discussion'.

> Humble rules of hygiene turn out to be rationally constructed with the way that the Lele cosmos is constructed . . . (Douglas, 1975:4)

Douglas's point, therefore, about what exceeds discussion, or is made absent from it, is fundamental to her consumption view, not trivial. She is not suggesting that there is something merely exotic in the Lele refusing to believe that contagion *cannot* spread by food cooked in a fire tended by a menstruating woman. Her point is that this is a belief which the Lele *must* refuse, since entertaining this possibility would require their whole cosmos to collapse. Other people's theories *are* rubbish.

It is at this 'critical moment' of refusal, a moment of key insight, that Douglas nevertheless appears temporarily to be abandoning the consumption thesis. By establishing persons as *having* beliefs *and* acting on them, she is either constituting persons *as* individuals, in contradiction to her arguments against 'theoretical individualism' (Douglas & Isherwood, 1980:62–4), or she is abandoning her ambition to surpass Durkheim's notion of the collective conscience, and creating society in the form of what Strathern (1992:14) calls an 'authorless text'. To move her analysis forward, she is either falling back on what I take to be a 'production' view of self, or, more likely, she is obviating self as a 'speaking subject'.[6]

Whatever Douglas's position is on this matter, it is clear that others, claiming to follow her, have theorized in ways that are more aligned to a production view of self. For example, McCracken (1986), in an influential and widely referenced paper, defines the culturally constituted world in terms of individuals holding beliefs:

> This is the world of everyday experience in which the phenomenal world presents itself to the individual's sense fully shaped and constituted by the beliefs and assumptions of his/her culture. (McCracken, 1986:72)

McCracken goes on to write that culture is the 'lens' through which the individual views phenomena. Although McCracken, in focusing on the circulation of meanings, provides a distinctively consumption view, goods nonetheless turn out to be no more than intermediaries; 'way-stations of meaning', in the transfer of meanings from the 'culturally constituted world' to the 'individual consumer' (1986:71). So, as with many writers on consumption, a consumption view of the social still spins on a production view of self.

Returning to Douglas, as already stated, consumption 'uses goods to make firm and visible a particular set of judgments in the fluid processes of classifying persons and events'.[7] Yes, but what is left ambivalent in Douglas's analysis is whether exclusion is an intrinsic activity of persons, or is it a part of their conduct that is consequent on their beliefs? Or, more interestingly, is it because 'exclusion' lies at the core of belonging? Is it, for example, only through an extrusion of others that we can both sense our membership and advertise it to those to whom we see ourselves as the same?

Powerful as her analysis of consumption is, I do not think these questions of belonging are resolvable within Douglas's analyses. Indeed, as fast as it clarifies the matter of belonging, I suspect that the consumption view, for all its undoubted insight and merit, empties out a notion of self. For this reason, I now turn to the work of Marilyn Strathern to explicate her novel views on the relations between exchange and extension.

Extending exchange

In her magnificent and provoking book, *Partial Connections* (1991), Marilyn Strathern elaborates a notion of extension. Ostensibly the book is a meditation on the problem of scale, a problem for anthropological researchers engaged in comparative studies. However, as Strathern weaves her way through the writings of anthropologists on exchange and appropriation, the theme of extension comes to dominate her text.

In beginning to understand Strathern's position, it is helpful to contrast extension with prosthesis. The notion of prosthesis, conventionally, is seen as a matter of adding parts. Picking up on this, Strathern makes a turn on the phrase 'adding parts'. For her, extension is not merely a matter, say, of the surgeon adding a wooden leg. Outwardly, yes, the notion of a part depicts the mechanical, the adding of material to material. But there is more than a facile production view at work here. Inwardly, for the subject, the notion of part is dramatic and elicits the opportunity for another form of extension, that of *performance*. The addition of a part (object) extends the possibilities for cultural performance as a 'part' (subject). Object and subject, as effects, move hand in hand.

Explaining that magnitude is a significant dimension to the dances Wantoat people put on at the time of the festivals, Strathern explicates this doubling of 'parts'.

> Performers literally magnify themselves. They wear barkcloth and bamboo extensions . . . carried by being tied on to the body of the dancer . . . In some cases, such figures triple the dancers's height . . . The whole edifice gives the appearance of a tree with a man at its base. (1991:63)

Those watching at the festival move *between* two figures; between a focus that on the one hand keeps body and bamboo apart and a focus on the other hand that sees the trees. There is at one moment a recognition of a mechanical attachment and in another moment a seeing of 'towering trees'.

Strathern's point is that we move *from* figure *to* figure and only this. Back and forth, in watching we can move between the extension as a figure of dancer plus bamboo and a catching of the image of 'towering' trees:

> If one looks at the dancer with the tall effigy one can see him
> as attached to/detached from the waving bamboo above, and in
> that sense created or revealed by it (1991:65).

This moving between figures by a process of attaching and detaching are part of the performance. Crucially, as in a gestalt switch, the seeing of the second figure involves a 'forgetting' of the parts of the first figure.

Although somewhat elusively presented, Strathern's point here is that extension, the adding (or exchanging) of parts, involves an *exchange* of 'identities'. Use values and exchange values therefore move hand in hand. This insight gets to the heart of traditional ideas of choice which assume a knowing subject indifferent to position. As watchers at the festival, or wherever else we are, what we see is neither determined, nor do we simply choose the figures we see. Instead, drawing on the artefacts of dress, bamboo and movement we *exchange* figures, one for another, through a process of attachment/detachment.

Affiliation and exchange, in their very possibility, are thus set up as implicit in any process of prosthesis. And, importantly, other artefacts, such as myth, may enter and prefigure this process. For example, these figures might appear differently if we are Wantoat. Drawing on material by Schmitz (1963), vividly depicting the Wantoat story of huge lengths of bamboo being filled to the brim with the blood of an old man after his being wounded as a bird by a boy, Strathern extends anthropology into its most telling. The myth speaks of how, as the boy and man sit in the hellish heat of an unbearable fire, there is suddenly a deafening report as the bodies of a man and a woman burst from the towering bamboo covered in blood.

In the sway of the dancers beneath their edifices, those watching—typically a sweating initiate who has been made to sit uncomfortably close to a huge fire all night—move between both ends of this tale, sometimes seeing the 'towering' bamboo trees as 'the spirits' and sometimes seeing in the dancers the birth of 'the first people'.

To see and experience *both* 'parts'. Crucially, Strathern registers how a movement of the dancers, in their doubling of 'parts', keeps in view this movement of experience between figures elicited by the myth:

> In coming into existence, the new dimension both realizes the
> pre-existing relationship and in giving it a specific (material,

substantial) form encapsulates the prior relationship in a new one. (1991:103–4)

Familiarity with the myth can be considered as effectively 'talking up' more physical aspects to extension. As Wantoat, our myth becomes 'attached' to what we see in ways that lead us to move, back and forth, between first the relations we enjoy with the 'spirits' through *their* relations to our ancestors, and second the bloodshot figure of our ancestors as the 'first people'.

Strathern here is giving full play to the term *attachment,* first as attachment, movement to and from something, and second as attachment, feelings of belonging to something. By keeping both meanings of attachment alongside each other, Strathern prevents the latter experience being made disjunct as (merely) subjective, or rejected as an emotion. Her image of attachment *as* detachment, and vice versa, tells us what is important about the relations between self and identity. Extension is always a 'doubling' of parts; a prosthesis of attachment/detachment that adds motility to performance.

Exchange and extension

So far we might be tempted to think of Strathern's analysis as a meditation on the production of a self. Indeed, the word 'extension' conjures up the very metaphor of a self that expands: first 'out', then 'in'. I now want to argue just how wrong this interpretation may be.

As I read *Partial Connections,* a key insight of Strathern's over culture arises out of the question of who or what travels. For example, in understanding community, she points to how in Elmdon, people travel, places remain in place.

Villagers define being a real Elmdoner according to who has travelled between places or who has stayed in one place. In this English view, persons acquire identity from the places they are at, modified by where they have come from and where they are going. Places stay, persons move, and a further cultural slip is made from geographical to class location. Classes are fixed, individuals mobile. (1991:117)

As Strathern captures it, moving between locations can seem an 'act of disorientation'. The fate of the upwardly mobile is pithily captured in the oft-repeated phrase 'a rolling stone gathers no moss'.

To travel, without repeatedly *coming back*, is to lose the relations between identity and belonging. One becomes estranged, a 'stranger', an 'outsider', an 'object' of distance. There is, then, something remarkably apt in the 19th century gunslinger's advertisement: Have gun, will travel. The person who offers themself for hire *as* a gun, who is ready to move 'to' the market, signals his lack of 'belonging'; his identity becomes sufficiently anonymous to be no more than a 'gun' for hire. This metonymy points to a further gap between notions of identity and self, perhaps just as the manual workers who travelled to the factory became known as 'hands'.

Strathern suggests that Melanesian examples show that none of this need be so. Places can travel:

If a person's identity is located in a shell valuable or encased in a bag or at the growing tips of a tree, it is these—the valuables, the bags, the trees—that travel out of sight, are put on and taken off, are turned upside down. A pearl is a place we might say, that walks between them. The centers of others become centers for oneself. Insofar as 'places' can appear now in one person and now in another, then it is the places that seem mobile. At least, Melanesians use locational devices to make this fact appear: travel out becomes travel back, inside becomes outside, top becomes bottom. (1991:117).

So how are we to understand these differences as affecting the vexing question of self?

A first reading of the sway of the dancers might dangerously prefigure it by imposing an idea of a prototypical 'identity'. The danger is of assuming a core self, one from which the 'real' person moves 'in' and 'out', to and from a range of 'identities' by appropriating artefacts which help 'create or reveal' these identities as extensions of this core self. But this is to fall back on prosthesis, the production view. It is to insist on a particular, and possibly parochial, view of extension. It is an image of persons taking on artefacts or 'roles' which either enlarge or diminish identity; and then retreating, hermit like to a 'true' self.

There is, however, a different reading of extension; one that I am suggesting is more in line with Strathern. First, in the process of extension, one is never travelling out from a place (the core self) and then returning. Rather, as indicated in the earlier section, the only movement is one of circulation: around and around from figure to figure - one figure picking up on what the other excludes. In the Melanesian imagery, as already noted, all movement is on this periphery of moving among 'figures'. As Strathern adds of the dancers at the festival: 'All are designed to sway and move'.

Second, it is arguable whether or not Strathern sees mutations of self as necessarily involved in this process of 'contraction and expansion'. Appropriation involves a surrender of possibilities for self, yes, but so might diminishment of identity involve appropriation. Here Strathern looks particularly at 'the pulsating moment' of Umeda festivals, where 'communities expand and scatter':

> . . . people become momentarily conscious both of their own centrality and of the necessity to maintain relations with other centres on the periphery—a contraction and expansion of focus. (1991:85).

Magnification is one direction, the most obvious. But we can also 'shrink'. Non-identity is also an accomplishment. One moment the 'big man'; the next moment 'anonymity'. Both involve prosthesis, yes, but both also accomplish extension through artefacts.

My interpretation of Strathern's position is that we are always in extension. *Indeed, extension is all that we are ever 'in'*. There is no 'core' self to which we retreat and come out again. Appropriation of artefacts makes possible 'performance' on a scale. This may be big or small, far or near; but we mistake the nature of the movement if we relate this diminishment, or 'anonymity' back to a *loss* of self. To suffer a 'loss of self' in moments of despair, or accomplish it as a form of meditation, is still to remain in extension.

Knowledge and extension

In her abandonment of notions of a 'core', Strathern's theorising of self seems to me to approximate the circulation metaphor inherent in a 'consumption view' of the social. Of course this does not dissolve all the difficulties. Difficulties in imagining 'self' follow from thinking of persons in terms of a prototype, as coming out *from* 'the' self and *into* 'society'. Yet a consumption view of the social could not have *as its origin* a consumption view of self.

The two views, that of society and that of self, are not additive. While Strathern (1992) speculates that, for 'twentieth century moderns', society has a metaphysics of presence similar to that of the person as individual subject, understandings of self and understandings of society have different genealogies. The importance of Strathern's (1991) reworking of extension stems therefore from providing a picture of experience that is very different from Western images of knowledge; where actual use is presumed to be a declension of universal truth. Weber, for example, has suggested that key terms are ideal typical and, in this respect, actual use of words must always stand in 'diminishment'. In that actual use always varys from the prototype, the actual use of a term is always a *deviation* from the ideal.

Strathern links this problem of prototypes with the attempt to distinguish key terms:

> If the prototype for an exchange partner is an affine, then why do we not classify all exchange partners as 'affines'—some being affines with women trafficked between them, and some being affines with masks or shells being trafficked between them? (1991:103).

Beginning with prototypes leads ultimately and inevitably towards the appearance of contradictions, an 'antagonism of parts' (1991:103).[8] Are persons self, or society? The question presupposes a division of mutual exclusion. It insists on persons being one thing or the other; otherwise the division would seem to collapse. But in the everyday, where categories never can be taken to be mutually exclusive, then divisions appear always to be falling in on themselves.

In addition, there will always be an 'empirical' problem in applying the ideal typical. As Strathern (1991) captures the difficulty for the ethnographer:

> By what prior knowledge do we in fact decide we are looking at the actions of affines on this occasion, of exchange partners on that? (1991:103)

Even if we were to agree on a principal or prime division, a founding 'pairing', how are we to agree on its application?

So in setting aside a time-honoured reliance on ideal-types as foundational, how might a theory of self begin to be mooted?

Perhaps the answer here is to begin with this undecidability, rather than end up with it. By seeing, for example, how *performances* can vary in respect of the making of distinctions. And working this undecidability right through the semiotic material of self—so that there are no foundations that are foundational. By recognizing that self, whatever else it does, has also to pick up on minute variations in what is being *made* foundational; say, in what is being made near and what is being made far. By self picking up and seeing what terms are being *made* near, as possible substitutes, and by studying what terms are being made incompatible, by being placed *as* opposites.

A theory of self as extension gets off the ground once we accept that all extension is exchange and that all exchange is partial and always provisional in its settlement. For example, in respect of the Hagen relations between affines and exchange partners, Strathern suggests:

> . . . the difference between affines and exchange partners is like the difference between a boy and a man or between a woman with a full and with an empty string bag down her back. (1991:103)

This image draws our attention back to a previous remark, where, in respect of the figures made up by the dancers, she notes: 'The man's figure embeds what the women's appear to have cut out.' (1991:64). Each is augmented by the other, not diminished.

She goes on to elaborate her image of what is happening to the woman who carries an empty bag, when once it was full:

> Yet the imagery of the bag misleads if it suggests that there is some prototype beyond which all is elaboration: on the contrary, the empty bag is as 'full' of significance as the one heavy with produce. Relationships always appear in the signifying dimension of enlargement, for that is how they are made to appear, taking specific form and presence from the enactment of people's intentions and obligations. (1991:103–4)

Movement among figures, for Strathern, is not, as Plato had it, a will to recover the magnificence of a prototype from its diminishment as a shadow on the wall. An endless process of 'repair' between an ideal and practice. Between the core self and its diminishment in a 'role'; a vain process of 'recovery', where the appearance is created of particulars that travel (badly) and a universal that always remains 'in place' as the same.

Since we are always 'in' extension (and remembering that is all we are 'in'), any movement, and hence magnification, remains within the limits of what can be attached and what is detached. In this respect, it is important to see that artefacts, however they are made or produced, are not necessarily 'goods'; artefacts may never be so anonymous. To insist on treating artefacts *as* goods is to exactly miss the point in Strathern's theme of extension:

> Appropriated or not by men depending on one's perspective, Telefol string bags are hardly anonymous products with a value only for exchange purposes: they do not exist apart from the relationships out of which they are made and for I which they either bear women s produce or men s personal paraphernalia. In fact their manufacture is elicited by known others. (1991:102)

Strathern takes this 'elicitation' itself as 'an act of elaboration or exaggeration'. As she goes on to say, 'the acts of specific persons are elicited in the social acts of others.'

We are still 'in' extension; and also a 'doubling' of parts. The manufacture of the bag is elicited in the same way as 'specific forms appear through the juxtapositioning of figures in a masquerade'.

> The form an act takes . . . acquires a specific substance and materiality in its being made present. . . The man who begs a bag from his sister finds that he also carries on his back a permanent memorial of her features. (1991:102)

As Strathern goes on to add, it can hardly be surprising that a widespread interest in the elaboration of relationships accompanies individuals' enhancing and enlarging their own spheres of influence under favourable demographic or economic circumstances.

Reworking self

In this chapter I have argued that a consumption view of the social is complicit with importing, on occasions of convenience, a production view of self. That, too easily, the circulatory spin of consumption is mooted on a false economy that shifts between a conflation of 'identity' with 'self' one moment, and a register of their difference in the next. At first blush, as Strathern (1992:9) phrases it, it might look like the individual subject and society at large each provide a perspective on the other. But, as she adds, 'there is no mutuality or reciprocity in their regard'.

In working through this lack of reciprocity, I have drawn attention to differences between three concepts; self, identity and belonging. One way for theorists to proceed is to flatten these distinctions altogether. Or at least one of these distinctions, as I have suggested is the case with Mary Douglas. Her emphasis on a production and reproduction of systems of exchange, discussed earlier, privileges identity and belonging and stops short of an analysis of self. Although her emphasis on inclusion and exclusion makes active the categories of class, ethnicity and gender, the categories remain 'external'. Her analysis of identity *relies* on persons trading 'internally', but she fails to go on and *include* the effects of this exchange in her considerations of bed, board and cult.

In contrast, I have suggested how Strathern offers a more thorough-going picture of exchange; a picture in which exchange not only goes all the way down but, crucially, has to be fabricated at every point. Tentatively on this picture, identity and self can be understood as different ways of looking at belonging. Identity is always from the eyes of the other: a matter of difference, where the addition or deletion of a few artefacts may be sufficient to mark that difference. One can think here of an impressionist painting, or a sketch, where the lines are drawn this way, rather than that. Selves are never so flimsy, since an ability to make an attachment or detachment depends on a sedimentation of past additions and deletions, the material of previous affiliations and former exclusions. Self here can be thought of as being as large, complex and cumbersome as a shaggy dog story, where the attention to detail always overcomes any ambition to become a 19th century novel.

In considering Strathern's writings it is important to remember that my comments are drawn as a partial view of a complex set of texts. It is not clear that Strathern has set out to theorize self—at least theorize it away from specific cultures at specific times. The liberties I have taken in appropriating her writings have their justification solely in counterpoint. In particular, I have set out to challenge a prosthetic architecture of identity that, in its metaphors of 'building blocks', insinuates a 'lego self'. The result is necessarily patchwork. Elsewhere, Strathern captures the difficulty of totalizing views:

> Indeed, when interpretation is imagined as taking a view, then incompleteness is made manifest by the interpretative exercise itself. (Strathern, 1992:6)

Speaking 'as an anthropologist', Strathern (1992:6) wants to add 'the possibility that perspective—including the techniques by which persons take a view—will make a difference'.

So this is the theme I wish to end on—difference. It seems to me that one of the real contributions of late twentieth century thinking about society has been to explode the myth of reversibility. We cannot become 'social selves' without a displacement of self, whatever that is.[9] So an irreversibility of relations collapses images of selves as contracting and expanding. If we go out, so to speak, we cannot necessarily go back 'in'. But far from this making an understanding of self irrelevant, I suggest that matters of difference intensify the importance of understanding selves. This matter invites a final comment.

In magnifying 'identity', there are no doubt stabilities of simulation. Class, ethnicity, gender. All these refer to stabilities in effect. Just in the same way that Latour (1987) argues about how we put a man on the moon, or Law (1986) argues over the Portuguese sailors, our cultural performance can become more exact, more constant in appearance. In moments of diminishment, however, moments where we set up an appearance of 'retreat', we may never, so to speak, step in the same self twice. We remain in extension, in a 'supplementation' as identity. So, far from acting as an excuse to obviate the need for understandings of self, we can draw on Strathern's (1992:8) understanding of the 'double meaning of supplementation': that self is as much in 'surplus' as it is always in 'displacement'.

Conclusion

Postmodern writing, much of it in the guise of theorizing consumption, has begun to form its own 'nega-narratives', hollowing out positions that rail against those who, for example, hold onto unique or centred notions of self. Asleep in a hammock of their own incredulity, these 'nega-narratives' delete debate over self. For the moment, the membership stakes over postmodernism seems to make its writers oblivious to recent arguments, like those of Cohen (1994). Of course Cohen, in re-mobilizing a notion like that of 'self consciousness', still animates self at its autonomous and anonymous core. But he is still able to point to the vacuity of current assumptions about self, in a way that traces these to the modernist heritage of what passes for knowledge in anthropology and sociology.

Is there no alternative, then, but that of either centring or de-centring the subject? Perhaps. But we seem to be too quickly caught here into taking sides. On the one side, the end of culture, bringing in an 'anything goes' notion of identity that would so disperse self, as if to delete it altogether. (And does not this relativism of possibility perversely smuggle in a latter day voluntarism—you can be 'number one' in whatever you want to be?) And on the other side, essentialist versions of the human, notions of a core self that continue to delete materiality from agency? (Perhaps this leads to the 'interactionist' school who seem to want to only study movement when there are 'meanings' to animate it *as* the social?)

These are old riddles. But what if ridding thought of a 'logic of presence' does not quite entail embracing the roller coaster of identity? At least the concept of identity in its current form as an *abandonment* of self. In dispensing with humanist versions of self, perhaps we need not go as far as privileging material over meaning, or vice versa. Indeed, as we have seen, we can rethink a *movement* of meaning in terms of extension. We live in a 'surplus' of materiality, as well as a 'displacement' of meanings.

In contrast to the sterility of earlier debate, this chapter has attempted to draw out a more potent version of what it means for self to be 'de-centred'. At the expense of some gross reduction of Marilyn Strathern's recent work, it offers a new theorizing of self. Three matters stand out. First, as persons we are always in extension. Extension is all we are ever 'in'. There is no core self to which we retreat, and no core self from which we emerge. But there is still self, even if this amalgam varies from moment to moment and from place to place.

Second, there are only *partial* connections. Any 'attachment' is also a process of 'detachment'; and any 'detachment' is also a process of 'attachment'. So movement is never a travelling to and from a core self, but always movement *around* the 'surplus' of a rim: we move endlessly from 'figure' to 'figure', not so much inchoate as undecided and undecidable.

Third, is the matter of scale. A process of 'diminishment' is likely to be as complex as a process of 'magnification'. To 'cut' a figure of 'member' is a cultural performance as much contrived as is the figure of the 'big man' (see also Wagner, 1991). In a process of attachment/detachment, one includes what the other 'cuts out'. It is here, with this rather different image of reciprocity, that I suspect we can find some harmony in Douglas's insights on belonging and Strathern's meditation on self.

Acknowledgements

I am grateful to Robert Cooper, Kevin Hetherington, Joanna Latimer, Celia Lury, Martin Parker and Marilyn Strathern for their comments on an earlier draft of this chapter.

Notes

1 Reference to the postmodern need not entail a disruption with the modern. For example, experience in modernity is already fragmented:

> In Modernity individuals necessarily move between a great number of circles each of which only involves part of his [her] personality. This segmentation of allegiances and associations provides the individual with a greater sense of his uniqueness and freedom, a self-consciousness which favours individualism. (Featherstone, 1991, pp. 3–4)

This said, use of the term postmodern often suggests a shift in attitude away from involvement and lifelong commitment to work or play. Hence my borrowing of the term 'grazing' from the tendency of many people to switch television channels every few minutes.

2 Clearly I am talking about perceptions of empire here. As other notions imply, such as ideologies and truth regimes, a producing of selves is open to a process of colonization. However, as will become evident later in the analysis there are other reasons for questioning naive notions of producing selves.

3 Treating the everyday as a sum of deviations has a self-sealing effect on securing the logic of rationality. The daily experience of countless deviations 'proves' the irrationality of 'individual' persons.

4 Good here is relative. In what Foucault (1970) calls the 'counter-sciences', what is 'good to think' will be what others think of as bad: neurosis and disorders.

5 The argument here is asymmetrical. We perhaps also have to consider that goods 'share' persons. I am grateful to Robert Cooper for pointing this out.

6 I tend to see Douglas as failing to get past Durkheim over the problem of

'cultural dopes'. In the more humanist literature, selves usually are moved to the fore explicitly as 'individuals'; that is, persons are individuated While this may seem to avoid treating persons as residual to analysis, individuals tend to become theorized as having 'motives', having 'intentions', having 'desires', having 'beliefs', having 'values'. These entities are perceived as the motors to action. While Douglas's work is profoundly structuralist, I can't quite rid myself of the suspicion that, on occasion, Douglas resorts to thinking of meanings in this way: as 'things' our selves are built out of and which then govern individual conduct.

7 Compare Gudeman (1986) who sees Dobuans as having a circular sense of time. The past—in which everything was related to everything else—has to be brought back again:

> Far from providing a foundation or base for the social order, 'the economy' . . . is an enactment which refers to other social acts (quoted in Strathern, 1995, p. 16)

Strathern (1995, p. 16) suggests that this 'exemplary recurrance', is 'a replaying what already exists to make it appear again'.

8 Strathern finds, for example within the Hagen, no necessary antagonism of 'parts' in relations of exchange and affiliation:

> An affine is one of the forms in which an exchange partner in Hagen may appear, as an exchange partner is one of the forms in which an affine can appear. Neither is isomorphic with the other, neither a subtype. Rather each is a version of the other. But the one relationship seen from the perspective of the other, as we might imagine affines embarking on a moka sequence as exchange partners, is an elaboration or augmentation on the relationship. (1991:103)

Being an affine can augment exchange and being in exchange can extend affiliations. Relationships, as she adds, quoting Gillison (in press), 'are made up of the constant recapitulation of prior ones'.

9 Following Mead, 'moderns' think that becoming a self from the social, involves loss of that social.

References

Bloor, D., (1976) *Knowledge and Social Imagery*, Chicago: University of Chicgo Press.

Bourdieu, P., (1984) *Distinction: a social critique of the judgement of taste*, trans. R. Nice, Routledge: London.

Cohen, A.P., (1994) *Self-Consciousness: an alternative anthropology of identity*. London: Routledge.

Douglas, M., (1966) *Purity and Danger: an analysis of the concepts of pollution and taboo*, London: Routledge.

Douglas, M., (1975) *Implicit Meanings: essays in anthropology*, London: Routledge & Kegan Paul.

Douglas, M. & Isherwood, B., (1980) *The World of Goods: towards an anthropology of consumption*, Harmondsworth: Penguin.

Featherstone, M., (1991) *Consumer Culture and Postmodernism*, London: Sage.

Foucault, M., (1970) *The Order of Things: An Archaeology of the Human Sciences*, London: Tavistock.

Friedman, J., (1990) 'Being in the World: globalization and localization,' *Theory, Culture & Society* Vol. 8, No. 4, pp. 311–328.

Gudeman, S., (1986) *Economics as Culture: Models and Metaphors*, London: Routledge & Kegan Paul.

Latour, B., (1987) *Science in Action: how to follow scientists and engineers through society*. Milton Keynes: Open University Press.

Latour, B., (1993) *We Have Never Been Modern*, trans. C. Porter. London: Harvester Wheatsheaf.

Law, J., (1986) On the methods of long-distance control: vessels, navigation and the Portuguese route to India. In J. Law (ed.) *Power Action and Belief: a new sociology of knowledge?* Sociology Review Monograph 32 (pp. 234–263). London: Routledge.

McCracken, G., (1986) 'Culture and Consumption: a theoretical account of the structure and movement of the cultural meaning of consumer goods,' *Journal of Consumer Research*, Vol. 13, June, pp. 71–84.

Schmitz, C.A., (1963) *Wantoat: art and religion of the northeast New Guinea Papuans*, The Hague: Mouton & Co.

Strathern, M. (1991) *Partial Connections*, Maryland: Rowman & Little.

Strathern, M., (1992) *After nature: English kinship in the late twentieth century*, Cambridge: Cambridge University Press.

Strathern, M., (1995) *The Relation: issues in complexity and scale*, Cambridge: Prickly Pear Press.

Wagner, R., (1991) The Fractal Person. In M. Godelier & M. Strathern (eds) *Big Men and Great Men: the development of a comparison in Melanesia*, Cambridge: Cambridge University Press.

Social class, consumption and the influence of Bourdieu: some critical issues

Brian Longhurst and Mike Savage

Abstract

Bourdieu's work has been an important point of departure for recent analyses of the relationship between social class and consumption practices. This chapter takes stock of Bourdieu's influence and explores some problems which have become apparent—often in spite of Bourdieu's own hopes and general views. We point to the way that Bourdieu's influence has led to an approach to consumption which focuses on the consumption practices of specific occupational classes and on examining variations in consumption practice between such occupational groups. We argue that it this approach has a series of problems and suggest the need to broaden analyses of consumption to consider issues of 'everyday life', sociation, and social networks.

In the past decade the writings of Pierre Bourdieu have played a key role in the development of sociological research on consumption. His most important work, *Distinction,* which argues that the core mechanism governing the process of consumption is one based around struggles over 'distinction', has become one of the central theses governing recent debate. Critical to the importance of Bourdieu's writing is the fact that his analysis allows him to relate consumption processes to the traditional emphases of mainstream Marxist and Weberian sociologists—class, status, social closure—whilst at the same time reframing these theoretical ideas in ways sensitive to the complexity of cultural media and the specificity of different cultural fields. For this reason Bourdieu's work has become the main point of contact between orthodox stratification sociology and newer, more avant garde currents to the subject, notably those associated with researchers in cultural and media studies. This presence of Bourdieu can indeed be felt in many of the papers in this book,[1] and this general observation raises a crucial question which we will take up explicitly in this chapter. The question we pursue in this chapter is the extent to which Bourdieu's work continues to offer a coherent and adequate research agenda to the study of consumption as the subject itself 'matures' and develops. This chapter is a 'stock-taking' exercise aimed both at clarifying the sorts of arguments which can be derived from Bourdieu's work, and also in evaluating some of his broader arguments in the light of recent research.

This question is not amenable to any straightforward treatment. Bourdieu's work is extremely wide ranging, and it is difficult to detach Bourdieu's specific arguments surrounding consumption from some of his more general claims about social theory. Therefore, although we have no direct interest here in considering more general features of Bourdieu's theoretical framework, for instance his ideas concerning 'habitus' as a bridging device between structure and agency, his claims about practice, and his advocacy of a 'relational' sociology (see Bourdieu 1977, 1990b), there are times when inevitably these general issues do indeed intrude.[2] We should add that our discussion is based primarily, though not entirely, on debates surrounding perhaps his most famous book, *Distinction* (1984), and its English language popularization in the past decade. Even this more modest approach raises difficult issues since this book has been interpreted in different ways.

We therefore begin by briefly describing the appropriation of Bourdieu in British and American research on consumption during the 1980s, noting how his work has been taken up in rather different, and partial, ways by American and British writers, and exploring how Bourdieu's ideas were important in developing early research agendas in the sociology of consumption. We show how Bourdieu's ideas proved to be congruent with an 'occupationally driven' view of class and consumption. We argue in the second section that this leads to a series of problems in Bourdieu's work. We show that Bourdieu's focus on the new middle classes tends to reproduce a rather conventional, and increasingly outdated way of reflecting on social change. We claim that—despite his own intentions—his approach tends to lead to a stress on the uncovering of 'variation' in consumption practices rather than the parallel need to explore how commonality and solidarities are forged between people. In our view a more dynamic and complex notion of the habitus is necessary to recognize the tensions at stake and in the third section we tentatively sketch out some ideas which might contribute to a formulation of the habitus which is more sensitive to agency. Drawing upon recent research in media studies exploring the issue of 'everyday life' we argue for an approach to consumption focusing on sociation, social networks and context.

1: Bourdieu's consumption paradigm

The reception of Bourdieu's work in English speaking sociology has taken place in two main waves. In the 1960s and 1970s Bourdieu's concept of 'cultural capital' was introduced primarily into educational sociology, as an analysis of one of the main mechanisms whereby class advantages were reproduced in the educational system (see Bourdieu 1977; Bourdieu and Passeron 1977). Bourdieu's work rapidly came to be highly influential within educational sociology, his concept of cultural capital being especially important as suggesting the inter-play between 'home-based' and 'school based' mechanisms for the reproduction of class inequality in educational attainment. However at this time his work was little referred to in wider sociological discussion about inequality or cultural practices.[3]

This was to change rapidly in the early and mid 1980s, especially with the translation of *Distinction* in 1984 (the French edition having been published in 1979), and with the subsequent translation of a number of Bourdieu's earlier works on photography (Bourdieu 1990a) and art (Bourdieu and Darbel 1991). *Distinction* offered a series of 'middle range' concepts, notably that of differing forms of capital (symbolic, cultural, economic, social) as ways of exploring how diverse forms of consumer practice could be seen as attempts to claim distinction. Perhaps the most impressive aspect of this book was Bourdieu's ability to range over such a variety of different forms of consumption—dress, eating, furnishing one's house, speaking, appreciating art and representations in general—whilst exploring how they could be seen as tied up with basic struggles and conflicts.

Distinction was also instantly controversial and ambiguous. This is clear enough from the secondary commentaries by Jenkins (1992) who sees Bourdieu as trying to provide an 'objective' account of social divisions as they affect consumption, and Robbins (1991) who emphasizes that Bourdieu tries to avoid such an account. For our purposes, it is interesting to note that reception of Bourdieu's work tended to lead into two, rather different directions, which themselves link to one of the emergent tensions in the analysis of consumption itself. At one broad level the sociology of consumption is concerned with the study of consumption practices and cultures in any social setting, from the sorts of small-scale societies which Bourdieu had studied in the 1950s to the 'hyper-modern' societies of late twentieth century West. Here his work can be seen as concerned with 'the global social logic of distinction that controls consumption' (Laermans 1993:79). However, the sociology of consumption has also developed a series of rather more specific arguments and interests, as a particular commentary on the development of 'consumer culture' in contemporary capitalism, a set of arguments originating in Frankfurt School analyses of mass culture but which were given new prominence during the major economic and social transformations of the 1980s. Here stronger claims are frequently made about the social and cultural significance of consumption (compared to, say, work and employment). In this latter, narrower guise, the sociology of consumption was seen as a central component of emergent debates about ideas of 'post-modern' cultures, the flattening of cultural hierarchies, the development of new cultural media and so forth. It is clear that Bourdieu's work offers insights on both these broad and narrow ways of thinking about consumption (cf Warde 1990), but it is significant that two rather different emphases tend to have been developed in the American and British debates.

In American research, Bourdieu has largely been seen in the broader of these two senses, as a theorist of cultural *reproduction,* of how forms of social and cultural distinction tend to be preserved over long periods of history. Consequently, Bourdieu's work tends to have been adopted primarily by historical sociologists in the United States (eg Beisel, 1993; Emirbayer and Goodwin, 1994; Laermans, 1993, Calhoun ed., 1993; Biernacki, 1995) as a means of investigating the long term processes by which forms of cultural distinction are constructed and reproduced. Here the locus is on the relationship of exclusion between the 'high cultures' of the privileged cultural groups and the 'low cultures' of the working and plebeian classes. In *Distinction* Bourdieu relates these divisions to the development of a distinct 'Kantian aesthetic' in the early nineteenth century (which in an unusually precise statement elsewhere he argues was consolidated in the 1880s—Bourdieu 1993:22). Elsewhere, however, he seems happy to see these distinctions as part of a longer term, almost transhistorical tension between military and economic power on the one hand, and cultural and religious power on the other (eg Bourdieu 1993:24). The emphasis in American research tends to be on this emphasis on the 'long durée' in Bourdieu's writing. However, Calhoun (1993) critically argues that Bourdieu is actually rather weak in recognizing historical variability and temporal change, noting that relations of power' 'are remarkably stable' (Calhoun, 1993:83). Similarly, Wacquant, a collaborator of Bourdieu who is based at Harvard University, also notes how Bourdieu focuses on 'the extraordinary resilience of structures of power in France' (Wacquant 1993:11). In so far as attention is drawn within this perspective to innovation in consumption practice, the usual focus is on how apparent change is consistent with long term reproduction, as for instance with Binder's (1993) account of how new forms of rap music can be appropriated to traditional forms of 'cultural authenticity'.[4] As Calhoun (1993) notes, this type of analysis can lead to serious problems in registering the significance of agency and historical specificity.

It is therefore interesting to note that in Britain, by contrast, the focus has been more on using Bourdieu's work in debates about contemporary cultural change, and in particular on debates surrounding the emergence of 'consumerism'. Here the key influence has been the popularization of his work in the journal *Theory, Culture and Society*, and in particular Featherstone's use of Bourdieu. During the early 1980s Featherstone and his collaborators emphasised the growing importance of what they termed 'consumer culture' (eg Featherstone 1982, TCS 1983). Their work drew upon elements of Frankfurt School Marxism, as well as the early work of Baudrillard in order to theorize this phenomenon. Following the translation of *Distinction* in 1984, and subsequent secondary commentary on it (eg Honneth, 1986) Featherstone (1987) heavily reworked his account of consumerism. He used Bourdieu's ideas to develop three distinct themes which were not fully worked out in earlier views concerning consumer culture; that people were not passive consumers (in the way suggested by mass society theorists) but were actively engaged in consumer practices; that such forms of activism could be seen as related to class strategies and habituses (and hence that they were not part of an undifferentiated 'mass'); and that the term 'lifestyle' could be used to understand the dynamics of consumer cultures (as individuals exercised agency to mould their consumer practices into distinctive patterns). These broad currents were subsequently taken up by Lash and Urry (1987), and Lash (1990). These writers were of crucial importance in drawing on Bourdieu's work to find ways of relating different types of consumerist culture to social divisions, and subsequent theorizing of social class and stratification in English speaking circles has become more interested in considering what merit Bourdieu's analysis of various forms of capital has to offer (see Savage *et al.*, 1992; Crompton 1993).

Featherstone's and Lash and Urry's appropriation of Bourdieu's work is very different from that in the American tradition. Although they would accept in general some of the broad claims about cultural reproduction which Bourdieu makes, they have been primarily concerned with the more specific analysis of 'consumerism', using his general framework to reflect specifically on the emergence of new types of consumer culture which might entail the breaking down of traditional cultural hierarchies, and in particular considering the significance of different types of 'new middle classes'. The main thread here was the role of 'new cultural intermediaries' as the bearers of a distinct new form of consumer culture. These new groups, located in new sorts of service jobs, are held to be distinctive in rejecting established forms of high cultural practice and subjecting new forms of consumer practice to forms of cultural distinction. Rather than cultural distinction being based around the classic terrain of high culture (notably through the appreciation of classical music, 'great art' etc), it might be based around the right sorts of exotic holiday destination, new vegetarian cuisine, or hiking gear. New forms of consumerism were thereby related to the strategies of upwardly mobile occupational groups. Admittedly the precise social groups held to be in the vanguard of these changes varied, and were indeed frequently unclear. In Lash and Urry's (1987) formulation they appear to be the entire 'service class' of professionals and administrators'. In Lash's (1990) formulation it is the post-industrial middle classes, involved in the manipulation of images, who are made central.[5] At other times non-class processes are also invoked. Nonetheless, Lash's summary indicates the broad direction of this body of research:

> the emergence of new class fractions within the professional managerial classes, as well as the increased internal stratification of the working classes, not to mention the heightened

importance of age and gender stratification within and without all classes will be integral to the shift towards specialized consumption' (Lash 1993:206).

In both American and British research, Bourdieu's work could be drawn upon to develop an occupationally driven view of the relationship between class and consumption, with consumption practices being seen as ways by which occupational groups reproduced and challenged class power. Just as parts of *Distinction* appeared to sanction claims about the relationship between specific occupations and forms of consumer practice, so the same period witnessed considerable debate about what sort of occupations 'fitted' into specific social classes, and this allowed a considerable congruence in debates about class and interests in consumerism to be generated, especially in the work of Savage *et al.* (1992), Crompton (eg 1993), and Warde (eg Warde and Tomlinson, 1995). In short, Bourdieu's work could be appropriated to an occupational class based approach to consumption, in a similar way that some commentators claim that behind Bourdieu's general sophistication lurks a fairly conventional Marxist approach to social analysis (notably Alexander, 1995). Bourdieu's analysis might be seen in this context as the most subtle attempt to relate consumption processes to occupational divisions and can therefore be seen a key test case for examining the adequacy of such a general framework for analysis.

2: Bourdieu, consumption and occupational classes: a critical survey

'These 'new intellectuals' who adopt a learning mode towards life (Bourdieu, 1984: 370) are fascinated by identity, presentation, appearance and lifestyle. Indeed their veneration of the artistic and intellectual lifestyle is such that they consciously invent an art of living in which their body, home and car are regarded as an extension of their persona which must be stylized to express the individuality of the bearer' (Featherstone 1991:60).

In some of the chapters of *Distinction* (notably pages 365–371) Bourdieu considers how new forms of cultural practice might be related to the rise of the 'new petite bourgeoisie'. He notes the growth of new forms of 'petty bourgeois' culture which have turned the ethic of 'duty' into that of 'fun' (Bourdieu 1984: 366). He is characteristically cautious in linking this group to specific social locations, but nonetheless does state that

> 'the new petite bourgeoisie comes into its own in all the occupations involving presentation and representation (sales, marketing, advertising, public relations, fashion, decoration and so forth) and in all the institutions providing symbolic goods and services. These include various jobs in medical and social assistance (marriage guidance, sex therapy, dietics, vocational guidance, paediatric advice etc) and in cultural production and organization (youth leaders, play leaders, tutors and monitors, radio and TV producers and presenters, magazine journalists) which have expanded considerably in recent years; but also some established occupations, such as art craftsmen and nurses' (Bourdieu 1984:359).

Bourdieu's focus on this group can be seen as rather unoriginal. The importance of these groups seemed to be that they fitted uneasily with established and traditional class divisions, because they are transient, occupying 'liminal' class positions. In some respects such ideas can be seen as the correlate of the commonplace arguments of stratification sociologists from the early 20th century (see Vidich, 1995) and which reached a peak in the 1970s and early 1980s. Writers such as Gouldner (1979) talked about the rise of the 'new class', Poulantzas (1973) analysed the 'new petite bourgeoisie', and Wright (1979, 1985) studied the middle classes in 'contradictory class positions'. Bourdieu was taking up a well worn theme in claiming that such liminal fractions of the middle classes played a crucial role in developing new forms of consumerist culture (see generally Lury, 1996).

It is therefore interesting to note that although during the early 1980s there were some parallels between Bourdieu's work and currents in class analysis pointing to the rise of 'new classes', in more recent years the focus of stratification writers has been very much on the consolidation of existing class relations, and there is currently considerable doubt about the supposed rise of 'new middle classes' of various types. The research here is varied and differences of opinion can readily be detected. Nonetheless, there is much to be gleaned from Brint's (1993) critique of the 'new class' hypotheses which argues that American professionals are not attracted to the distinctive radical politics which Gouldner had supposed. Goldthorpe (1995) has also emphasized the consolidation of 'service class' power, focusing especially on the ability of professionals and managers to pass on their advantages to their offspring. Savage *et al.* (1992) have a rather different account and prefer to talk of the consolidation of professional power (thus acknowledging the declining significance of the managerial middle classes—on which see further Scase and Goffee, 1989; Butler and Savage, 1995). Notwithstanding some differences of opinion, the focus of all these accounts concern the maturation of the established middle classes. Much secondary evidence is congruent with such an emphasis on social polarization. Gershuny (1993) claims that British male work histories are becoming increasingly divided between professional workers on the one hand and manual workers on the other. The majority of professional workers spend their entire careers in professional jobs whilst manual workers find it ever more difficult to move away from such forms of employment. Even where it is possible to point to distinctively new occupational groupings it is by no means clear that they adopt the various characteristics of the 'new middle classes' suggested by Bourdieu. Thus, in the expanding alternative health field, chiropractors, for instance, can command high incomes (an average of £90,000pa) and recruit the established middle classes from exclusive private schools (Cant, forthcoming).

Although it therefore seems unwise to focus on the rise of new middle classes, it is clear that the middle classes are fractured in many ways, and that it is a meaningful project to explore the implications of such axes of differentiation (see especially Butler and Savage, 1995). However, it is by no means clear that forms of consumer practices can readily be mapped onto middle class fractions. Savage *et al.* (1992) used a market research survey to examine patterns of spending on given consumer services and products, in order to see if a distinct 'yuppie' culture could be detected, and if so whether there were particular groups which appeared to be its main supports. They argued that there were indeed three distinct middle class cultures anchored in different occupational bases: an ascetic culture, found especially amongst public sector professionals; a 'post-modern' culture which 'mixed and matched' elements of high culture with a hedonism of excess, which seemed to be based in the private sector professional middle classes, and a conventional, undistinctive middle class culture found especially amongst managerial groups. This does seem compatible with

Bourdieu's and Featherstone's account in some ways, except that it suggests that the older established professions as well as the 'new cultural intermediaries' may also be active 'consumerists'.

Warde's analysis of food consumption also offers important insights into the applicability of Bourdieu's ideas. He shows that independent professionals spend more money on food, and that whilst at one level they eat healthily, they are also more likely to eat lavishly: 'eating out in stylish restaurants, experimenting with domestic cuisine and eating more healthily probably are features of the food experiences of this class' (Warde, 1997:194). This account is compatible also with the idea that the affluent professional middle classes are bearers of new forms of consumer culture. However, at this point a limitation of the sort of survey analysis used by both Savage *et al.* (1992) and Warde (1997) needs to be noted. Both approaches involve measuring forms of consumer spending amongst those in different occupational categories. Because private sector professionals appear both to spend above average amounts on 'lavish' items, and also on 'healthy' food, they assume that individuals within these groups are characterized by a kind of 'pick and mix' culture. However, a deduction of this sort would be wrong since it assumes that the actions of individuals mirrors those of wider groups. It may be that some individuals within this occupational group favour the healthy lifestyle/ and others favour the lifestyle of excess, hence that two different cultures are being detected, not one contradictory or post-modern culture as Savage *et al.* (1992) suggest. We here see some of the limitations of the occupationally driven approach to class. Occupational class differences can often be detected, but the decision to measure differences and variation in terms of occupation does not in itself demonstrate the real salience of such factors. This point raises crucial issues of methodology which we discuss more fully below.

Before moving on, it is important to note that the preceding discussion raises the real possibility that individuals do have more complex and contradictory forms of consumer practice than is suggested by Bourdieu's focus on the habitus as the 'practice-unifying and practice-generating principle . . . the internalized form of class condition and of the conditionings it entails' (Bourdieu, 1984:101). It might in fact be argued that the tension between ascetic consumer practices and hedonistic ones is actually of very long standing, as might be suggested by a comparison of Weber's claims about the Protestant Ethic and Campbell's (1987) emphasis on the parallel development of a romantic ethic. The point to bring out might be that far from these two axes having distinctive occupational bases, they may exist in tension with each other. This point is suggested by Wynne and O'Connor (1995) (and see also O'Connor and Wynne, 1996). Their analysis of consumer attitudes in central Manchester claims that there is no direct social base to the consumer practices they detect, even though the central Manchester location was specifically chosen to attempt to allow the salience of yuppie urban residents to be manifest. They conclude by noting that 'our subjects, then, represent nothing that could be structurally understood as a rising class fraction' (p. 10). More radically, they go on to question Featherstone's emphasis on lifestyle and the extent to which people adopted a 'heroic' approach to consumer practices at all. The reason that their respondents appear to engage in a variety of apparently disconnected consumer practices is not due to their adoption of a creative 'post-modern' lifestyle which heroically stitches together otherwise discrete lifestyles into a new pastiche. It is simply that people themselves do not attempt to synthesis or link together their consumer actions in the way that Bourdieu's notion of the habitus would suggest as being fundamental. Indeed, their respondents did not seem terribly concerned with 'performing' cultural distinction in any clear way.

What is needed, we would claim, is a way of focusing on the contradictions and dynamics of individuals and class habituses. Although Bourdieu himself would appear to recognize this by referring to the specificity of different cultural 'fields' in which habituses exist, he nowhere provides a systematic account of how fields are related to each other. In our view it is important to find a perspective which does not reduce consumption practices to one axis, nor which simply lists descriptively that people do different things in various contexts, but which explores more systematically the internal tensions of different habituses. One point which is particularly important to address here is the need to explore how habituses do not simply establish differences between people, but also how they construct identity and solidarity. In this latter enterprise, Bourdieu's ideas have little to say.

The reason for this is the way that Bourdieu's methodological procedures gear him towards focusing on need to uncover and explain *variation*. Therefore, despite his powerful jibes against positivist approaches to sociology, and his invocation of 'reflexive' methods (eg, Bourdieu, 1996), he cannot but situate himself very much within the terrain of positivist approaches to social inquiry. It would appear that Bourdieu sees his approach as non-positivist because it does not concentrate on specifying the importance of individual variables but recognizes the necessary inter-connection between them (Bourdieu, 1984:103, 106). Bourdieu thus spends some time emphasizing that class and gender are intrinsically interrelated, rather than separately constituted 'variables' (Bourdieu, 1984:107). It would be possible to question Bourdieu's adherence to his own stated principles, in that he not infrequently invokes the singular power of specific variables over others ('a socio-occupational category . . . derives a major part of its effects from the secondary variables *it governs*' (p. 112), 'the *primary differences* . . . derive from the overall volume of capital . . .' (p. 114) (our italics). However, leaving this aside, we would suggest that it is wrong to see positivism as being based around the assumption that variables need to be understood as isolated. Nearly all forms of multivariate quantitative analysis now recognize the need to consider the interlinkages between independent variables (using methods such as multilevel modelling) rather than attempting to specify the causal weight of particular, uncontextualized variables. What is crucial to defining an approach as positivist is the assumption that causality is understood by accounting for variance in the dependent variable (see Lieberson 1985). Therefore, although it is true that the method Bourdieu uses in *Distinction*, correspondence analysis, is a sophisticated multivariate technique which allows the interlinkages between independent variables rather than their independent effects to be examined, it is still based around the need to look for correlations between dependent variables (types of consumption practice) and clusters of independent variables (occupational positions, gender, age groups etc) and then measuring the association between them.

The main issue is that by focusing on the explanation of variance Bourdieu directs attention to only one, partial, process at stake. For, as Lieberson (1985) emphasizes, not all processes need vary significantly for them to be significant. Indeed, the most powerful processes, precisely because they are so powerful, tend not to vary very much. Of course there is always some variance which can be measured, and possible correlates of whatever variation exists sought after, but this might draw attention to a relatively uninteresting question. Thus it is always possible to find some sort of variation (even the effect of the earth's gravity, for instance, varies somewhat according to the position of the moon) but this variation need not be the most important or interesting thing to consider (we are never able to float into space because the moon reaches a certain position!).

In this context consider, for instance, the example of contemporary television viewing. By 1990, 95 per cent of British households had at least one colour television set (59 per cent had a video cassette recorder with a remote control and 32 per cent had two television sets) (*Cultural Trends*, 1992:2). By 1993 80 per cent of households had a video cassette recorder of one kind or another (*Cultural Trends*, 1994:25). This rises to 90 per cent when households with children are considered (*Cultural Trends*, 1994:12). Virtually everyone in Britain therefore has direct access to television broadcasts and, increasingly, VCRs. There is some variation in the amount of television watched by age, gender and social class. Thus in 1993, 4–15 year olds watched an average of 18.9 hours of television per week, whereas those 65 and over watched 35.4 hours per week. The variation across the ages 25–34, 35–44 and 45–54 was small, averaging 25.2, 24.5 and 25.2 hours per week respectively. There are also differences by gender. In 1992 for example, men watched on average 23.4 hours of television a week while women watched 26.2 hours. Some variations by class are also apparent. In 1992, social classes AB watched on average 18.6 hours per week, class C1 23.8, class C2 25.6 and classes DE 29.3 (*Cultural Trends*, 1994:38).

Nonetheless, the important point is that these variations need to be placed in the context of relatively 'heavy' viewing. Furthermore, 'Social groups DE appear to be watching rather less television *vis-a-vis* the population as a whole than in the second half of the 1980s, in contrast to groups ABC 1 which are watching rather more' (*Cultural Trends*, 1994:38). Our suggestion is that these differences in viewing patterns which do give evidence of differential consumption of television in class terms, and which could be hypothesized also to relate to some degree to differential possession of cultural capital, are potentially overshadowed by the overall total consumption of television by the population as a whole. Thus even the lowest watching groups (people under 16 and social classes AB) are still watching over 18 hours per week. This is reinforced when data about what people watch are considered. As Abercrombie (1996:48) explains: 'The proportions of time spent watching different types of programme are almost constant across the different groupings within the audience. In many ways this is a remarkable finding. In other fields of activity, generally speaking, one finds that different social groups have very different social behaviours'. However, this introduces an important point about the distinction between *what* is viewed/done and *how* it is viewed/done in a wider context.

Our aim is not to reinstate mass society theories such as those of Adorno concerning the universalizing effects of given economic and social processes. Rather, our point is that the search for variation needs to be placed in direct relationship to the related need to examine patterns of commonality. Bourdieu himself however frequently neglects this point, in his at times obsessive search for cultural 'difference'. One interesting demonstration of this point is Halle's (1993) examination of interior decoration in the homes of working and middle class Americans. Halle emphasizes that although there were important differences in the decoration of these homes there were nonetheless some general patterns which spanned classes, ethnicities and genders. All groups, for instance, tended to like pastoral ('non-peopled') landscape paintings and photographs. And, although the upper class residents were more likely to hand abstract art on their walls than were working class residents nonetheless, only a small proportion of the decorations of even the upper classes (13.9 per cent) were of this character (see Halle 1993:61). To be sure Halle does discuss a number of salient and important differences between the tastes of social classes (for instance, the middle class appreciation of 'primitive art' or the working class appreciation of religious iconography), but only by placing them in broader contexts.

This same broad point is also evident from many of Bourdieu's own analyses. Bourdieu shows that, certain 'high cultural' practices such as going to the opera, theatres etc.) are much more likely to be indulged in by the professional middle classes than by other social groups. However, it may still be the case that even the professional middle classes rarely engage in these practices. Lamont (1992) shows that most American middle classes rarely show much direct interest in high cultural practices. Bourdieu's study of variations in musical taste points to undeniable gradients by social location. However, taking one example, appreciation of the 'Well tempered clavier' varies from 1 per cent (of clerical and commercial employees) to 33.5 per cent (for higher education teachers). One important point, not made by Bourdieu, is that this music is generally unpopular, even amongst the most culturally privileged groups. To take another example, every occupational group found a 'sunset over the sea' much more beautiful than 'a snake' to look at (see Bourdieu, 1984:38). There were no groups where even a fifth of respondents thought that a 'car crash' 'would make a beautiful photo' (Bourdieu 1984:526). Contemporary data on album purchases tell a similar story. Thus 41 per cent of classical music albums are purchased by those in social classes AB, pointing in the direction of a Bourdieu distinction paradigm, however, only 17 per cent of the albums purchased by AB social classes are of this type. They are far outnumbered by the purchase of rock and pop albums which constitute 52 per cent of purchases (*Cultural Trends*, 1993—see further Longhurst 1995).

A further point here, following on from this, is the fact that variations have differing degrees of meaning or significance. Some literature on consumption fully acknowledges this point. Mennell's analysis of changing patterns of eating, for instance notes that 'the main trend has been towards *diminishing contrasts and increasing varieties* (quoted in Warde, 1997:35). Some forms of variation are not always of any real substantive point. This is of course a major theme of Frankfurt school critics, one of whose major claims is that the apparently different forms of popular music on offer can actually be seen as essentially similar. The really significant point therefore is not just to note that variation exists but to bring out the relational character of such variation, or in other words that the existence of particular tastes is directly related to the absence of given tastes elsewhere. Bourdieu however appears to be confused here. He equates the demonstration of variation in taste with the demonstration that such variation is meaningful. It is precisely for this reason that we argue that it is important to focus on questions of 'everyday life' in order to gauge the significance of specific cultural practices in their context.

This leads us to final general point. By focusing on variation in consumption practices, Bourdieu tends to reproduce a view of consumption which emphasizes the struggle for difference. But this perspective does not allow us to find ways of examining how solidarities and bonds are formed. It is for this reason that occupational identifiers become so central to Bourdieu's account since these are the sole surrogates which can stand in for this process of identity formation. We would argue that it is essential to consider how consumption practices allow common identities to be established between people, as well as considering how they are used to distinguish between people. Such an exercise involves considering, sociologically, how patterns of uniformity and common-ality are constructed. One possible way of developing our under-standing of this issue would be to take up some of the arguments of American network theorists who point to the way that differ-ent types of social networks facilitate identity formation (see Savage, 1996 for a general discussion of some of these issues). This again leads us to consider debates about 'everyday life', which we take up in the next section.

3: Consumption and 'everyday life'

In this section we want to indicate that a focus on 'everyday life' can offer ways of taking forward analyses of consumption that are more sensitive to the interplay between individual subjectivity and context; which allow the question of the 'meaningfulness' of variation to be addressed; and which are more flexible and soph-isticated in their rendering of agency in consumption practice. Part of the promise in the emphasis on 'everyday life' is simply for a fuller analysis of the context in which consumption practices take place, and as permitting us to find ways of exploring the nature of consumption divisions in ways which are less concerned to base such practices in occupational class divisions. Turning back to our example of television, some qualitative evidence on the nature of the audience for television does introduce important dimensions of variation. Research has tended to show that there are important gender differences in the way that men and women watch television (for example, Morley 1986; Gray, 1992). However, it has also been shown that level of educational attain-ment can lead to a significant narrowing of the gap between men and women. Gray (1992) shows that at higher class levels, the dif-ference between men and women in television watching are decreased where the possession of educational capital plays a sig-nificant role in bridging the gap between the genders. On first sight this seems like important evidence to support a thesis derived from Bourdieu on the role of educational capital within the middle classes. The problem however, is that it is not at all clear how these patterns of television viewing (in terms of viewing preferences) articulate with the range of other activities which occur in the rest of the viewers' lives. This has led much recent research on media audiences to seek to locate television and media use within the patterns of everyday life more broadly (for example Silverstone and Hirsch, 1992; Silverstone, 1994).

Silverstone ambitiously seeks to develop an overall account of the place of television in contemporary everyday life. For present purposes two strands of his argument are particularly important: his general theory and discussion of consumption. In attempting to provide a general theory of television, Silverstone points to three important aspects: the generation of 'ontological security', the construction of the contemporary individual and routinization. We shall consider each of these areas in turn. First, Silverstone connects his argument to those advanced by such as Giddens (1990) concerning the role of trust in contemporary society. Television, he suggests, is critically important in the construction of contemporary 'trust from a distance'. Moreover, television can play this role in the generation of trust as it plays a core role in contemporary constructions of notions of self and individuality. Silverstone uses the work of Winnicott on the separation of the child from its parents through the use of 'transitional objects' to argue that television importantly plays such a role in many households today. Television acts for the infant in the same way as the blanket or the teddy bear. Children are often 'baby-sat' by the television during busy periods and so on. This role, in Silverstone's argument, continues through into adult life. Television as an contemporary transitional object mediates between different psychological and social spheres. Routinization is thus inherent in households and the everyday media use.

Silverstone develops this discussion through examinations of different concepts of the home and the household and the appropriation of different media technologies by different sorts of households, and in so doing draws on much previous research on media audiences (for summaries, see Moores, 1993; Lewis, 1991; Morley, 1992). In the course of this argument he specifically examines the process of consumption, identifying a 'cycle of consumption' where goods move through the spheres of commodification, imagination, appropriation, objectification, incorporation and conversion. In Silverstone's argument, then, consumption is 'at the heart of mobile privatization' and is 'both the oil and glue of structure and agency within everyday life' (p. 131).

The points made in rather abstract and theoretical terms by Silverstone are confirmed by some recent empirical research. Thus, Gillespie (1995) examines the fine grain and complexities of the interaction with television within the Asian community in

Southall in West London, pointing in particular to the role of television in the construction and reconstruction of local identities in the global, diasporic context. Further, Hermes (1995) has examined the complex position of womens' magazines in the everyday lives of women. Beginning from an analysis of the audience, rather than the text or 'concern' about the effects of these texts on women's consciousness, Hermes shows that on one level these magazines are not that important to the women studied, in the sense that they expressed no great enthusiasm or anger about them. However, at particular stages in their lives, especially where time was short, they became far more important and heavily used. Hermes argues that these uses are importantly related to the maintenance of a particular identity. She shows how the magazines help to form (or imply) bonds between women through the repertoire of 'connected knowing' and how practices such as the clipping of recipes from magazines do not imply the necessary use of the recipes in cooking, but rather may be an important component in the maintenance of the identity of a home-maker at a particular point. Significantly, she also examines the way in which men use these magazines in their lives. Like television, these magazines tend to be consumed in households.

Thus, we want to suggest that this sort of approach is potentially helpful in overcoming some of the issues developed concerning class in the earlier parts of this paper. This research suggests that while there are clear differences in the patterns of consumption of media, these can only be properly understood within a fuller understanding of the 'everyday life' of the consumers. This has been a significant move made in cultural studies and accounts of the media audience in recent years. Drotner (1994:346) has also shown how the development of more qualitative and ethnographic work on the media audience has led to a stress on the idea of everyday life. She argues that: 'To date, no media ethnographer has defined what he or she means by this concept' (p. 346). Drotner attempts to rectify this omission.[6] She identifies pessimistic (in the work of Lefebvre) and optimistic (in de Certeau) theorizations of everyday life. The importance of Lefebvre in her view is that:

> he makes a crucial connection between modernity and the development of the everyday, and he emphasizes that the everyday infuses all aspects of life, not merely the family or leisure. These aspects are timely reminders also to scholars of

media reception who all too often fail to situate their investigations in a specific historical perspective, and whose emphasis on one mass medium tends to obscure the influence of other media (Drotner 1994:348).

Drotner suggests that Lefebvre's follower de Certeau is far more optimistic in his approach to contemporary everyday life,[7] but that he tends to idealize resistance in everyday life and overplays the carnivalesque (Drotner 1994:349). An important antidote to this more celebratory approach can be found in some of Grossberg's publications. Grossberg (1992) offers a distinction between everyday life and daily life. In broad terms everyday life is the province of the better off (most of the population in the advanced capitalist societies of the west). Everyday life is also routinized and in important senses mundane: 'there is a real pleasure and comfort in its mundanity, in the stability of its repetitiveness. Not only its practices but also its investments are routinized. In a sense, one need never worry about living within the maps of everyday life. Instead, one gets to "choose" how one insubstantiate the maps, what matters, where one invests. In everyday life, one has the luxury of investing in the mundane and the trivial, in the consumption of life itself. To offer the simplest example, there is a real security and pleasure in knowing when and where and exactly for what (including brands) one will go shopping next' (Grossberg 1992:149).

Grossberg distinguishes 'everyday life' from the 'daily life' of those whose do not possess the economic, political and social resources to generate an everyday life. Grossberg uses the example of the place of rap music among blacks in contemporary US. Rap in his view addresses the concerns of those who are excluded from everyday life and constantly emphasizes political and economic matters. Moreover the everyday life of the better off is renewed and 'spiced up' by the appropriation of forms from others daily lives.[8] A constant cycle in the appropriation of various forms of music and one which is consistent with the broad issue of social polarization which we discussed above.

Grossberg thus tends to move the idea of everyday life away from concepts of opposition and resistance in a way similar to that derived from Schutz by Drotner (1994:350). Drotner attempts to break with the notion of the everyday as resistant through adapting two terms from Schutz: repetition and recognition. Thus everyday life is both repetitive in its established patterns (like Grossberg) and based on the recognition of texts and the giving of them meaning. It is possible to adapt these terms for a fuller consideration of the nature of everyday life which goes beyond the explicit concern with media texts and which allows us to form links with Bourdieu's concept of habitus so that the temporal and contextual nature of consumption gains fuller recognition than in existing work in this area.

Bourdieu's notion of the habitus draws attention to the way that the 'self' and the 'social' are mutually constitutive. The habitus cannot be evaded by the individual. 'The schemes of the habitus, the primary forms of classification, owe their specific efficacy to the fact that they function below the level of consciousness and language, beyond the reach of introspective scrutiny or control by the will;' (Bourdieu, 1984:466). Of course, Bourdieu recognizes that the habituses only operate in different 'fields', and hence can generate quite different sorts of practice, but his stress nonetheless is on the unifying role of the habitus, the way it integrates consumer practices into a coherent lifestyle. One of the problems faced by Bourdieu here is his approach to the individual and his account of agency. Bourdieu's account is extremely persuasive in its ability to emphasize the 'performative' significance of consumer actions, the way that such actions are directed towards impressing others. However, consistent with our emphasis on 'everyday life', it can be argued that consumption practices should be placed in the context of both individual as well as social dynamics, as a way of bringing out how habituses may be subject to contradictory rather than consistent dynamics By individual dynamics, we refer to the tendency for individuals to engage in consumption practices which are consistent in their own eyes with their life narrative. Such a project may not always lie squarely with the more outward looking, externally directed impression management which is the main target of Bourdieu's analysis. This point is raised, in interesting ways, in Alan Warde's examination of social and cultural 'taste' for food in contemporary Britain (Warde, 1997; Warde and Tomlinson, 1995). Warde uses both survey data and documentary analyses of the presentation of food and eating in magazines to explore the processes which govern the consumption of food. He shows that there more variation can be detected in single person households than in multi-person households ('better models are achieved because food patterns are more class distinctive than for individuals than they are for households allocated to classes on the basis of the occupation of the head of household'—Warde and Tomlinson, 1995:243). And yet, one of the striking things about single person households is that most of their spending will be for food which they consume alone and will therefore not be subject to any 'performative' need to impress others (except, perhaps, the check out operator or shop assistant). Of course, Bourdieu's emphasis on the habitus draws attention to the way that dispositions are internalized and cannot be taken up or discarded according to particular social settings (in the way that Goffman and other interactionist sociologists might emphasize). But it is precisely in this sense that Bourdieu's approach can be accused of being insensitive to the different ways in which performances are managed according to context (see generally Mouzelis 1995).

Here it can be suggested that it is essential to distinguish two rather different types of consumption action, that geared towards impressing others and that directed at reassuring oneself. Somers (1994) has argued for the need to make the analysis of narrative central to the study of identity. Narratives, she emphasizes, 'are constellations of *relationships* (connected pasts) embedded in *time and space*, constituted by *causal employment* (Somers, 1994:616). Emplotment refers to the way that particular events need to be integrated into a meaningful 'plot' in order for them to allow identity to be constructed. Thus, she emphasizes that a particular individual needs to see specific life happenings as linking together in a coherent manner. In this sense, we could argue that there is an important distinction between consumption action directed towards emploting one's own narrative and that directed directly towards others in particular social settings. Thus, the reason that a middle class professional man living by himself may still buy expensive and well prepared food when cooking for himself (rather than just buy fish and chips), may be due to his need to organize events consistent with a narrative he can identify with and which reassures him. Of course, some people in this category may not find it important to systematize their consumption habits in this way to maintain a recognizable life narrative, or 'life script'. And of course, outward looking and inward looking activities are associated, in that personal narratives are inextricably involved with public and social activities, but they nonetheless draw attention to two rather different processes which may affect consumption patterns—how to impress distinction on oneself as well as on others.

Bourdieu would argue that an argument along these lines

would be to valorize a particular, class specific, way of thinking and relating to the world. This is because it accepts the *a priori* validity of the individual voice when in fact the ability to reflect in such a way can only be seen as the product of a habitus based on forms of social and cultural exclusion. The 'right to speak' (and relatedly, we might add, the right to think of one self in narrative terms) cannot be taken for granted (Bourdieu, 1984:411). Nonetheless, Bourdieu's point raises problems. It is well known that there is a great difficulty in his work in acknowledging the cultural dynamics of working class and plebian cultures. It is a common critique of Bourdieu's position that his account of working class culture is patronising and élitist (eg Jenkins, 1989; Fowler, 1994). This is because since Bourdieu seems to see the right to agency and individuality as the product of prior battles over distinction, it is therefore intrinsically associated with privileged social classes and therefore it is difficult for him to acknowledge—despite his own intentions—how excluded groups can be agents.

One of the attractions of thinking about consumption as being governed by these different axes is that it allows us to more fully register the contradictory processes which lie behind consumption, and also allows us to see how different practices are taken up according to context. One of the important implications of this argument is also to suggest the need to focus on the *temporal* dimensions of consumption activity, to note the significance of *individual subjectivities* and to situate consumption more generally in the context of *everyday life*. This of course perfectly consistent with the general orientation of Bourdieu's work although they have not fed through as yet to studies of consumption.

Conclusion

We have argued that Bourdieu's general approach to consumption has in the past decade been appropriated to a form of 'occupationally driven' approach to the subject. This has had the virtue of allowing a cross fertilization of ideas and insights between sociologists of stratification and those working in newer areas of consumption. Nonetheless, there have been serious losses. In this paper we have concentrated on two of these. Firstly, it is important to focus not just on variation in consumption practices, but also processes which bind people together. We have suggested that a focus on everyday life, sociation, and on social networks is a valuable way of taking debates further here. Secondly, it is important to take further the complexity of different 'fields' of consumption and to stress the systematically fractured nature of habituses. It is not enough simply to say that there are a variety of 'fields' in which battles over distinction are waged. Such a formulation allows no ready way of integrating analysis and tends either to lead to a descriptive listing of different fields, or an ultimately reductive approach in which some form of priority is ultimately posited (see Alexander 1995). In our view, an important step forward is to recognize that consumption processes are driven by performative processes directed at impressing others, processes directed at reassuring oneself, and also processes forming links and bonds with significant others. This formulation hints at the complexity of the process of consumption whilst also recognizing the possibility that habituses may be synthesized, and also emphasizes the role of agency.

In our view, the general argument we have sketched out is that the sorts of interconnections between class and culture, posited by those authors who have adopted a correlative stance derived from Bourdieu, are importantly deficient in their inattention to the dynamics and complexities of everyday life. This argument has methodological implications in that we would argue that these processes cannot solely be investigated through survey data, but rather call for a more qualitative approaches. Of course, this move has been made by a number of media researchers in the contemporary period. However, the success of this has been limited by four problems: the research has tended to be insufficiently ethnographic, relying on a small number of relatively short interviews; discussion has focused on media consumption within households and in particular in families; the approach concerns itself overmuch with television rather than with the interconnections between the use of different media; and finally, research has been over-general in that it is neglected the differential patterning of everyday life along established lines of social division—which may be re-patterned through media relationships themselves.

Methodologically, our preferred solution for further research is to examine the patterning of routinized networks of sociation, which may have households as their nodes but which draw in a number of other social institutions such as voluntary associations. In some respects this entails a return to more ethnographically based studies of interaction within specific 'localities'. However, it seems to us that there is at least one clear difference from earlier studies of community; the hypothesized crucial role of the media of diverse kinds in the contemporary patterning of social relations This means taking seriously as a prompt for research the sorts of hypotheses about the aestheticization of everyday life and performativity discussed above. However, we would want to remove these ideas from the Bourdieu paradigm and to examine them empirically through extended qualitative research.

Acknowledgements

We would like to thank Kevin Hetherington and Alan Warde for comments on a first draft of this chapter.

Notes

1 Examples include Allatt, Bagnall and Werbner. Other papers given to the series 'Conceptualising Consumption Issues' were also influenced by Bourdieu, for example Miller (1995) and Thornton (1995a). In particular, Thornton's innovative development of the concept of 'subcultural capital' draws heavily on Bourdieu, see also Thornton (1995b).

2 We might make it clear here that in general terms we are sympathetic to many of the broad currents of Bourdieu's social theory and see our paper as a sympathetic critique of his general project which aims at developing the potential of his ideas.

3 Though his ideas were taken up by Parkin in his attempt to develop Weberian closure theory—see Parkin (1979)

4 In anticipation of our later arguments it can be argued that rap music is actually important in shifts in the organization of everyday life through the stimulation of inter-racial dialogue, see for example Stephens (1992) and Cross (1993). Others (for example Swendenberg 1992) have suggested that rap is involved in the subversion of commodified mass culture from within.

5 This development was not restricted to Britain or those associated with *Theory. Culture and Society*. Thus, in the US, Pfeil (1990) argued for the association of new forms of culture with the 'baby boom PMC' and in Britain McRobbie (1994) also commented on the social location of new forms of culture. The significance of Jameson's (1984) pioneering essay on postmodernism and late capitalism would also figure in a fuller account of these developments.

6 It is important to note that Drotner was writing in advance of the publication of Silverstone's book as discussed above. However, this general point still holds in important outline senses.

7 An optimism which has fed into studies of the media and the audience through the work of John Fiske (for example 1987) and most importantly in the studies of fans carried out by Jenkins (1992), whose debts to de Certeau include the extended use of the idea of poaching in everyday life.

8 See Rose (1994) for an important argument which connects the development of rap to black music traditions, technological innovation and the disruption of daily life brought about by the Cross-Bronx Expressway in New York.

References

Abercrombie, N., (1996), *Television and Society*, Cambridge: Polity.

Alexander, J., (1995), *Fin-de-Siecle Social Theory*, London: Verso.

Allatt, P., (1996), 'Consuming Schooling', this volume.

Bagnall, G., (1996), 'Consuming the past', this volume.

Beck, U., (1992), *Risk Society*, London: Sage.

Beisel, N., (1993), 'Morals vs Art: Censorship, the politics of interpretation and the Victorian nude', *American Sociological Review*, 58, 145–162.

Biernacki, R., (1995), *The Fabrication of Labor: Germany and Britain, 1640–1914*, Berkeley: University of California Press.

Binder, A., (1993), 'Constructing Racial Rhetoric: media depictions of harm in heavy metal and rap music, *American Sociological Review*, 58, 753–768.

Bourdieu, P., (1977) *Outline of a Theory of Practice*, Cambridge: CUP.

Bourdieu, P., (1984), *Distinction*, London: Routledge.

Bourdieu, P., (1900a) *Photography: a middle-brow art?*, Cambridge: Polity.

Bourdieu, P., (1990b) *In other words: towards a reflexive sociology*, Cambridge: Polity.

Bourdieu, P., (1993), 'From ruling class to a field of power: an interview with Pierre Bourdieu on "La Noblesse d'Etat" ', *Theory, Culture and Society*, 10, 19–44.

Bourdieu, P. and A. Darbel, (1991), *The love of art: European art museums and their public*, Cambridge: Polity.

Bourdieu, P., (1996) 'Understanding' *Theory Culture and Society* 13:17–38.

Bourdieu, P. and Passeron, C., (1977), *Reproduchon in Education, Society and Culture*, London: Sage.

Butler, T. and Savage M., (eds) (1995), *Social change and the Middle Classes*, London: UCL Press

Brint, S., (1993), *The New Class*, Berkeley: University of California.

Calhoun, C., (1993), 'Habitus, Field and Capital: the question of historical specificity' in Calhoun *et al.* (eds).

Calhoun, C., LiPuma, E., Postone, M., (eds) (1993), *Bourdieu: critical perspectives*, Oxford: Polity.

Campbell, C., (1987), *The Romantic Ethnic and the Spirit of Modern Consumerism*, Oxford: Blackwell.

Cant, S., (forthcoming), 'Homeopathy and professionalization in late modernity', PhD thesis, University of Manchester.

Crompton, R., (1993), *Class and Stratification*, Oxford: Polity.

Cross, B., (1993), *It's Not about a Salary . . . Rap, Race and Resistance in Los Angeles*, London: Verso.

Cultural Trends, (1992), 13, London: Policy Studies Institute

Cultural Trends, (1993), 19, London: Policy Studies Institute

Cultural Trends, (1994), 23, London: Policy Studies Institute.

Drotner, K., (1994), 'Ethnographic Enigmas: "The Everyday" in Recent Media Studies', *Cultural Studies*, 8, 2, 341–357.

Emirbayer, M. and Goodwin, J. (1994) 'Network analysis, culture and the problem of agency' *American Journal of Sociology*, 99(6), 1411–54.

Featherstone M., (1982), 'The body in consumer culture', *Theory, Culture and Society*, 1, 2, 18–33.

Featherstone, M., (1987), 'Lifestyle and Consumer Culture', *Theory, Culture and Society*, 4, 55–70.

Featherstone, M., (1991), *Consumer Culture and Postmodernism*, London: Sage.

Fiske, J., (1987), *Television Culture*, London: Methuen.

Fowler, B., (1994) 'The hegemonic work of Art in the age of Electronic Reproduction: An assessment of Pierre Bourdieu' *Theory, Culture and Society*, 11:129–54.

Gershuny, J., (1993), 'Post-industrial career structures in Britain' in G. Esping-Andersen (ed.), *Changing Classes: stratification and mobility in post-industrial societies*, London: Sage.

Giddens, A., (1990), *The Consequences of Modernity*, Cambridge: Polity.

Gillespie, M., (1995), *Television, Ethnicity and Cultural Change*, London: Routledge.

Goldthorpe, J.H., (1995), 'The service class revisited' in T. Butler and M. Savage (eds), *Social Change and the Middle Classes*, London: UCL Press.

Gouldner, A., (1979), *The future of intellectuals and the rise of the new class: a frame of reference, theses, conjectures, argumentation and historical perspective*, London: MacMillan.

Gray, A., (1992), *Video Playtime: the gendering of a leisure technology*, London: Routledge.

Grossberg, L., (1992), *We Gotta get out of This Place*, London: Routledge.

Halle, D., (1993), *Inside Culture: Art and Class in the American Home*, Chicago: University of Chicago Press.

Hermes, J., (1995), *Reading Women's magazines*, Oxford: Polity.

Honneth, A., Kocybu, H., Scwibs, B., (1986), 'The struggle for the symbolic order: an interview with Pierre Bourdieu', *Theory, Culture and Society*, 3, 3, 35–52.

Jameson, F., (1984), 'Postmodernism or the cultural logic of late capitalism', *New Left Review*, 146, 53–92.

Jenkins, H., (1992), *Textual Poachers: Television Fans & Participatory Culture*, London: Routledge.

Jenkins, R., (1989), *Pierre Bourdieu*, London: Routledge.

Laermans, R., (1993), 'Leaning to Consume: early Department stores and the shaping of modern consumer culture', *Theory, Culture and Society*, 10, 79–102.

Lamont, M., (1992), *Money, Morals and Manners: the culture of the French and American upper-middle class*, Chicago: University of Chicago Press.

Lash, S., (1990), *The Sociology of Postmodernism*, London: Routledge.

Lash, S., (1993*)*, 'Pierre Bourdieu: cultural economy and social change', in Calhoun *et al.* (eds).

Lash, S. and Urry, J., (1987), *The End of Organised Capitalism*, Oxford: Polity.

Lash, S. and Urry, J., (1994), *Economies of Signs and Spaces*, London: Sage.

Lewis, J., (1991), *The Ideological Octopus: An Exploration of Television and its Audience*, London: Routledge.

Lieberson, S., (1985), *Making it Count*, Berkeley: University of California Press.

Longhurst, B., (1995) *Popular Music and Society*, Cambridge: Polity.

Lury, C., (1996) *Consumer Culture*, Cambridge: Polity.

McRobbie, A., (1994), *Postmodernism and popular culture*, London: Routledge.

Maffesoli, M., (1994), *The Time of the Tribes*, London: Sage.

Miller, D., (1995) 'Shopping: Why an Ethnography', Paper to ESRC Seminar Series, Conceptualizing Consumption Issues, University of Keele.

Moores, S., (1993), *Interpreting Audiences*, London: Sage.

Morley, D., (1986), *Family Television: Cultural Power and Domestic Leisure*, London: Comedia.

Morley, D., (1992), *Television, Audiences and Cultural Studies*, London: Routledge.

Mouzelis, N., (1994), *Sociological Theory: what went wrong?*, London: Routledge.

O'Connor, J. and Wynne, D., (1996), 'Left Loafing', in D. Wynne and J. O'Connor (eds), *From the Margins to the Centre*, Swindon: Arena.

Parkin, F., (1994) *Marxism and Class Theory: A Bourgeois Critique*, London: Routledge & Kegal Paul.

Pfeil, F., (1990) *Another Tale to Tell*, London: Verso.

Poulantzas, N., (1973), *Political Power and Social Classes*, London: New Left Books.

Robbins, D., (1991), *The work of Pierre Bourdieu*, Milton Keynes: Open University Press.

Rose, T., (1994) *Black Noise: Rap Music and Black Culture in Contemporary America*, Hanover: Wesleyan University Press/University press of New England.

Savage, M., (1996), 'Space, networks and class formation', in N. Kirk (ed.), *Social Class and Marxism: challenges and defences*, Aldershot: Scolar.

Savage, M., Barlow, J., Dickens, P., Fielding, A.J., (1992), *Property, Bureaucracy and Culture: middle class formation in contemporary Britain*, London: Routledge.

Scase, R. and Goffee, D., (1989), *Reluctant Managers*, London: Allen and Unwin.

Silverstone, R. and Hirsch, E., (eds), (1992), *Consuming Technologies: Media and Information in Domestic Spaces*, London: Routledge.

Silverstone, R., (1994) *Television and Everyday Life*, London: Routledge.

Somers, M., (1994), 'The narrative constitution of identity: a relational and network approach', *Theory and Society*, 23, 5, 605–650.

Stephens, G., (1992), 'Interracial Dialogue in Rap Music: Call-And-Response in a Multicultural Style', *New Formations*, 16, 62–79.

Swendenberg, T., (1992), 'Homies in the Hood: Rap's Commodification of Insubordination', *New Formations*, 18, 53–66.

TCS (1983), 'Special Issue on Consumer Culture', *Theory, Culture and Society*, 1, 3.

Thornton, S., (1995a) 'Hipness: The Logic of Subcultural Capital' Paper to ESRC Seminar Series, Conceptualizing Consumption Issues, University of Salford.

Thornton, S., (1995b) *Club Cultures: Music, Meaning and Subcultural Capital*, Cambridge: Polity.

Vidich, A.J., (1995), *The New Middle Classes: lifestyles, status claims, and political orientations*, Basingstoke: MacMillan.

Werbner, P., (1996) 'The enigma of Chrismas', this volume.

Wacquant, L.J.D., (1993), 'On the tracks of symbolic power: prefatory notes on Bourdieu's "State Nobility"?', *Theory, Culture and Society*, 1–17.

Warde, A., (1990), 'Introduction to the Sociology of Consumption', *Sociology*, 24, 1.

Warde, A., and Tomlinson, M., (1995), 'Taste among the middle classes, 1968–88', in Butler and Savage (eds).

Warde, A., (1997), *Taste and Food*, London: Sage.

Wright, E. O., (1979), *Class, Crisis and the State*, London: New Left Books.
Wright, E. O., (1985), *Classes*, London: Verso.
Wynne, D. and O'Connor, J., (1995) *City Cultures and the New Cultural Intermediaries*, paper presented to BSA Annual Conference, Leicester.

Afterword: the future of the sociology of consumption

Alan Warde

No longer can it be said that consumption is a neglected area of study: the collection of review articles edited by Miller (1995) cite a vast amount of literature on the topic within different social science disciplines—marketing, political economy, geography and psychology, as well as sociology and anthropology. But it also demonstrates that the field of consumption is still widely dispersed and highly fragmented. Disconcertingly, given the extent to which the British social scientific community currently pays homage to the virtues of interdisciplinary work, there is little overlap among the sources identified by practitioners in different disciplinary areas. Each discipline still has much to learn from dialogue with the others, this volume hopefully being a testament to fruitful conversation between sociologists and particularly anthropologists. It seems unlikely, indeed even inappropriate, to expect cross-disciplinary synthesis of approach; rather we might hope for mutual appreciation of the effective range of the research programmes of different disciplines and much improved internal theoretical clarity. It therefore seems appropriate to conclude this monograph with a prospective glance at the sociological research agenda, bearing in mind Campbell's (1995) authoritative overview of key themes in the development of the sociology of consumption over the last decade in the UK which identifies many unresolved tensions.

The sociological approach to consumption

Two topics have dominated recent sociological analysis of consumption; the attempt to understand the ramifications of an intensified commercial consumer culture and the consequences of the commodification of services previously supplied through alternative modes of provision, primarily the state and the household. Sociology was involved in an encounter with cultural studies on the first issue, with political economy on the second. (The extent to which these concerns are potentially different can be appreciated by comparing the chapters here by Falk with that of Dowding and Dunleavy.) While both provoked intense and sometimes unproductive controversy, some progress has been made.

Consumption is a process concerned with the acquisition and use of goods and services. Economists are particularly interested in one form of acquisition; that which involves the transfer of money in exchange for ownership of, or access to, commodities. Sociologists cannot afford to neglect such matters: the consequences of acquisitiveness and the unequal distribution of resources are issues to which sociological analysis has traditionally contributed and remains relevant. Though there are exceptions like Ford and Rowlinson, much recent theoretical discussion of consumption has assumed that now survival is assured, the means of physical and social reproduction guaranteed, the practices of consumption have become more diverse in their purposes, more expressive in intent. Basic material and instrumental imperatives to select efficiently and economically the means to satisfy 'needs' have been overcome, superseded by more elevated or elaborate purposes. Some chapters in this volume demonstrate that neglect of the earlier concerns with survival is premature: severe problems in ensuring survival remain for substantial segments of the population, for the sick, the poor and the socially deprived. Particularly instructive is Baldock and Ungerson's demonstration that shortage of money is not the sole source of the inability of many stroke sufferers to obtain adequate care.

The remit for sociological investigation must, however, be wider. Not only were goods and services never solely a matter of survival, but it is generally accepted that other, particularly expressive, purposes have increased in importance. The current phase of inquiry has been much influenced by the 'cultural turn' in social theory, two effects of which are particularly worthy of note. First is the depiction of the way that notions of the consumer are socially constructed; to the hegemonic model derived from economics of a sovereign consumer making autonomous decisions in the light of individually chosen desires and goals have been added models of the consumer as communicator, identity-seeker, rebel, and so forth (see Gabriel and Lang, 1995, for a full catalogue). Second, and related, is an appreciation of the complexity of the use to which goods and services are put, raising questions about the functions and purposes of consumption. Consumption comprises a set of practices which permit people to express self identity, to mark attachment to social groups, to accumulate resources, to exhibit social distinction, to ensure participation in social activities, and more things besides. Among issues still subject to debate is the extent to which consumption practices respond to these different social objectives. This provides some potentially rich sources of theoretical disagreement.

The purposes of consumption

Self-identity and its others

Discussion in the 1990s occurs under the shadow of a rampant and theoretically naive notion of consumer choice, part of a discourse deriving from the abstract model of the consumer in economics, adapted and popularized as political principle by the New Right, which insinuates that the maximum level of personal freedom is found in the market place. Sociological accounts of consumption have always challenged the worst excesses of individualistic explanations of how and why people select what to consume among the immense range of products and services available. Nevertheless many have succumbed to the temptation to accept the vocation of market research by seeking to isolate the essential characteristics of the abstract figure of '*the* consumer'. Others have adopted an implausibly exaggerated version of what Munro calls the production view of the self which sees choices in the field of consumption as an instrumental and unconstrained strategy for the construction of personal identity. As Campbell (1995) observes, an implausible account of consumer behaviour arises from giving excessive weight to a notion of consumption as the communicative action of the individual.

The theme of increasing individualization drives many analyses of contemporary social change and thereby focuses attention on the means by which a person can intentionally and actively express a sense of personal distinctiveness. It is debatable the extent to which the individual is in control of this process; as Allatt shows, in important respects identity is, at very least, coproduced. If the mechanism of socialization is no longer, alone, a satisfactory explanation of the formation of identity, it is still a conditioning force in creation and maintenance of a sense of self. Nor is it clear that consumption itself is paramount in identity formation: we lack the experiential and phenomenological evidence, from autobiography for instance, to support the claim. Other sources of identity, particularly of identification with national, ethnic, occupational and kin groups remain strong without being dependent upon shared patterns of commercial consumption. Identities are achieved through affiliation to groups but the processes by which this occurs in a late modern age deserve more attention. While acknowledging that in some part the artefacts of consumer culture are deployed performatively in the attempt to differentiate the actor from others within and beyond a given relevant social circle, a more measured analysis will maintain that the answer to the question 'who am I?' is closely bound to that of 'who are we?', and that the answer to both these questions is likely to involve consideration of social location, involvement in social networks, involuntary exposure to persuasive communications, and so forth. The production view of the self not only underestimates the social context of identity formation but also overemphasizes the role of cultural products (particularly media outputs and icons of fashion) at the expense of the variety of practices which create and sustain social relations of kinship, friendship and association.

Participation and solidarity

The concern with self-identity, in the context of a historical tendency for studies to focus on the significance of the personal ownership of goods, has obscured collective aspects of consumption associated with social participation. Many consumption practices are major sources of social solidarity, entailing joint activities which, while involving financial expenditure, can scarcely be attributed to consumerist motivation. Subscribing to clubs and associations, or engaging in hobbies and sports which require purchasing, and sometimes the collecting, of goods, often entail investment of vast amounts of time and attention which is easily misunderstood, and indeed belittled, if considered through the lens of consumerism. A considerable proportion of household expenditure is directed towards two kinds of service: securing opportunities to meet other people thereby to share an experience; and having sufficient information to engage with them.

305

A wide range of commercial services exist to permit face-to-face social interaction. Some interactions are routine, others special occasions. Arguably, meaning is increasingly attached to being present at some special place or event. Being with others at a particular site or at a 'live' performance, say a concert or a sports contest, is a source of satisfaction in itself. This is partly because participation enhances a longed for sense of belonging, in many ways the neglected 'other-side' of personal identity-formation, and its associated sentiments of obligation, camaraderie and communion. The hierarchical bonding within families through gift-giving rituals on the occasion of Christmas (Werbner) is one example. Another is the cultural reaffirmation achieved through the symbolic content of a shared meal for members of a migrant group: Harbottle shows that consumption may seem dangerous and risky, but that through intervention and skill a potential threat may be annulled and consumption turned to positive effect in generating solidarity and enhancing cultural identity. The ways in which solidarity is enhanced by social consumption is still not comprehensively appreciated.

Even less well understood is the significance of another important way in which consumption facilitates participation. In television broadcasting, for example, information and entertainment which is communicated is bought, but is not easily subsumed under the term consumption: it is not natural to talk of 'consuming' a programme or a book, although the relationship between producer and audience is one that apparently parallels other modes of commercial provision. Yet to have a relevant knowledge deriving from such media sources is often essential for the process of social participation. Perhaps concepts like Thompson's (1995) notion of 'mediated quasi-interaction', which implies action at a distance, needs to be aligned with other understandings of consumption. Similarly, the way in which architecture and urban design structure public space and thereby convey collective meaning upon those subject to it, impersonally through mere presence as it were, could be subjected to more profound theoretical analysis. Bagnall's study of behaviour at tourist sites, which documents the way that meaning is derived from visits to places which have been constructed to represent the collective past, is indicative of the way that consideration of spaces of consumption might be integrated.

Distinction

Sociological approaches to consumption are closely identified with notions of group differentiation and social distinction. In particular sociology has concentrated extensively on mechanisms of social status and social class. Thus for Fine and Leopold (1993), Veblen and Bourdieu are the prototypical representatives of a sociological approach. Almost certainly this resulted in comparative neglect other social groupings, particularly gender and generation; but also of ethnic, local and national differences. Processes of closure and exclusion operate in situations where groups identify themselves through their valued performances and classify others on the basis of their taste and judgment. Bourdieu still offers the most elaborate and nuanced analysis of the processes of classification, and it is not surprising that his work is so prominent. Yet there are grounds for reservation; not only is his writing interpreted inconsistently, as Longhurst and Savage indicate, but many doubt the survival of a social hierarchy of taste and whether distinction in consumption can be mapped onto class structure or indeed onto any system of social positions. I suspect, following Crompton, that the death of social class is much exaggerated, as is its effect on consumption (see also Butler & Savage, 1995), but existing explorations in the social mapping of taste are not a sufficient basis to resolve the question. Among the reasons for uncertainty are: that much individual consumption behaviour is contextually determined; that there is insufficient sophisticated empirical inquiry; and the descriptions of the systems of difference that are supposed to have superseded class are imprecise and therefore inestimable.

Some problems of method and measurement

The methodologies and techniques of data gathering deployed in the study of consumption have been appropriately varied, ranging from random sample survey to semiotic analysis of texts to detailed ethnography. All have made their particular contributions; none can be dispensed with. Some legitimate questions about, say, patterns of ownership of goods or differential rates of participation in leisure activities can only be derived by sampling the population statistically. Understanding the impact of advertisements will never be complete without the detailed and systematic examination of examples. And the meanings ascribed to goods and services will never be established without talking extensively with, and observing people engaged in, the practical activity of consumption. Arguably the last is still the least exploited method and the one that will offer the greatest immediate intellectual returns. As some studies in this volume demonstrate, the use of identical products and the reception of the same media messages vary very significantly; having a need for care, buying food, attending a museum or listening to a broadcast elicit different responses and interpretations from groups and categories within society. If *understanding* consumer practices is the objective then it is the broadly ethnographic techniques that are most likely to pay dividends.

A principal reason for this is that consumption is contextual. The use and display of goods and services by any individual occurs on many different sites in front of many different audiences. In this regard, consumption is sequential and amenable to fragmentation, inconsistency and inconstancy. Consequently methodological difficulties arise when the objective is to understand individual consumer behaviour. If consumption practices comprise a perpetual series of short performative episodes, the opportunity for the social scientist to estimate the coherence of any individual's behaviour is severely restricted. And if taste and judgment vary between situations, it is only by keeping close company with the consumers in question that their behaviour can be evaluated. Inventing unobtrusive measures for such circumstances constitutes a real challenge. However, if the sociological concern is more one of understanding the various 'social worlds' (eg Becker, 1982) that individuals inhabit, whether their immersion is deep or fleeting, then ethnographic attention to interaction situations is especially appropriate.

Substitution between modes

Much recent theorizing about consumption has focused almost entirely upon the commodity sector. Why an individual purchases one item rather than another is a question to which many powerful organizations have an overriding practical interest in finding an answer. That social science so readily accepts this, the vocation of market research, as its own problem is probably a side-effect of political discourse in the last couple of decades.

Excessive focus on the purchase of commodities ignores the fact that much of what is consumed is not acquired, delivered or enjoyed in commodity form. Not only are many items channelled through other institutions for provision—the state, the community, the household—but even most of the items bought in the market require further labour on the part of the purchaser in order to make them useful and/or meaningful. Conceptual frameworks, like that of Warde (1992), which separate out analytically the modes and cycles of provision, and relate them to the rules of access and forms of enjoyment involved in episodes of consumption, offer a means to more comprehensive appreciation of complexity.

Debate about the replacement of state provision by markets has concentrated on how the price and quality of services is affected. A practical and political issue of profound importance, the debate on the consequences of the privatization and marketization of utilities and welfare will continue unabated. The restructuring of welfare, so instructively dissected in essays in the first part of this volume (eg Baldock & Ungerson, Clarke), has significant, and varied, effects for citizenship as well as for individual customers and clients. Generally, however, less attention is paid to the consequences for social relations of substitution of one mode of provision for another.

The social relations surrounding consumption practices vary by the mode of their provision, as is made transparent by Werbner's analysis of gift giving at Christmas which is simply one instance of the way that people weave wonderful rituals, to which they attribute great inter-personal and collective significance, from consumption opportunities. An identical object will often have a different meaning for its owner if it was received as a gift. Obligations of reciprocity and symbols of affect attached to gifts cement social relationships in particular ways. But the process is complex, partly because several modes may be called upon simultaneously. Christmas festivities involve both the exchange of presents, which are a mixture of commodities and home-made goods, and the delivery of domestic services of hospitality and entertainment. Similar complexity was apparent in Allatt's description of the way that parental purchase of private schooling increased the sense of obligation and commitment of children and involved other family members in the co-production of educational performance. The combination of different ways of obtaining services, and the complex effects of provision on social relations, remains to be fully understood. But this is part of processes of developing and maintaining public and private trust, entrenching local and national solidarities, altering the balance between egoism and altruism, and so forth. Consumption practices have a key role in establishing, maintaining, transforming and displacing social relationships.

Substitution, viewed as historical process, might additionally serve as a useful frame for analysing the connections between consumption and social change. The commodification of some fields of consumption has been charted (eg Cowan, 1983 on the industrialization of the home). But study of the comparative development of consumer societies is in its infancy; the coincidence between industrial development and consumer demand for particular goods and services, which varied in timing and extent from country to country, is little examined (though see Therborn, 1995:139–46) The differential onset of mass consumption, and the effect of the uneven persistence of alternative modes of provision, promises a new perspective on the history of modern societies, particularly if combined with insights from the comparative analysis of welfare states (eg Esping-Andersen, 1990). Processes of commodification and de-commodification, of bureaucratization and informalization, of centralization and de-centralization in the realms of consumption together are capable of charting some of the critical dynamics of 20th century social formations.

The need for more empirical case studies

Theoretical progress is unlikely in the absence of more extensive empirical analysis of the different facets of consumption processes. One promising avenue for further progress in understanding consumption is the undertaking of more case studies of specific social practices. The tasks are to study the way that different groups operate in particular fields and the ways that fields themselves differ in their logic. More studies like those in the second part of this volume, on processes and experiences of consumption, might eventually accumulate into a body of analyses of particular practices sufficiently encyclopaedic for effective comparison and generalization. Ultimately the aim must be to compare both the behaviours of different social groups and the behaviours entailed by different types of activity.

Towards theoretical development

Notwithstanding the bold and speculative attempt of Miller (1995:1–57), the field of consumption remains one of partial, competing perspectives. The subtle engagement of Featherstone with postmodernism (1991) and the rigorous application of the concept of 'systems of provision' by Fine and Leopold (1993), two of the most important recent contributions to theoretical debate, reflect a continuing stand-off between approaches indebted to cultural studies and political economy respectively. A sociology of consumption might bridge this chasm, drawing on its traditional capacity to appreciate both the instrumental imperatives of material life and the normative grounding of all social action. Attention to the definition of the specificity of the field of consumption, and charting its boundaries with the studies of popular culture, everyday life and material culture, seems necessary. The increasing interest in Bourdieu's socially grounded aesthetic approach, which reasserts the importance of social relations and associations and deploys concepts of different sorts of capital, thereby keeping the unequal distribution of resources in focus, may be amenable to further development. Also, systematic application of analytic frameworks which isolate and specify the modes and cycles of provision and enjoyment involved might help to better specify the complex connections between production and consumption. Though comparatively modest, such ventures, by helping to reduce the separation between understandings of the production of consumption and the processes of consumption, offer more promising immediate means of theoretical clarification than would the search for some grand post-disciplinary synthesis.

Bibliography

Note: those items referred to in this chapter which are not accompanied by bibliographic details are essays in this volume.

Becker, H., (1982) *Art Worlds* Berkeley: University of California.
Butler, T. & Savage, M., (1995) *Social Change and the Middle Classes* London: UCL Press.
Campbell, C., (1995) The sociology of consumption in Miller, D., (ed.) *Acknowledging Consumption: a review of new studies* London: Routledge 96–126
Cowan, R.S., (1983) *More Work for Mother: the ironies of household technology from the open hearth to the microwave* New York: Basic Books.
Esping-Anderson, G., (1990) *Three Worlds of Welfare Capitalism*, Cambridge: Polity.

Featherstone, M., (1991) *Consumer Culture and Postmodernism* London: Sage.

Fine, B. and Leopold, E., (1993) *The World of Consumption* London: Routledge.

Gabriel, Y. & Lang, T., (1995) *The Unmanageable Consumer: contemporary consumption and its fragmentation* London: Sage.

Miller, D. (ed.) (1995) *Acknowledging Consumption: a review of new studies* London: Routledge.

Therborn, G., (1995) *European Modernity and Beyond: the trajectory of European societies 1945–2000* London: Sage.

Thompson, J.B., (1995) *The Media and modernity: a social theory of the media* Cambridge: Polity.

Warde, A., (1992) Notes on the relationship between production and consumption in R. Burrows & C. Marsh (eds) *Consumption and Class: divisions and change* London: Macmillan, 15–31.

Notes on contributors

Pat Allatt is a Professor of Sociology in the School of Business and Management, University of Teeside. Her research and publications include evaluations of crime prevention and drugs awareness education programmes, popular culture, family and youth. She is currently engaged in transnational research on young people's orientation to the future. She is co-author of *Youth Unemployment and the Family* (1992).

Gaynor Bagnall is a postgraduate researcher in the Institute for Social Research/Department of Sociology at the University of Salford and is currently completing a PhD thesis examining the consumption and production processes at two north west heritage sites.

John Baldock is a Reader in Social Policy at the University of Kent, He has conducted research and written widely on issues to do with care of the elderly, particularly in a European context.

John Clarke is a Senior Lecturer in Social Policy at the Open University. He has a longstanding interest in the politics and ideologies of social welfare. His recent work has focused on the role of managerialism in the reconstruction of the welfare state. His publications include *New Times and Old Enemies* (1991), *Managing Social Policy* (1994), and *The Managerial State* (1996).

Rosemary Crompton is a Professor of Sociology at the University of Leicester. Her recent publications include *Class and Stratification* (1993) and *Changing Forms of Employment* (1996).

Keith Dowding is a Reader in the Department of Government at the LSE. He is the author of *The Civil Service* (1995) and *Power* (1996).

Notes on contributors

Patrick Dunleavy is a Professor in the Department of Government at the LSE. His recent publications include *Democracy, Bureaucracy and Public Choice* (1991).

Stephen Edgell is a Professor of Sociology at the University of Salford. His current interests include the social theories of Thorstein Veblen and the sociology of consumption. Recent publications include *Class* (1993) and *Debating the Future of the Public Sphere* (1994).

Pasi Falk is a Senior Research Fellow at the Department of Sociology/Research Unit, University of Helsinki. His recent publications include *The Consuming Body* (1994) and *The Shopping Experience* (1996).

Janet Ford is the Joseph Rowntree Professor of Housing Policy at the University of York. Her interests include the provision, use and management of mortgage and consumer credit by both institutions and households and she is currently researching the changing relationship between the housing and labour markets.

Lynn Harbottle is a Nutritionist and Medical Anthropologist at Keele University. Her recent publications include articles on *Feminism and Medical Anthropology* (1995) and *Towards a Culturally Sensitive Research Approach* (1996).

Kevin Hetherington is a Lecturer in Sociology at Keele University. His main research interests include the sociology of space as well as the sociology of consumption. Forthcoming publications include *The Badlands of Modernity* (1997).

Brian Longhurst is a Senior Lecturer in Sociology at the University of Salford. He is currently completing a book on *Media Audiences* and his most recent publications include *Popular Music and Society* (1995).

Rolland Munro is a Reader in Accountability in the Department of Management, Keele University. He is also founder member of the Centre for Social Theory and Technology. He has recently co-edited *Accountability: Power, Ethos and the Technologies of Managing*, 1966.

Karen Rowlingson is a Senior Lecturer in Sociology at the University of Derby, and was previously a Research Fellow at the Policy Studies Institute.

Notes on contributors

Mike Savage is a Professor of Sociology at the University of Manchester. His main research interests are in the study of social divisions, historical sociology, and urban sociology. His recent publications include *Property, Bureaucracy and Culture* (1992) and *Social Change and the Middle Classes* (1995).

Clare Ungerson is a Professor of Social Policy at the University of Southampton. Her recent research is concerned with social care and payment for care, largely from a feminist perspective. She is author of a number of studies including *Policy is Personal* (1987).

Alan Warde is a Professor of Sociology at the University of Lancaster. He was editor of a special edition of *Sociology* (1990) on Consumption and his recent research has explored the topic with particular reference to food. His forthcoming publications include *Consumption, Food and Taste* (1997).

Pnina Werbner is a Senior Lecturer in Social Anthropology at Keele University. She is director of an ESRC project on 'South Asian Popular Culture: Gender, Generation and Identity'. Her recent publications include *Black and Ethnic Leadership in Britain* (1991), *Economy and Culture in Pakistan* (1991), and *Debating Cultural Hybridity* (1996). Her forthcoming publications include *The Politics of Multiculturalism* (1997).

Index

Abercrombie, N., 286–7
access, to goods and services, 19–20, 22–4
activism, 81–2, 84, 85, 278
advertisements, for patent medicines, 193–5
altruism, 156–7
Anderson, B., 151
Anthias, F., 151
attachment/detachment, 261, 267, 270, 271
Audit Commission, 15
authenticity, of heritage site experiences, 238–40, 243–44

backgrounding, 173–4
Baudrillard, J., 136
Bauman, Z., 154
Beard, G., 200n
Beck, U., 120
Bourdieu, P., 136, 137, 157, 160n, 166, 307; on class and consumption, 118, 274–97; *Distinction*, 274, 276–8, 280–2
Braverman, H., 119
Brint, S., 281
Bulkley, M., 92

Calhoun, C., 278
Campbell, C., 136, 239, 304
Caplow, T., 138
care in the community *see* community care
Caring for People, 15
Carrier, J., 149–50
Castells, M., 42, 43, 44
centralization/decentralization, in social welfare, 74–5
charitable giving, 139–40, 141, 152–3
Cheal, D., 138, 143
Cheyne, George, 188, 200n
choice, 78, 136; in community care, 16–17, 27; and consumption, 173–6, 179; micro-choices, 173, 179; of school, 167–71
Christmas 138, 156–9; and moral economy of the nation, 151–3; myths of, 142–5; non-Christians at, 153–4; as potlatch, 138–40, 152
A Christmas Carol, 158–9
class: and consumption, 113–14, 117–29, 280–1, 281–90, 307; and

culture, 287–8; and identity, 115, 118–25, 126, 128; and museum visiting, 231–2
class analysis, 114–17, 127
clerical workers, 118–19
clientalism, 32–3
code of conduct/relations of substance, 145–6, 147–8
Cohen, A. P., 270
collective consumption, 36, 37, 42–8, 60–1
collective goods, 48–60, 61
commodification processes, transformations in, 39–41
communitarianism, 79–88
community, 80, 82–3, 87; monoculturalism in, 84–5
community action, 81–2, 84
community care, 11–33, 85–6; consumption of 18–27; participation in provision of, 28–33
Community Development Project, 84
compliance, 149, 156–9
Condorcet, A-N. de, 189
confirmatory emotional map, 236–9
conspicuous consumption, 138, 139, 180n
consumerism: Bourdieu and, 279–80; and community care, 16, 29–30; in social welfare, 74–6
consumption, 163–4, 165–7, 303; conditions of, 19–21, (in community care, 21–7); purposes of, 304–7; sociology of 18–19, 277; *see also* collective consumption
consumption aggregates, 115–17
control over schools, 170–1
Cooper, D., 47
credit agents, 102–7; recruitment of women as, 99–102; relationships with customers, 97–9
credit market, 97–107
crowding, 53–4
culinary triangle, 223
cultural capital, 148, 232, 245, 276
cultural heritage, and choice of school, 168–9
cultural reproduction, 277–8, 279
culture, 259, 260; class and, 287–8; sharing of, 256–8
cycles of production and consumption, 2–3, 290–91

Index

De Certeau, M., 291
decentralization, in social welfare, 74–5
default, credit agents and, 108–9
delivery of services, 20, 24–5
Dennis, N., 80, 81
diet, 208; British, 219–20, 223; Iranian, 214–16, 223–4; morality and, 218
dietetics, classical, 187, 188
difference, 269, 284, 288; *see also* distinction
diminishment of identity, 263–4, 265, 267–8, 271
disaggregation, 41
discreteness, of collective goods, 53
distinction, 278–9, 280, 307
domination, through giving, 137, 157–8
Douglas, M., 173, 255–6, 257–59, 272n
Drotner, K., 291, 292
Du Gay, P., 122–3
Duke, V., 45
Dunleavy, P., 41, 43, 45

economic cost, of education, 176–7
economic settlement, of welfare state, 67, 70
Edgell, S., 45
education, as site of consumption, 163–80
educational attainment, of visitors to museums, 232, 233
Edwards, J., 146, 147
elderly, care of *see* community care
emplotment, 294
employment, class identity and, 115, 118–25, 126, 128
employment aggregates, 115–17, 125, 127, 128
enjoyment, social environment of, 20, 25–6
Erdos, G., 80, 81
ethical socialism, 80–1
ethnic consumption, 154–5, 204, 206
Evans-Pritchard, E. E., 148
everyday life, consumption and, 289-95
exchange, 268; extension and, 262–4
exchange value, 250, 261
exclusion, 154, 307; from collective goods, 49, 53, 54–5; self and, 258–60
expenditure: at Christmas, 152; on community care, 17; public, 69–70
extension, 260–2; exchange and, 262–4; knowledge and, 264–7

family, 71, 83, 154; giving within, 150; morality and, 80–1; New Right and, 156

family life, consumption of education and, 164–5, 172–6, 176–8
Father Christmas, 142–3, 144, 151, 157
fear: of growing old, 191–3; for health, 190–1
Featherstone, M., 278, 311
Finch, J., 145, 156
Fine, B., 307, 311
Finland, vitamin consumption in, 197–8
Fischler, C., 206
flexible working, 120
flows, 139; of kinship, 145–50, 156
food, 293–4; class and, 283; and identity, 206–7, 224; medicinal properties of, 210–13; and nutrition, 214–15; transformations, 223–4; and well-being, 205–7, 222–4
Fortes, M., 157
Frankfurt School, 277, 288
Frenkel, S., 124
Freud, S., 200n
Friedman, J., 249, 250, 251

Game, A., 238
Germany, care of the elderly in, 14
Gershuny, J., 283
Ghormeh-sabzi, 204–7
Giddens, A., 150
gift: economies, 135–7, 139–40; education as, 172, 175, 176–8
Gillespie, M., 290
giving: charitable, 139–40, 141, 152–3; as sacrifice, 137, 155; scales of , 150–3
global strategies, 250, 251
Goldthorpe, J. H., 282
goods, 37, 49–50, 250; access to, 19–20, 22–4; artefacts as, 267; collective, 48–60, 61; culture and, 255–6, 259
Gouldner, A., 281
government intervention, 48, 50, 61; and new public management, 57–60
Granovetter, M., 18
Gray, A., 289
Green, D., 81
Grossberg, L., 292, 293

habits of the heart, 28–33
habitus, 284, 293
HADACOL, 195, 196
Hall, S., 242, 244
Halle, D., 287
Halsey, A. H., 80
happiness, and choice of school, 169–70

318

Index

Murray, C., 81
Museum of Science and Industry, Manchester, 230, 231, 235, 237, 239; visitors to, 231, 232
museums, as sites of leisure consumption, 227–8

narrative, and identity, 294
nation: as family, 151, 153; as moral community, 155–6
National Trust, 227
nativity, 143
neo-conservatism, 76, 79, 83
neo-liberalism, 76, 79
new middle classes, 283
new public management (NPM), 37, 41, 47, 57–9
New right, 70, 72, 74, 76, 77–9, 156
NHS and Community Care Act 1990, 15–16, 85
nostalgia, 239–40

obligations to reciprocate, 177–8, 309
occupational classes, 115; and consumption, 118, 280–89
O'Connor, J., 284
Offe, C., 120
organizational settlement, of welfare state, 68–9, 71–2

pantomimes, 144–5
parental choice, 6, 167–71
Parsons, T., 157
participation, 305–6
passivity, 32–3
patent medicines, 193–9, 201–2n
'people': New Right and, 72, 76, 77; state and, 68, 70–1
performance related pay, 124, 130n
police services, divisibility of, 52
positivism, 285
postmodern consumption, 135–7; Christmas and, 138
potlatch, 166; Christmas as, 138–40, 144
Poulantzas, N., 281
poverty, credit in management of, 92–4
preservation, 192–3
Preteceille, E., 36
prevention, health and, 184–5, 190–1
preventive medicine, 195, 197–8
private health care, 59
private sector, in community care, 23–4
privatism, 30–1
production, 19, 21–2; and consumption, 2–3, 44, 59–60, 290

professional class, and consumption, 279, 282–3, 287
professionalism, in state welfare, 69, 71–2, 73, 75, 78
prosthesis, 260–1
prototypes, 265
Provident Financial Services, 95
public/private spheres, education and, 164, 166
public services, 4, 22; dispersal of, 78, 309; purchaser/provider roles in, 41–2; marketization trends in, 40–1
purchaser/provider roles, 41–2

Quicke, J., 180
Quinn, J. B., 38

reassuring oneself, 294, 296
recipients of gifts, 143
reciprocal giving, 139, 149–50
reciprocity, 177–8
regulated credit, 92–3, 94–5
regulation, 57–8, 59
rejective emotional map, 238–9
reminiscence, 240–1
representation, in advertising, 185, 194–5
reproduction, and consumption, 166, 179, 277
responsibility, 83, 85, 87; transfer of, 174–6
Riesman, D., 123, 189
risk, in credit markets, 97, 107–9
Robbins, D., 276

sacrifice, 140–2; education as, 172, 174, 177; giving as, 137, 139, 141, 155
Samuel, R., 229
Samuelson, P., 48, 52–3
sarde-garme (hot-cold) beliefs, 208–13
Saunders, P., 114, 116–17
Savage, M., 233, 283
Savas, E. S., 55, 57
Schmitz, C. A., 261
Schneider, D. M., 145–7, 150
Scott, J., 127
sectoral conflict, 45–7
self: consumption view of, 249–52, 255–7; exclusion and, 257–9; production of, 252–5, 267–8, 304; reworking, 267–9
self-completion, 190, 191, 193, 200n
self-concern, 189–90
self-identity, 304–5
services: employment in, 121–5; growth of, 37–8; *see also* public services
Sharma, U., 149

320

Silverstone, R., 290
Singapore, 44
social environment of enjoyment, 20, 25–6
social relationships, 309–10; and community care, 13, 27; in credit markets, 97–9, 102–7; education and, 166, 179
social settlement, of welfare state, 67–8, 70
socialization of consumption *see* collective consumption
solidarity, 305–6
Somers, M., 294
state, 72, 73–4; and collective consumption, 44, 45, 47; dispersal of power of, 86; *see also* public services
Stoker, G., 81
strangers, at Christmas, 153–4
Strathern, M., 145, 146, 249, 260–9, 272n
subordination, through giving, 137, 157–8
subsidization, 57, 59
substance, relations of, 145–6, 147–8
surrogate mothers, 146–7
Sweden, welfare reform in, 14
symbolic violence, 137, 157–8, 160n

taste, 136; variations in, 287–8
Taylor, R., 97
Tebbutt, M., 93
television, 286, 289–91
Terrail, J. P., 44
total quality management (TQM), 124, 125, 127
trust: in credit markets, 97, 107–9; role of television in, 290

unilateral giving, 137
unregulated credit, 93

Urry, J., 120, 128, 163, 228, 240, 279
use value, 250, 261

variations, 285–9
Veblen, T., 139, 180n
Vesselitsky, V., 92
visitors, to museums, 231–4
vitamins, 184, 193–4, 197–9; advertising, 194–6, 201n; magical character of, 185–6, 194, 199; marketing of, 184–5; and preservation, 192–3
voluntary sector, in community care, 25
volunteering, 85, 87

Wacquant, L. J. D., 278
Warde, A., 19, 128, 163, 283, 293–4
Weber, M., 37, 115
weekly collected credit *see* money lending
weight loss, 215–17
welfare state, 66–9; crisis of, 69–73; dispersal of, 78, 309; reform of, 73–6
welfarism, 31–2
Wigan Pier, 230, 233–5, 236–7, 238–9; visitors to, 231–3
Williams, F., 67
women: as credit agents, 94–6, 98–9, 100–2, 107–10; and family health, 204–24
women's magazines, 291
work/non-work, 121–3
work organization, 123–5, 126–7, 128
World Health Organization (WHO), 205
worthy goods, 55–7
Wright, E. O., 281
Wynne, D., 284

Young, S., 81
Yuval Davis, N., 151

The Sociological Review

Edited by Denis Smith

The Sociological Review provides comprehensive coverage of all areas of sociology, social anthropology and cognate subjects such as cultural and women's studies, social policy and industrial relations. The journal has a flexible approach to both its content and style. No social topic is considered irrelevant, innovative subject matter and style are welcomed, and articles are always topical and current.